SECURING THE FUTURE OF MANAGEMENT EDUCATION: COMPETITIVE DESTRUCTION OR CONSTRUCTIVE INNOVATION?

REFLECTIONS ON THE ROLE, IMPACT AND FUTURE OF MANAGEMENT EDUCATION: EFMD PERSPECTIVES

Recent Volume:

REFLECTIONS ON THE ROLE, IMPACT AND FUTURE OF
MANAGEMENT EDUCATION: EFMD PERSPECTIVES,
VOLUME 2

SECURING THE FUTURE OF MANAGEMENT EDUCATION: COMPETITIVE DESTRUCTION OR CONSTRUCTIVE INNOVATION?

BY

HOWARD THOMAS
*Lee Kong Chian School of Business,
Singapore Management University, Singapore*

MICHELLE LEE
*Lee Kong Chian School of Business,
Singapore Management University, Singapore*

LYNNE THOMAS

ALEXANDER WILSON
*Loughborough University, UK; Singapore Management
University, Singapore*

United Kingdom – North America – Japan
India – Malaysia – China

Emerald Group Publishing Limited
Howard House, Wagon Lane, Bingley BD16 1WA, UK

First edition 2014

Copyright © 2014 Emerald Group Publishing Limited

Reprints and permission service
Contact: permissions@emeraldinsight.com

British Library Cataloguing in Publication Data
A catalogue record for this book is available from the British Library

ISBN: 978-1-78350-913-3

ISOQAR certified
Management System,
awarded to Emerald
for adherence to
Environmental
standard
ISO 14001:2004.

Certificate Number 1985
ISO 14001

INVESTOR IN PEOPLE

To the Thomas, Lee and Wilson families who are the foundation of our lives

Contents

Acknowledgements

This book would not have been completed without the collaboration and help of a number of key people.

To Eric Cornuel and Matthew Wood of EFMD, we owe our immeasurable gratitude for encouraging Howard and Lynne Thomas to undertake the research work that informs the content of this book. They have also offered constant encouragement and support throughout the research and writing phases of this volume.

We wish to thank the 39 individuals listed in the appendix who gave us two to three hours of their time and were highly supportive, open and frank in answering our questions. Their professionalism, expertise and willingness to share their viewpoints increased the depth and quality of the insights about management education presented here.

We also owe a high debt of gratitude to colleagues at the Singapore Management University (SMU), particularly Professor Arnoud de Meyer and Provost Rajendra Srivastava, who have provided the stimuli and enthusiasm to push this project through to fruition. In particular, our sincere appreciation goes to Susan Chong Oi Yin (HT's deputy PA at SMU) for cheerfully and professionally executing the typing and revision of various earlier drafts of the book; to Gillian Goh Cheng Cheng, Ho Yan Yan and Yun Si Min for outstanding research assistance and finally to Dorasen Khoo Ban Yie (HT's PA at SMU) for her constant encouragement and organization of HT's time.

As authors we would like to acknowledge the financial and academic support offered by SMU and particularly to Alex Wilson who visited Lee Kong Chian School of Business, SMU as Lim Kim San Research Fellow in Strategy and Organisation in Summer 2011, Summer 2012 and Summer 2013. We also appreciate the help and advice of Michael Thomas of Blue-eyed Digital Marketing and David Thomas at Lancaster University.

Finally, the quality and exposition of the written argument, has been considerably improved by the excellent and tireless efforts of George Bickerstraffe, the Consultant Editor of EFMD. We are extremely grateful to him for his professionalism and expertise, but recognize that we alone are responsible for the content and structuring of the argument in the book.

— Howard Thomas, Michelle Lee,
Lynne Thomas and
Alexander Wilson

Foreword: Discussing the Future

Volume I – *Promises Fulfilled and Unfulfilled in Management Education* by Howard Thomas, Lynne Thomas and Alex Wilson (Emerald, 2013) provided interview and other evidence about the challenges, issues and unfulfilled promise of management education. It adopted a retrospective view of the evolution of business schools since 1990. It noted the strong and continuing growth of business schools, particularly in new areas such as Europe and Asia, and pointed out the increasing criticisms and concerns about both the value and legitimacy of management education.

Volume II now focuses much more closely on the emerging trends, and uncertain futures in management education. It explores, using an open-ended interview research process, the lessons not learned and the on-going challenges in management education. It outlines a set of future scenarios for management education for the next 10 years and examines potential future patterns, "tipping points", blind spots and critical issues for the future. It also discusses the need for changes and innovations in business models, and highlights areas that must be resolved in the future, for business schools to continue their strong positioning in higher education.

Chapter 1

Introduction: Success and Failure in Management Education

Preface

The past five decades have seen business schools grow globally following their successful initial growth in the United States and Western Europe.

In Volume I of this book (Thomas, Thomas, & Wilson, 2013, p. 9), Noorda (2011, p. 520) says: "In many aspects business schools are perfect proof of what you get when universities are doing what they are supposed to do and doing it well. They are fit for purpose because they are serving the specific needs of the communities they relate to."

However, not all commentators agree with this assertion. More recently, and particularly since the financial crisis that began in 2007/2008, business schools, and management education in general, has been heavily criticised. They have been charged, for example, with having some complicity in the events leading up to the financial crisis because of their perceived strong focus on financial engineering and "casino capitalism" (Locke & Spender, 2011).

Others argue that they must also bear some responsibility for not emphasising the need for a moral and ethical compass and thus contributing to ethical failures involved in the collapse of large companies such as ENRON and WorldCom (Gregg & Stoner, 2008).

The key question, therefore, is what is the current status and legitimacy of business schools? Are they at new turning point in their evolution? Are they now on a downward spiral of conservatism and inertia that avoids change? Or, more hopefully, are they in a period of reinvention in which they will create a new sense of identity and partnership with their key stakeholders in business, government and industry?

If business schools are indeed in the process of reinventing and rethinking their curricula frameworks and programme logics, it is important to encourage debate about the issues and challenges they will face.

In this volume we examine the opinions on relevant evolutionary issues offered by a set of global leaders in management education (see the appendix for their names). This is based on an analysis of their responses to

> If business schools are indeed in the process of reinventing and rethinking their curricula frameworks and programme logics, it is important to encourage debate about the issues and challenges they will face

questions posed in a recent series of extensive semi-structured interviews about management education carried out by Howard and Lynne Thomas.

Exposing these ideas and frameworks to further critical examination can be extremely valuable in confronting and rethinking models of management education.

Indeed, as Eric Cornuel, the Director and CEO of the European Foundation for Management Development (EFMD), notes in the foreword (Thomas et al., 2013, p. xvii) to Volume I: "The very fact that the management education 'industry' can examine so openly and forensically the challenges it faces and its own shortcomings only reassures me that it will ultimately respond positively and with eventual success."

We believe that such a detailed examination of challenges, blind spots in decision-making, lessons to be learned and conjectures about new models/pathways and future scenarios can be a valuable input for business school deans and university administrators as they reflect on and propose new approaches to management education.

In this chapter, we first examine debates in the current literature, including the question of where management education now stands from the perspective of key stakeholders, particularly the professional bodies such as the Association to Advance Collegiate Schools of Business (known as AACSB International and sometimes described as the American Association of Collegiate Schools of Business) and EFMD.

We also point out some of the existing evidence of decline and then re-examine unresolved issues, evidence and critiques of management as identified in a series of recent books focusing particularly on the evolution and reform of management education. We then summarise the main areas of criticism and suggestions for improvement as a framework for addressing the issues raised by our interviewees in some of the subsequent chapters of this volume.

Where does Management Education Stand? What is Its Current Positioning?

Introduction

Prior to the financial crisis of the early 2000s the business school had achieved widespread, if sometimes grudging, acceptance in higher education.

For example, Wilson and Thomas (2012, *JMD*) note that EFMD leader Professor Cornuel wrote in the pre-financial crisis environment that "in the future, the legitimacy of business schools will no longer be questioned". Further, he argued that they had become "legitimised parts of society" and that "their role was clear" (Cornuel, *JMD*, 2005).

Close to a decade later, however, it would appear that the role, acceptance and legitimacy of business schools are all very much in the "melting pot".

A news story in the *New York Times* in March 2009 makes the point clearly (see Wilson & Thomas, 2012). It discusses how economic pressures in higher education have led to a decline in the teaching of humanities. Responding to this chapter, a series of readers' letters argued strongly that students exposed to the humanities (such as arts, culture, history, literature and philosophy) are better prepared to develop their capabilities in areas such as moral and ethical reasoning and critical thinking that are growing in importance in society.

The correspondents also pointed out that business schools rarely develop those capabilities and skills adequately. They suggested that this absence of a moral and ethical compass may in turn have caused some MBA graduates holding senior management positions to make a series of short-sighted, perhaps greedy and self-serving, decisions. Decisions that contributed to both the financial crisis and organisational crashes and failures such as Parmalat in Europe and ENRON in the United States (as also pointed out by Gregg & Stoner, 2008).

Further, Joel Podolny (2009), a former dean at Yale School of Management and now CEO of Apple University, has expressed a series of concerns about business schools and their faculty. In his view, many business school academics are not really aware of, or interested in, organisations and their problems.

Podolny noted that generally they are not curious about what really goes on in business and government and many of them have little or no experience in the corporate or governmental sphere. He argues that they prefer to develop theoretical models and approaches that may do little to clarify the way organisations operate or indeed contribute to improving management practice.

This attitude among business academics in turn generates a belief among key business and governmental figures that business schools are somewhat divorced from practice and hence not useful as sources for policy guidance.

Equally worrying for business school deans and university administrators is that there is recent evidence of a decline in student enrolment in MBA and other master's programmes. To quote *The Economist* (8 May, 2010, p. 65): "The business school boom depended largely on the idea that MBAs were entry tickets to the world's two most lucrative professions: investment banking and consulting … But banks and consulting firms are increasingly recruiting people without MBAs, particularly mathematicians and computer scientists. They are also getting keener on growing their own."

> The quality of teaching in business schools is also increasingly dictated by a school's ability (or otherwise) to recruit high-quality academic staff and "clinical" faculty i.e. those with practical management experience who can complement and enhance the quality of the teaching process

There is also a perceived diminution of quality in postgraduate management education offerings including the criticism that less time is spent by students on mastering their academic subjects and more time is committed to networking and finding a job or future career path.

The quality of teaching in business schools is also increasingly dictated by a school's ability (or otherwise) to recruit high-quality academic staff and "clinical" faculty, that is, those with practical management experience who can complement and enhance the quality of the teaching process.

New directions are necessary — business schools should either change and adapt more rapidly to stakeholder demands for relevance and quality or face the daunting prospect of their management degrees being usurped by the models and curricula frameworks of the more traditional social science schools of economics, psychology and sociology.

As pointed out by *The Economist* (8 May, 2010, case studies, p. 66): "The new generation of deans will undoubtedly preside over dramatic changes. But the changes already made have produced one huge benefit: a much more variegated environment. Business schools are offering a greater variety of courses taught in a greater variety of ways than ever before. Perhaps they are finally becoming as vibrant as the subject they study."

AACSB Concerns

AACSB's concerns about the future of management education were evident to Howard Thomas when he served on the AACSB Board as a member and subsequently as Vice-Chair and Chair of the Association

> [AACSB felt] that continued demand for management education and associated market growth was not in itself an adequate indicator to assess the value and success of management education

(2010). The board regularly spent part of its meetings discussing a series of pressing management education issues.

The feeling in the AACSB Board, shared by many of the members of AACSB, was that continued demand for management education and associated market growth was not in itself an adequate indicator to assess the value and success of management education. They were motivated to identify, in particular, the impact of business schools on organisations and society.

Since much of the data about the value of individual business schools to their communities, alumni and organisations is not widely shared, it is sometimes difficult to assess the contributions and impacts business schools in aggregate have on organisations, societies and even countries.

As a consequence, it was argued that AACSB needed to examine more closely the value and impact of management education and *The Impact of Research in Business Schools* report (AACSB, 2008) emerged from this thinking. It focused on identifying the relevance and impact of business schools research output and followed on from an earlier AACSB publication, *Why Management Education Matters* (2005), which stressed the importance and value of management education to individuals, organisations and society.

The observations and conclusions of this preliminary examination are strong warning signals that must be addressed in designing future pathways for management education.

First is the limited impact of management research. The report concluded that only a small fraction of management research, mainly focused on organisational, strategic and financial topics, could be considered to have had an impact on practice (and, therefore, be considered important).

Indeed, Birkinshaw and Mol (2006), who have studied management innovation extensively, concluded that few, if any, significant management ideas had their origin in academic journals. Those that did generally had less impact than ideas that arose in management consulting firms or in innovative management practices.

Further, the considerable level of business school research into financial engineering and stock prices, such as asset pricing, derivatives, stock options and so on, has been somewhat devalued in recent years. It has also created the perception that business schools may need to modify their overarching focus on financial economics and shareholder capitalism as anchoring philosophies. (Note that the eminent financier Warren Buffett had described derivatives as "weapons of mass destruction".)

This has prompted other prominent academics (Schoemaker, 2008) to suggest that large-scale multi-disciplinary research may have had the greatest impact on business. Schoemaker's analysis of impactful research differs significantly from the list in the AACSB research impact report.

He favours examples such as the long-term research on behavioural decision making (such as Cyert & March, 1973; Simon, 1997; Tversky & Kahneman, 1974); the MIT report on lean production in the automotive industry (Altshuler et al., 1984); the multi-disciplinary study of the resource allocation process (Bower, 1986) and Mintzberg's (1973) classic book on the nature of managerial work – all of which had avowedly multi-disciplinary perspectives.

Second, the limited research impact of business schools suggests that the broad relationships and linkages between business schools and their stakeholders in business, government and industry have not been adequately forged and developed.

> **The limited research impact of business schools suggests that the broad relationships and linkages between business schools and their stakeholders in business, government and industry have not been adequately forged and developed**

In a large sample study of 4,000 manufacturing firms, Bloom and Van Reenen (2007) found a strong correlation between good management practices and strong business performance, suggesting clearly that improvement in management practices is an important research topic (see Bloom, Sadun, & Van Reenen, 2012, for similar findings, but in the context of schools and hospitals).

However, the authors did not study the important linkages between business school education and research and better higher-value management practices. The dominant belief in business schools is that business education improves managerial capability and quality yet relatively few studies (Delbridge, Gratton, & Johnson, 2006; Staw & Epstein, 2000) have identified whether management practices are influenced by management education and research.

Third, the world has witnessed a rapid global expansion of management education (e.g. the unprecedented, and planned, expansion of MBA programmes in China over the last 20 years). Research on the *Global Management Education Landscape* (GFME, 2008) indicates that there are over 12,000 business schools currently in existence with around 1,000 accredited by either AACSB or EFMD – the two leading accreditation agencies.

The key issue then is whether the extent and quality of management education influences the global competitiveness of a country.

Michael Porter's influential work on the *Competitive Advantage of Nations* (Porter, Free Press, 1990) points out the importance of a strong human resource base, particularly in the area of managerial and scientific talent, as one of the critical input conditions that influence the level of innovative capacity and growth of competitiveness in a national economy.

Another study (Martin & Milway, 2007) hypothesises that a strong focus on management education must be a significant element in the development of innovative capacity in Canada.

However, innovation researchers (e.g. Bhide, 2008) argue that in this modern, interconnected world, new innovations, inventions and ideas are quickly transmitted. Their view is that innovative companies are critical to competitiveness in any growing global economy for their focus on the rapid adoption and commercialisation of new ideas. This, in turn, suggests that the development of strong managerial capability in such areas as entrepreneurship, strategy, marketing and operations in innovative companies are important in order to exploit any potential competitive advantages.

> It is argued that management education in the form of MBA curricula may be the managerial catalyst for strong economic growth and in reinforcing the competitive edge offered by innovative companies.

Hence, it is argued that management education in the form of MBA curricula may be the managerial catalyst for strong economic growth and in reinforcing the competitive edge offered by innovative companies.

Ultimately, the research proposition is that high-quality management education and the availability of managerial talent will increase the global competitiveness of a country.

Yet few, if any, empirical studies have confirmed the validity of this suggestion. It is possible, as Porter says, that the quality of human resource factor inputs, including management education and talent, is but one of a series of factors that interact to produce high-quality business competitiveness and growth in a particular economy.

This multi-factor explanation of global competitiveness is consistent with the multiple criteria perspective of the World Economic Forum's Global Competitiveness Index (Schwab & Martin, 2012), which includes the quality of management schools among the criteria for judging competitiveness.

Fourth, one way of judging the performance of business schools, particularly for MBA programmes, has been the salary level of graduates. The proposition generally has been that MBA education has a positive

> The proposition generally has been that MBA education has a positive and significant effect on the salary of graduates. The post-MBA salary, taken as the return on the investment, thus justifies pursuing an MBA

and significant effect on the salary of graduates. The post-MBA salary, taken as the return on the investment, thus justifies pursuing an MBA.

However, students can attend MBA programmes for other reasons including career change, developing an enhanced knowledge base and personal challenge. Hence, salary level can be an inappropriate measure of career success despite the fact that influential MBA listings, such as the *Financial Times* ranking of global MBA programmes, devote up to 40% of the rankings on post-programme salary levels and graduates' increases in salary supposedly due to the MBA degree.

These rankings, therefore, may give a distorted view of the quality of various business schools, particularly since MBA programmes represent around 15% (Jessica Brown, 2012) of the enrolment of business schools – in fact, most of the enrolment is in undergraduate education (around 75%), with a gradual disincentive to invest in doctoral programmes to feed the collective shortage of doctoral faculty in the field (AACSB, 2003), largely because of their cost and lack of influence on business school rankings.

EFMD Concerns

Taken together, the current literature and AACSB evidence highlight a lack of research and allied data about the impact of business schools on organisations and on the global competitiveness of countries/regions.

The challenge of an interconnected, globalised world has led EFMD reflecting a more European style and model of management, to produce a manifesto (*The Future of Management Education*, 24 January 2012) of change that offers a framework of strategic options for management education in an increasingly complex, global environment.

It makes clear that, in contrast to the positioning of the dominant US business school model, management education should adopt a wider stakeholder purpose and address the needs of society more broadly. Thus, their source of legitimacy would involve educating students about the key skills and competencies for managing in society and not focusing narrowly on shareholder value and business interests.

This legitimacy would be achieved through five principles for addressing the key elements in a new approach to management education. These principles are (EFMD, 24 January 2012):

- Transformational change
  Business schools will have to change the way they operate. They should take a multiple stakeholder perspective in the design of their programmes and research activities. Schools should be transformed into moral institutions that perpetuate strong values, a clear vision and open processes in governance and strategic change.
- A more holistic approach to management education
  Business schools should incorporate a more integrated and liberal view of management education in which knowledge of the humanities, culture and history can be integrated into the principles of responsible management and form a framework for cross-disciplinary thinking. This implies that issues of ethics, moral responsibility and sustainability "should be embedded in the core curricula of management education as well as in the broader practices of schools".

- Sustainability
  "Sustainability, with its ecological, social and economic dimensions" requires those in management education to "carefully consider cultural and developmental differences when dealing with sustainability issues".
- Critical thinking and whole person learning
  Critical thinking must be designed to emerge from the tension between learning about humanistic principles and the more professional, analytic business subjects, such as accounting, finance and marketing. Students must learn how to absorb skills of both analysis and synthesis but also develop a personal willingness to reflect on issues and incorporate self-criticism into the learning process.
- Accreditations (such as EFMD Quality Improvement System)
  Accreditations must be updated to reflect the advent of multiple stakeholder perspectives and a more holistic approach to management education. They must also recognise that 75–80% of all business school students are participants in *undergraduate* programmes. The focus on the MBA by many business schools (largely because of MBA-based reputational media rankings) has diverted attention from undergraduate business education.

Colby Report Concerns

Anne Colby, author of an important study of undergraduate business education (*Rethinking Undergraduate Business Education: Liberal Learning for the Profession*, 2011; sponsored by the Carnegie Foundation

> Undergraduate business programmes are the largest undergraduate business major in both the UK and the US and, arguably, much more significant in the education of future managers than post-graduate programmes

and the Aspen Institute), also emphasises that undergraduate business programmes are the largest undergraduate business major in both the United Kingdom and the United States and, arguably, much more significant in the education of future managers than postgraduate programmes.

She believes, from a US perspective, that the liberal arts education tradition is in danger of being lost and usurped by a business school curriculum that has become too technical and narrowly instrumental.

While she sees the strengths of undergraduate business education in teaching analytical skills and substantive knowledge of the key business fundamentals such as accounting, finance, marketing, organisational behaviour, operations and strategy, she identifies a series of curricula weaknesses that make the application of analytical and business knowledge to management practices more difficult and problematic.

The weaknesses that she identifies are outlined in summary fashion as:

- while some teaching attention is focused on global perspectives, the treatment of globalisation is largely shallow and unsophisticated
- there is very little, if any, attention given to the effective teaching of how to handle ambiguity and complexity in business decision making
- while students absorb analytical and business concepts well, they apply them uncritically and treat them as objectives in themselves rather than as frameworks that can be used to develop an appropriate dialogue about strategic options and strategic choice
- more worrying is the fact that students are often taught not to question the underlying assumptions, or indeed the business reality, of the main business and economic models they are exposed to
- students were found to have a narrow focus and they stressed immediate instrumentality in their approach to education – jobs, careers and grades dominated their approach to different courses
- there was little curricular emphasis on the cultivation of ethical and moral dimensions. The nurturing of managerial judgement, managerial purpose and professional identity was noticeably absent
- students are not taught to think in an integrative fashion. Integrative thinkers (Dunne & Martin, 2006; Kelley & Littman, 2005) possess skills to evaluate and trade-off alternative strategic options in order to create viable strategic solutions to problems
- integrative thinking also requires skills of creativity, imagination and innovation, which are often overlooked in teaching. Students are not challenged to generate new ideas, to improve their problem-framing skills or their self-reflection on the meaning of problems and their ultimate solution
- there is a gap and a missing link that integrates humanities courses in history, arts and so on with the knowledge students gain from their business courses. Students see the relevance of business courses but are often very sceptical about the value of humanities courses

As Schoemaker (2008) and Khurana and Spender (2013) point out, the agenda of the Ford Foundation/Carnegie Foundation reports (Gordon/Howell, 1959; Pierson, 1959, on management education) was gradually hijacked over time so

Skills of analysis (the model of logical positivism) have been prioritised. This has been at the expense of skills necessary for managerial judgement and the process of managing organisational environments of increasing challenge, complexity and ambiguity

that skills of analysis (the model of logical positivism) have been prioritised. This has been at the expense of skills necessary for managerial judgement and the process of managing organisational environments of increasing challenge, complexity and ambiguity.

In summary, management education currently is clearly at a crossroads. Many of the observations made by AACSB, EFMD and the Colby Report point to a series of consistent weaknesses in the development of a range of managerial capabilities from creative, critical thinking to integrative problem-framing and solving that would enhance the basic knowledge of business and analytic skills.

Recent Books on the Strengths and Weaknesses of Management Education

This section focuses on the literature presented by an increasing number of eminent authors who follow similar themes in exploring the roots and pathways in the development of management education – its evolution, history, growth, curricula and associated problems.

The Evolution and History of Business Schools

The first group of authors – Khurana (2007), Locke, and Spender (2011), Augier and March (2011), and Starkey and Tiratsoo (2007) – concentrate primarily on the history and evolution of business schools. Khurana and Augier and March anchor their analysis and observations mainly on the US experience while Locke and Spender and Starkey and Tiratsoo take a somewhat broader and perhaps more global perspective (the latter, however, primarily from a UK perspective).

Khurana's (2007) book is an important and extremely thorough institutional, intellectual and social history of the growth of US business schools with a provocative title – *From Higher Aims to Hired Hands*.

As noted by Thomas, Lorange, and Sheth (2013), the original impetus for the business school arose from the perceived need of wealthy 19th-century US industrialists such as Joseph Wharton and Amos Tuck to legitimise management activity as respectable and meaningful – that is, the idea of management as a profession together with the simultaneous creation of a new industrial, socio-economic order.

To achieve their goals they advocated the creation of university-based management education and subsequently funded the Wharton School at the University of Pennsylvania and the Tuck School at Dartmouth College as pioneering university-based business schools at the end of the 19th and the beginning of the 20th centuries.

The weaknesses of this plan, however, were, first, the absence of an accepted management curriculum (knowledge base) and, second, hostility towards management as an appropriate subject by other university departments.

> **Khurana's argument is that there have been three phases in the evolution of American business school: the professionalisation phase, the managerialist phase and the marketisation/commercialist phase**

Indeed, Khurana notes the difficulties in the following quote (Khurana, 2007, p. 7): "The logic of professionalism that underlay the university-based business school in its formative phase was replaced first by a managerialist logic that emphasised professional knowledge rather than professional ideals, and ultimately by a market logic that, taken to its conclusion, subverts the logic of professionalism altogether."

Khurana's argument is that there have been three phases in the evolution of the American business school; namely, the professionalisation phase, the managerialist phase and the marketisation/commercialist phase.

In the professionalisation phase, the manager was conceptualised as having higher aims, such as developing professional norms and values, which encouraged both the attainment of personal profit and a duty to be socially responsible and ethical. The manager was seen as a professional steward of the firms' resources.

This phase, often labelled the "trade school" era (Thomas et al., 2013, p. 10), was more vocational in its orientation, with schools acting mainly as "teaching" schools (often operating simply at the undergraduate level) with a relatively small number of faculty producing research about management issues.

The vocational model was the dominant model until the Second World War. Indeed, many new business schools, using Harvard Business School, Tuck and Wharton as models, were founded in the United States in the first half of the 20th century. The founding of AACSB in 1916 as a professional body to promote business and business schools closely followed the growth of these new business schools (Thomas et al., 2013, p. 10).

The professionalisation phase suffered because the subject of management never achieved any lasting legitimacy or respect in the academic environment.

Consequently, foundations, such as those established by Ford and Carnegie, became interested in improving management education, particularly after the Second World War explosion of deep scientific approaches to management such as operations research.

The two foundations commissioned the Gordon and Howell (1959) and Pierson reports (1959). They recommended the establishment of a cohesive, broad-based business school curriculum and professional body of knowledge, which encouraged the intelligent and appropriate use of university disciplines such as economics, psychology, sociology and statistics but also stressed the importance of research, sometimes of an interdisciplinary character, in the management field.

This vision of a more "scientific", academic and research-backed management discipline was the beginning of the managerialist phase – managerial capitalism – in which the managers become the owners' "hired hands", operating mainly on the basis of contractual relationships.

In this environment the business schools emphasised "scientific research". New high-quality research-oriented journals, such as *Administrative Science Quarterly, Journal of Finance* and *Journal of Marketing*, were created to reinforce the "science of management" approach and encourage faculty to produce academic management research. In this process the more practical side of management and more applied, action-oriented research was largely crowded out of the business school environment.

In the third phase, shareholder capitalism is seen as the dominant purpose of schools and a great faith is placed in efficient markets and economic and financial fundamentals. This marketisation phase emphasises market logic, competition and the accretion of financial resources.

The academic writings of agency theorists, Jensen and

> **[Developing] a professional class of managers akin to doctors, lawyers or accountants, [requires] first, a real, accepted and meaningful body of knowledge about management; second, a consensus about managerial status and legitimacy; and third, an effective professional organisation that sets polices, managerial standards and appropriate examinations for final entry into the profession**

Meckling (1976) in economics, which treat managers as "agents", further diminished the scope of managerial autonomy, thus "subverting the logic of professionalism altogether" (Khurana; 2007, p. 7). But there are questions about whether the professionalisation project would ever have succeeded.

Is the purpose of a business school to develop a professional managerial caste? Clearly, in order to develop a professional class of managers, akin to doctors, lawyers or accountants, you need, first, a real, accepted and meaningful body of knowledge about management; second, a consensus about managerial status and legitimacy and third, an effective professional organisation that sets polices, managerial standards and appropriate examinations for final entry into the profession.

Arguably, management education has only achieved one of these – the body of knowledge criterion – and this is only based on the continued acceptance of management education models advocated by the Gordon/Howell and Pierson curriculum reports in the late 1950s/early 1960s.

These disrupted the vocational models of management education and set the course for the scientific, analytic business school model (often labelled logical positivism), which became the dominant design for the US business school in the second half of the 20th century.

Spender (2008, AMR, pp. 1022–1026) in a very insightful and positive review of Khurana's book finds fault with his analysis on two grounds. First, in its ethnocentric focus on American management education and business schools (see also Knights, AMR, 2008, p. 1021) and, second, in its treatment of the role of the university in the development of the university-based business school.

In the first case, he believes that there is insufficient attention and recognition given to the role of Europe in the evolution of the business school, with schools in France, Germany and the United Kingdom acting as catalysts.

> **The managerial transition from a role involving "higher aims" to that of "hired hands", i.e. the era of de-professionalisation has diminished and demoralised managers. Self-interest has replaced a proper ethical and moral compass and has resulted in a lack of trust in managerial actions**

For example, the role of the German "cameralist" schools of administration (who had a strong sense of duty to the German state) in the founding and creation of the early elite business schools in Chicago, Harvard and Wharton is not formally acknowledged. As Thomas et al. (2013) note, the founders of Harvard (Edwin Gay) and Wharton (Joseph Wharton) both visited Germany and closely studied the cameralist models of education in framing the conceptual base of their own schools.

In the second case, history shows that the universities themselves, and their presidents, used commercialisation and marketisation tactics and funded a significant proportion of university budgets from the growth of their business schools. Hence, they abandoned the professionalisation project – the search for higher goals – and used management education as a "cash cow" and a means to fund other departments and projects within their universities.

Khurana also emphasises that the managerial transition from a role involving "higher aims" to that of "hired hands", that is, the era of de-professionalisation (see also Thomas et al., 2013, p. 16), has diminished and demoralised managers. Self-interest has replaced a proper ethical and moral compass and has resulted in a lack of trust in managerial actions.

Augier and March (2011) provide an extremely scholarly and equally rich treatment of the evolution of US business schools in the post-war period.

Indeed, they regard the 1950s and 1960s as a "golden age" for business schools in which reinvention and restructuring of the business school model created a period of excitement and energy in elite US schools.

Augier and March (2011, p. 28) note that Herbert Simon, the Nobel Laureate and Professor at the Graduate School of Industrial Administration (GSIA) at Carnegie-Mellon University, described the state of business schools immediately after the Second World War as "wastelands of vocationalism". He described them as generally having weaker faculty, undemanding vocational syllabi and weaker students than those present in other university departments.

The 1950s were, therefore, a period when the leading business schools endorsed the view that well-thought out scientific, knowledge-based approaches could be applied to the solution of organisational problems.

For example, Augier and March point to the work of the RAND Corporation in demonstrating successfully how operations research and other analytic approaches could be applied to organisational problem solving.

In addition, the highly regarded interdisciplinary, scientifically oriented research work on management at the GSIA at Carnegie Tech (now Carnegie-Mellon University) was extremely influential. According to Augier and March (2011, p. 128), Carnegie Tech (with Richard Cyert, Jim March and Herbert Simon as key faculty members) became the "poster child for change" and an important model in the design of the curriculum for the new model of management education.

As already noted, the wealthy foundations such as Ford, Carnegie and Rockefeller stepped in to put some order and serious funding into these fast-changing, newly emergent business school environments

> The 1950s and 1960s saw business schools becoming strongly influenced by clear principles of academic scholarship and the adoption of serious academic disciplines in their curricula

(through programme investments in Carnegie, Chicago, Columbia, Harvard and Stanford). Indeed, as noted by Thomas et al. (2013, p. 7), Gordon and Howell (1959) and Pierson (1959) set a broad but challenging agenda for business schools.

"Gordon and Howell (who wrote the Ford report) advocated the study of all business operations and functions from a broad, integrated managerial perspective and championed education about the political, economic and social environment. They stressed analytical rigour and problem-solving ability, scientific method, research and knowledge creation and placed a strong emphasis on graduate education and doctoral education for business."

And: "Pierson's report further emphasised the scientific rigour element by endorsing the innovative quantitative methods (including statistics, simulation and operations research) of the GSIA at Carnegie Tech" (Thomas et al., 2013, p. 8).

Together these reports formulated a number of policy suggestions that led business schools to consider a more cohesive, research-grounded and academic model (perhaps with a discipline-led focus). As a consequence, the 1950s and 1960s saw business schools becoming strongly influenced by clear principles of academic scholarship and the adoption of serious academic disciplines in their curricula.

The educational philosophy of this US model (logical positivism (Grey, 2005)) involved analytic approaches, scientific rigour and discipline-focused scholarship. However, Khurana and Spender (2013) believe that the vision of broad intellectually robust and relevant research with an educational agenda of balanced academic excellence and effective interdisciplinary scholarship embedded in the Gordon and Howell framework has largely been hijacked by faculty publishing in narrow, discipline-defined, peer-reviewed A-journals in each of the management disciplines.

Augier and March (2011) also indicate that another objective of the 1950s/1960s reports was the attempt to create an autonomous body of knowledge for management education. Arguably, they may have succeeded in producing such a knowledge base. But with no socially regulated, institutional framework (as in law, medicine, engineering, accountancy and so on), they could not create a "profession" of management with a more trustworthy management cadre.

Augier and March (2011) believe that the energy of the 1950s and 1960s golden age did not result in a more balanced business school model. They feel that subsequent decades have revealed the limitations of logical positivism and have positioned business schools as more utilitarian and useful, instead of promoting a more balanced, liberal view of management education.

> **Manageralism (the creation of a managerial elite) and the managerialist phase in the evolution of the business school adopts the principles of modern capitalism in the separation of organisational ownership from managerial control**

They hope that a new business school model may result from closer exploration of the tensions between academic and experiential knowledge. And they yearn for a situation in which academic faculty produce rigorous, meaningful research and managers feel more motivated to read and apply that research, echoing the sentiments in Hambrick's (1994) article "What if the academy really mattered?".

Locke and Spender's (2011) book confronts one aspect of post-war changes in business schools by highlighting the advent of managerialism and "management mystique" in business schools. As noted earlier in the discussion of Khurana's book, manageralism (the creation of a managerial elite) and the managerialist phase in the evolution of the business school adopts the principles of modern capitalism in the separation of organisational ownership from managerial control.

From that viewpoint, organisations are now run by a managerial class (elite) on whom we depend for the effective performance of organisations.

Locke and Spender worry about how managerialism, with its emphasis on the analytic and quantitative culture embedded in neo-classical economics, can come to grips with the practical aspects of the organisational environment.

Indeed, as Thomas et al. (2013, p. 16) point out, Locke and Spender argue that "the business school focus on numbers, mathematical modelling and theories, and specifically those based on financial economics can lead to rational choices that ignore important issues of culture, managerial behaviour and ethics. They conclude that market capitalism has evolved into 'casino capitalism', largely absent of a moral and ethical compass, in which the lack of financial morality and ethical leadership partially fuelled the global economic crisis of 2008."

Interestingly, they also argue that managerialism is not only culpable in the 2008 crisis but, more importantly, in the decline of Western capitalism (the Anglo-American business school model) as it faces strong global challenge and competition in regions such as Asia.

Starkey and Tiratsoo (2007) concur with Locke and Spender's arguments and point out the evidence of rising levels of managerialism and commercialisation in the UK higher education environment, partially necessitated by the decline in government funding for education.

UK business schools have, therefore, been pressured more by market demand (and by the university administration's expectation of excess cash flow) than by offering a model of management education that presents the best insights from the academic world.

They contend that existing business school models − essentially adaptations of the logical positivist US "dominant design" for management education − fuelled both the corporate scandals of ENRON, PARMALAT and others and, through financial greed and ethical lapses, the global financial crisis of 2008.

While they do not offer a detailed history of the evolution of the UK business school, they nevertheless point out that UK business schools have lost their way since the "heady" days of change for UK business schools

> **In the 1960s-1980s, UK schools followed very closely the US-dominant design of logical positivism. Only in the last 25 years or so have they really acknowledged important contextual and cultural differences**

in the 1960s as they transitioned from more vocational schools of management to US-style business schools.

This was an era when reports on business schools and higher education (The Robbins report (1960) and the Franks report (1965)) heralded the creation of business schools in London (London Business School) and Manchester (Manchester Business School) within a university setting.

These schools were charged, in a similar fashion to the prescriptions offered by the Gordon/Howell and Pierson reports in the United States, to become more rigorous in research and teaching. The ultimate aim was to encourage the professionalisation of UK management at a time when the country was beset by a perceived lack of competitiveness relative to other major trading nations.

It is nowadays argued more coherently that business schools should mirror the societies in which they are created. However, in the 1960s–1980s, UK schools (London, Manchester, Warwick, Lancaster and others) followed very closely the US-dominant design of logical positivism. Only in the last 25 years or so have they really acknowledged important contextual and cultural differences and to favour the driving purpose of socially responsible capitalism and the adoption of strong linkages between business schools and business, government and society (Thomas et al., 2013, pp. 12–13).

This represents a more balanced and somewhat less analytically rigorous framework for management education, in which experiential learning and action-based and interdisciplinary research can thrive.

Starkey and Tiratsoo worry that the current business school model presents a business school dean with a range of different challenges beyond collegiate academic leadership and setting a clear strategic direction for a school. They depict the complexity and increasing commercialisation of the role of the business school dean over time (Fragueiro & Thomas, 2011, p. 9; Starkey & Tiratsoo, 2007, p. 55) in the following terms:

"Forty years ago running a business school was something that a senior professor might well take as a matter of duty shortly before retirement. Nowadays deans almost constitute a profession in their own right, a cohort with unique and specialist skills …. Deans may be likened to sports coaches, hired to improve performance, fired at will, but with one eye always on building their own careers …. The truth is that financial performance largely makes or breaks a dean's reputation."

However, Starkey and Tiratsoo (2007) share the same hope and vision for the business school as Augier and March (2011) in seeking to achieve a balance between academic research and practice. They favour a movement away from its current strategic positioning of being responsive to markets and adopting economic and financial models as underlying logic frameworks. They seek a shift towards the academy (and knowledge production) as critical and important for the revival of the business school:

"It is time for the business school to define what it stands for in a new way that will position it centrally in the evolving world of knowledge. Indeed, it is our contention that the business school must clearly live the principle that the business of the business school is knowledge" Starkey and Tiratsoo (2007, p. 211).

In summary, the historical reviews of business school evolution by Khurana, Augier and March, Locke and Spender and Starkey and Tiratsoo reveal disquiet about current business school models particularly in terms of purpose, context and culture and in achieving "balanced excellence" across the academic and practical fields involved in managing in public, private or voluntary organisations.

We now turn to an examination of key books on the reform of the management education curriculum.

Reform of Management Education

Henry Mintzberg (1973, 2004) is recognised as a deep thinker and scholar on management and management education. He has consistently criticised curricula and particularly the process and content of management education for many years (at least the last 30!).

His PhD thesis was "The Nature of Managerial Work" and this excellent study richly described what managers do and neatly catalogued the practice of management. Indeed, he argues that the majority of MBA programmes stress analytic approaches to the detriment of explaining the process of management including the role of context and the "soft skills" of managing such as engaging, sharing and facilitating the effectiveness of individuals in an organisation.

In his book *Managers not MBAs*, Mintzberg (2004) explains clearly that "I was simply finding too much of a disconnect between the practice of management that was becoming clearer to me and what went on in the classrooms" (2004, ii). In thoroughly reviewing the history of management education, he notes that particularly after the Gordon/Howell reports, "A 'dominant design' [for an MBA programme] established itself in the 1960s and continues to hold most of this education firmly in its grip" (2004, p. 6).

In this respect Khurana, Augier and March, Locke and Spender and Starkey and Tiratsoo would agree with Mintzberg's "dominant design" hypothesis and the urgent need for serious revision in models of management education, particularly the view of the MBA as management by analysis. Mintzberg notes, "The genius of the original GSIA was its work across the disciplines and functions" but this was hijacked by the discipline-focused MBA.

Mintzberg (2004, pp. 10–11) also argues that management is neither a science nor a profession in the following terms:

"Management is not even an applied science, for that is still a science. Management certainly applies science: managers have to use all the knowledge that they get, from the sciences and elsewhere. But management is more art, based on 'insight', 'vision', 'intuition' .... Put together a good deal of craft with a certain amount of art and some science, and you end up with a job that is above all a practice."

Further, in a discussion that management is not a profession (echoing Khurana's view of the early death of the professionalisation project in management education), he points out:

"Little of its practice has been reliably codified, let alone certified as to its effectiveness. So management cannot be called a profession or taught as such."

He believes that MBA programmes train people in the wrong ways with wrong consequences ultimately lending to "corruption of management practice".

Mintzberg's well-written book has three phases.

In the first, he berates MBA programmes for being trapped

> **Inevitably, Mintzberg's book is a manifesto preaching the necessity for change in management education**

by a "dominant design" and demonstrating little innovation in pedagogy and not much differentiation in approach.

In the second phase, he assesses the practice of management itself (and the important managerial "mindsets"), drawing on his book on managing managerial work as a background framework.

In the third phase, he outlines his own preferred postgraduate programme – the International Masters Program in Practicing Management (the IMPM) – which rests on the premise that MBAs should be restricted to practising managers only and indeed questions whether managers without experience can benefit from management education.

The implementation of the IMPM has involved a collaboration across a number of global management programmes, including McGill (Canada), Lancaster (United Kingdom), Renmin (China) and IIM Bangalore (India).

Inevitably, Mintzberg's book is a manifesto preaching the necessity for change in management education. Teaching management in discipline-related "silos" – the "dominant design" – in his view fails to deliver on principles of practice critical to integrated management education and puts the onus on students to fulfil the task of integrating their own learning.

Moldoveanu and Martin (2008) discuss the future of the MBA and their core belief that MBA graduates do not know how to think and act clearly. They also argue for the development of integrative thinking and they stress, following Mintzberg, that it must be a strong feature of the MBA curriculum. Thus, the focus is on developing the thinking styles and capacities of MBA students rather than on the explanation of a series of analytic tools and approaches.

Their vision is that senior managerial decision makers should be viewed as "integrators" who possess characteristics and skills of openness, clear reasoning, imaginative inquiry, reflection and possess problem-framing, mapping and solving capabilities.

This integrative thinking approach is at the core of their revised MBA programme at the Rotman School, University of Toronto, in Canada.

Three elements are included in this programme:

First, a focus, through two core courses, on integrative thinking, on challenging students to criticise and understand the assumptions and limitations of concepts, models and theories of management process.

Second, forcing students to recognise the complexity and multiple factors of business problems and to learn how to solve "messy" multi-disciplinary issues involving topics such as corporate citizenship, sustainability and demographic changes in ageing and health-associated polices.

Third, through exploration of principles of design thinking and innovation, encouraging student creativity and imagination in developing new and better approaches to handling complex business and organisational problems.

Hence, the overall aim is to produce a holistic student perspective on management (not a silo-oriented one) that will encourage the development of integrative thinkers who, in management careers, will be more likely to make decisions with integrity, reflection and an ethical and moral compass.

> **The overall aim is to produce a holistic student perspective on management (not a silo-oriented one) that will encourage the development of integrative thinkers who will be more likely to make decisions with integrity, reflection, and an ethical and moral compass**

Professors Datar, Garvin, and Cullen (2010) also focused on the limitation of the MBA programme in their book *Rethinking the MBA*. They review many of the current critiques and evaluations of MBA programmes and use these as an anchor for an ambitious and extensive study of the MBA involving interviews with deans, business and management leaders and an exhaustive review of MBA programmes at the Center for Creative Leadership, Chicago, Harvard, INSEAD, Stanford and Yale.

Their findings point to a series of important gaps that should be evaluated by schools in rethinking their programme curriculum. They focus on a series of promising innovations and changes to MBA programmes.

These include the following: gaining a global perspective; developing leadership skills; honing integrative skills; recognising organisational realities and implementing effectively; acting creatively and innovatively; thinking critically and communicating clearly; understanding the role, responsibilities and purpose of business and understanding the limitations of markets (particularly in different contexts, countries and cultures).

These gaps and needs are, however, only useful guidelines for action. Most MBA schools are still trying to determine how to plug these gaps and how to adapt their pedagogies in developing the "soft skills" of innovation, creativity and integrative thinking in their student bodies.

Datar et al. (2010) conclude that while there are strong similarities between MBA programmes, particularly in subject coverage and core curricula (reinforcing Mintzberg's observation that there has been little change in innovation and pedagogy in MBA programmes), there has nevertheless been some differentiation in MBAs relative to their programme structures, course sequencing, and programme requirements.

Santiago Iniguez (2011, pp. 52–54) argues that we are on a new learning curve in management education as we seek to reinvent its structure and content.

He highlights five trends shaping the new learning curve:

- increased global competition (and competitive differentiation) and commoditisation of standards for programmes (often mandated by accreditation agencies and media rankings)
- multi-polar competition (for example the growing number of multinational companies in emerging economies)
- consolidation of the era of university-based business schools
- hybridisation involving, for example, cross-disciplinary courses and building a balanced and integrated academic/clinical (or practice) faculty
- the need to achieve critical size and scale as evidenced by mergers and acquisitions (e.g. Aalto University in Finland, SKEMA in France and Henley/Reading in the United Kingdom) and closure of some management faculties.

Iniguez believes strongly (2011, pp. 180–181) that "education delivered at business schools can, and should, be a personal transformation process … two of the most promising avenues for deepening this transformation process are: first, the systematic training of management students in what might be called the 'managerial virtues', and, second, integrating the study of management and the humanities".

In summary, the focus of Mintzberg, Moldoveanu and Martin, Datar et al. and Iniguez has been largely on the redesign of the MBA. While they find common weaknesses in the overemphasis on analytic skills and the underemphasis on the

> While [commentators] find common weaknesses in the overemphasis on analytic skills and the underemphasis on the 'soft skills' of managing, they all recognise that there is now a lively debate about adapting to changing environments and expectations

"soft skills" of managing, they all recognise that there is now a lively debate about adapting to changing environments and expectations.

In addition, despite Colby's (2011) impressive work on rethinking undergraduate management education, it is surprising that relatively less attention has been devoted to reassessing undergraduate management programmes despite the fact that they typically represent 75–80% of business school activity.

Interestingly, many of the critiques of MBA programmes can be found in the list of strengths and weaknesses of current undergraduate management programmes found in the Colby report.

Addressing the Gaps in Specific Skills in Management Programmes

Specific Skill Gaps

Common to all the critiques of MBA and undergraduate management programmes is a plea to address the specific skill gaps — often about so-called "soft skills" — in existing programmes. Khurana and Spender (2013) ask "What skills do MBA students really need?" The aim of the critics is to influence the balance between the academic skills of analysis and scientific rigour and more practical skills in order to develop a more holistically trained, integrated and rounded management graduate.

Typically problems occur in addressing the following questions:

- Can creativity and innovative thinking be taught?
- Is leadership too innate a concept to be taught? Are management and leadership the same thing?
- Can ethical and moral perspectives be taught effectively?
- How can critical thinking and skills of reflection and integration be introduced?
- Can a management curriculum teach skills in cognitive and emotional intelligence?

According to Robinson (2011), creativity is at the heart of all the work we do. It is important to get individuals (in our case management students) to recognise the extent of their creative abilities and to break out of cultures of standardisation and conformity.

Robinson notes, however, that creativity and imagination are not the same. While imagination is about bringing into an individual's mind things and issues not immediately sensed by them, creativity involves doing something about that imagination. It is in that sense that he conceives of creativity as "applied imagination" and as the process of creating original ideas that have value.

Robinson argues (2011, p. 41) that business in the 21st century operates in a fast-changing economic and technological environment with an ever-present need for adaptation and change. For example, he regards changing environments, such as e-commerce and the Internet, as stimuli that can release the imagination and creativity of individuals:

"The evolution of the internet has been driven not only by innovations in technology but also by unleashing the imaginations and appetites of millions of users, which in turn are driving further innovations in technology."

He goes on to say:

"We can't predict the future. But some things we do know. One is that the nature of work will continue to change for very many people ... The emergence of e-commerce and internet trading in the 1980s swept away long-established ways of doing business."

As a consequence, new industries (such as the creative sector) and job opportunities have emerged globally in not only the financial sector but also the intellectual property sector. Robinson (2011, p. 43) points out that:

"The creative industries ... include advertising, architecture, arts and antiques, crafts, design, fashion, film, leisure software, music, performing arts, publishing, software and computer services, television and radio. The intellectual property sector is even more significant when patents from service and technology are included ... The creative industries are labour intensive and need many different types of specialist skill."

All of these changes can only happen if diversity and a readiness to innovate are embraced in organisations. Indeed, organisations need diversity in groups and design teams so that through collaboration and sharing ideas, differences in viewpoints or opinions become strengths not weaknesses.

Robinson believes that diversity and diverse perspectives generate a dynamism, which is a strength because creativity cannot simply be turned on like a light switch. Often, human

> **Business schools must foster the development of unstructured learning as a route to teaching skills in creativity, reflection and imagination**

talent is buried beneath the surface in organisational contexts and the creative spark must be tapped to unlock the non-linear pulse of human achievement.

From an educational viewpoint, it suggests that business schools must foster the development of unstructured learning as a route to teaching skills in creativity, reflection and imagination. In such an environment, perhaps 50% of the time would be spent in classroom sessions and 50% directed towards group projects, self-generated studies, and approaches such as brainstorming and lateral thinking.

Studying creative people such as architects is also a viable option. The book *Conceptual Blockbusting* (Adams, 2001) by Stanford architecture professor James Adams, unearths the skills of imagination, creativity and problem-framing necessary to design space for an individual or organisational living environment.

The connection between creativity and innovation is clear – innovation is about putting good ideas into practice and in that sense, may be considered "applied creativity". A necessary condition for innovativeness is an organisational context that promotes a culture of innovation.

Tom Kelley's books *The Art of Innovation* (Kelley & Littman, 2004) and *The Ten Faces of Innovation* (Kelley & Littman, 2005) together with Tim Brown's *Change by Design* (2009) map the work of the IDEO frameworks for innovation. (IDEO is regarded as one of the best design and innovation consulting companies.)

Both Brown and Kelley stress that a culture of organisational innovation is essential for driving creativity through an organisation. IDEO's work is built around its five-step innovation methodology:

- understand the market, the client, the technology and the perceived constraints on the given problem
- observe real people in real-life situations
- literally visualise new-to-the-world concepts and the customers who will use them
- evaluate and refine the prototypes in a series of quick iterations
- implement the new concept for commercialisation

But Kelley stresses that "innovation is a team sport" and a winning team requires the kind of diversity that Robinson also stresses.

Design thinking is also premised on the idea of a collaborative, interdisciplinary team of skilled individuals from diverse personal, cultural and emotional/cultural intelligence backgrounds.

Design thinking is also premised on the idea of a collaborative, interdisciplinary team of skilled individuals from diverse personal, cultural and emotional/cultural intelligence backgrounds

Kelley's ten faces of innovation lay out the characteristics of the ten types of individuals who can bring their diverse talents to a winning team.

As Robinson states (2011, pp. 235−236), "Creative teams are dynamic. Bringing people together is no guarantee of creative work ... Collaboration is at the heart of (Pixar's) creative process ... The purpose of collaboration is to benefit from the stimulation of each other's expertise."

However, Kelley and Brown stress that creativity takes time and that innovation − the creative implementation leap − is the single, most decisive organisational competitive advantage. How then can innovation thinking, and blended learning approaches, be taught in business schools?

Implications of Innovation for Educational Pedagogy

Christensen has written extensively about innovation and competitive advantage beginning with his book the *Innovator's Dilemma* (2000, first edition; 2011, paperback edition). In two more recent books, *Disrupting Class* (Christensen, Horn and Johnson, 2008) and *The Innovative University* (Christensen and Eyring, 2011), Christensen and colleagues discuss how higher education can adjust to disruptive technologies such as e-learning by re-engineering their institutional practices and structures.

Wessel and Christensen (*Harvard Business Review*, December 2012, pp. 56−64) note that disruption is not so much a single event as it is "a process that plays out over time" and for an organisation to survive a disruption with a sound strategic response, it needs to:

- Identify the strengths of the disruptor's business model
- Identify the organisation's relative advantages
- Evaluate the conditions that would help or hinder the disruption from co-opting your current advantages in the future

"To guide you in determining a disrupter's strengths, we introduce the concept of the extendable core − the aspect of its business model that allows the disruptor to maintain its performance advantage as it creeps upmarket in search of more and more customers."

They point out that "not all the advantages of a disruptor's extendable core are so overpowering; often they are offset by disadvantages" (2012, p. 59).

In the context of business schools, the current disruption is the onset of online, e-learning universities such as Apollo Group's University of Phoenix, which can grant degrees at lower cost than conventional university-based business schools.

While the initial value of such offerings was suspect they have improved the quality of their product while reinforcing their core advantages of lower cost and convenience. Wessel and Christensen (2012, p. 59) offer two cases in which these core advantages cannot be extended to overcome the relative advantages of high quality face-to-face learning.

> By gaining entry to, and graduating from, a highly reputable elite business school, a student might expect to obtain career placement in a leading organisation much more frequently than a graduate of an online university

The first case involves prestige and status. By gaining entry to, and graduating from, a highly reputable elite business school, a student might expect to obtain career placement in a leading organisation much more frequently than a graduate of an online university.

In the second case, the important factor for some students is the face-to-face learning environment whose social aspects – networking, interaction with peers, living away from home and proximity to faculty and business gurus – are seen as much richer and more rewarding than an online offering.

Some business schools – Warwick and Henley in the United Kingdom, the University of North Carolina in the United States and Instituto de Empresa in Spain (Iniguez, 2011) – have developed highly successful and well-regarded online, distance learning programmes. The United Kingdom's Open University Business School and Dean Iniguez's school in Madrid have developed hybrid blended learning programmes that seek to mix the advantages of distance and face-to-face learning.

But in this situation we have yet to observe the creation of sustainable alliances and partnerships between purely online universities and traditional university-based business schools. This may happen in the future but it is likely that the online learning disruptor's "extendable core" will not be sufficient to attract students who value face-to-face learning and the socialisation and prestige of attending a business school with a strong reputation and brand image.

The evidence to date shows that none of the "disruptors" has achieved a position in the reputational ranking of the Top 100 Global MBA programmes produced annually by the *Financial Times*.

The problem with business schools is that the disruptive innovation of technology-based learning is challenged by the inertia, conservatism and lack of willingness to change exhibited by both faculty and university-level administrators. Online learning is very often characterised as low-quality, second-rate learning relative to the "dominant model" of face-to-face high-quality instruction (Thomas & Thomas, 2012).

Christensen, Horn, and Johnson (2008) offer an explanation of this behaviour:

"In the language of disruption, here is what this means: unless top managers actively manage this process, their organisation will shape every disruptive innovation into a sustaining innovation – one that fits the processes, values, and economic model of the existing business – because organizations cannot naturally disrupt themselves."

This explains why both the IDEO consultants and Professor Robinson stress the importance of leadership in innovation and the development of a culture of organisational innovation led by those at the top. Leaders must understand the different elements of innovatory leadership and build a holistic mindset of change in which collaboration and a sense of vision/ direction and the future are clear to the individuals in the organisation.

Leadership and Innovations in Business Schools

How can business school leaders (deans) promote creativity, imagination and leadership in their staff and faculty colleagues? Their skills and capabilities can clearly be the catalysts for change and the impetus to persuade faculty colleagues to concentrate on addressing specific gaps in their management programmes. But what are the critical characteristics and skills that make a successful dean?

Surprisingly there are relatively few studies of the leadership characteristics and leadership styles of (exceptions are Davies & Thomas, 2009; Fragueiro & Thomas, 2011; Thomas & Thomas, 2011). Leadership in a business school context offers a series of significant challenges outlined by Lorange (2008), Mintzberg (1998), Fragueiro and Thomas (2011) and Thomas et al. (2013).

In particular, Mintzberg regards skills of imagination and creativity as critical. His metaphor of the leader as an "orchestral conductor" suggests a covert form of leadership that preserves individual autonomy and critical debate (Thomas et al., 2013, p. 151).

With this type of leader, innovation and insight are complemented by personal characteristics such as self-awareness, confidence, motivation, empathy, social skills and intuition (Thomas et al., 2013). These cognitive and emotional skills are necessary in order to cope with a range of tasks from politician and strategist to implementer and human capital manager.

Indeed, in business schools, contextual intelligence (Nye, 2008) is extremely important for both graduates and school leaders. Contextual intelligence means that individuals must possess a clear understanding of the changing environment and an ability to capitalise on emerging trends in management education – in short, effective business school leadership requires an understanding of the internal context of the business school and the university and the external context of multiple stakeholders such as business, media and governments.

That context is characterised by Crainer and Dearlove (1998) as schizophrenic – business school deans must operate their schools in a strong academic manner but simultaneously generate knowledge that can solve

> **Contextual intelligence means that individuals must possess a clear understanding of the changing environment and an ability to capitalize on emerging trends in management education**

the current practical problems in management and themselves operate their schools in a business-like fashion.

As Thomas et al., (2013, p. 154) note:

"This creates two general consequences. First, deans (leaders) are often unwilling to upset the basis of their existing revenue streams. Second, the rift between management edu-

> **Relatively few deans have the courage, determination and time to achieve path-breaking and path-bending leadership for their schools**

cation and management practice is exacerbated as faculty stress rigorous academic research rather than more practically oriented research: management education, and deans, are trailing behind in influencing management practice rather than taking an action and positive stance in shaping it."

Therefore, a leadership dilemma for deans is how to balance the twin hurdles of rigour and relevance (Pettigrew, 1997). Other problems result from attempting to handle the pluralism, inertia and conservatism that is endemic in academic cultures (Clark, 1998; Fragueiro & Thomas, 2011, pp. 10–11).

Davies and Thomas (2009) note that deans have variously been described as "jugglers", "dictators", "doves of peace" and "dragons", highlighting the stressful and multifaceted roles that they often have to play in a time-pressured and somewhat bureaucratic university environment.

It is not surprising that there is an unwillingness on the part of deans (who often have short tenures) to take risks and to be courageous enough to embrace change. More often, they will opt for minor, incremental changes to their existing approaches and programme offerings even if it is abundantly clear that instruction in "soft" skills, cultural, global and emotional intelligence should be added to their programmes.

Relatively few deans, however, have the courage, determination and time to achieve path-breaking and path-bending leadership for their schools. Leaders such as Borges at INSEAD, Bain at London Business School and Lorange at IMD exhibit the characteristics of strong, resilient leaders (Fragueiro & Thomas, 2011, pp. 199–203):

"For instance, Bain spent six months talking with everyone with some influence on the school's strategic agenda before he actually assumed the LBS deanship. This dedicated effort transferred into a significant asset when he set out to define and raise support around LBS's strategic deadlines. Based on his experience, leadership 'is more about having good ears than a good mouth' " (Fragueiro & Thomas, 2011, p. 199).

Equally important in inspiring a business school's progress were Antonio Borges' strategic programme at INSEAD:

"Especially revealing were Borges' breakthrough initiatives at INSEAD: his drive to turn the school into a research-oriented institution – when most faculty had a different background – and his bold initiative to open a new campus in Singapore in order to globalise the school ... Borges' ability to sell his initiatives to key faculty and board members, effectively engaging them as initiative sponsors, made it possible for INSEAD to overcome a multitude of obstacles and difficulties in both pursuits" (Fragueiro & Thomas, 2011, pp. 199–200).

Lorange's success in transforming IMD following the IMEDE–IMI merger is another good example of a strong, resilient President in action:

"Over his 15-year tenure as IMD's president, Lorange forged an organisational transformation that could only be brought about with unequivocal decision-making power. Moreover, Lorange believed that deans are not only meant to determine a school's strategic focus but that they should also decide which pathways are more effective in order to pursue that goal" (Fragueiro & Thomas, 2011, p. 203).

Lorange (2010, p. 63) also discusses a number of essential leadership characteristics, namely, integrity, agility, a broad stakeholder focus and pragmatic optimism. Manfred Kets de Vries also (2006, p. 263) suggests hope, harmony, humility and humour whereas Collins (2001) offers a "paradoxical combination of personal humility and professional will".

All of these direct our attention to the role of integrity, responsibility, humility and an ethical and moral compass in managing a business, or even a business school, effectively for the benefit of all stakeholders.

Prior to the financial crisis of 2008, Ghoshal (2005) pointed out the dangers of a lack of morality in business schools and charged business schools for undermining business practice through teaching "amoral" theories. Locke and Spender, following the financial crisis, concluded that the lack of ethical leadership – absent from serious consideration in business school curricula – had partially contributed to the crisis (Thomas et al., 2013, p. 16). Fragueiro and Thomas (2011, pp. 3–6) also charted the growth of the treatment of ethical issues in business school debates following the crisis.

They point out changes in both students and faculty in recognising the need for a stronger purpose and set of ethical values in their lives and careers. From a student viewpoint:

"Rather than having an image as 'resilient wreckers' who wreaked such havoc over the last two years (*The Economist*, 2009), MBA students are jumping aboard a campaign to turn management into a formal profession (*The Economist*, 2009; Khurana & Nohria, 2008). Recently a large group of Harvard's second-year students promoted an oath before their graduation to 'serve the greater good', 'act with the utmost integrity' 'and guard against'... 'decisions that advance my own narrow ambitions, but harm the enterprise and the societies it services'" Fragueiro and Thomas (2011, p. 5).

> **It is clear that deans and faculty are focusing much more on updating their courses on ethics, business, and society so that they stress the importance of the multiple stakeholders in society**

It is clear that deans and faculty are focusing much more on updating their courses on ethics, business and society so that they stress the importance of the multiple stakeholders in society.

They emphasise the following issues:

- long-term value creation not short-term
- leadership and corporate responsibility
- compensation systems and their impact on short- and long-term value creation
- a broad and "systemic" perception of risk
- corporate governance, board composition and responsibilities
- an awareness of shareholders' rights and obligations as ultimate company owners

(Fragueiro & Thomas, 2011, p. 5).

However, there is very little agreement on how ethics should be taught (Millar & Poole, 2010).

As noted in Thomas et al. (2013, p. 17), business school leaders also have to recognise the importance of catering more significantly to the needs of a wide range of stakeholders including society at large, business, government, students and employers.

This perspective calls for a more balanced relationship between business schools and business, government and society — this means that business schools need to reassert their influence and focus in the education process to satisfy the diverse interests of their stakeholders.

Recently, Muff et al. (2013) proposed the development of a more balanced business school curriculum organised around the so-called "triple bottom line" and derived from the philosophy of a socially responsible, social democratic form of capitalism (i.e. developing leaders who will make businesses more socially responsible and sustainable).

They argue that the underlying philosophy in most curricula today is that the sole purpose of

> **How should the business school develop and adapt to changing contexts and situations? What is the new framework with respect to its positioning and in designing the future evolution of management knowledge?**

a firm is to maximise shareholder wealth, which can lead to the creation of amoral business leaders who thrive on implementing "casino capitalism".

Current Views on the Future of Business Schools

The foregoing naturally leads to the question of where the business school and its curriculum should go in the future. How should it develop and adapt to changing contexts and situations? What is the new framework for the business school with respect to its positioning and in designing the future evolution of management knowledge?

Current suggestions and scenarios for change tend to follow Cheit's (1985) categorisation of business school models as either professional or academic.

For professional schools, the most commonly suggested options are either to mimic schools such as medicine and law (Khurana, 2007) or adopt a pragmatic, consultancy-oriented model more commonly found in applied management schools.

In the former case, the curriculum would emphasis subjects such as law, economics, politics, psychology and sociology with less emphasis on others such as marketing and operations management.

The latter case would be based on practitioner/academic networks that would become dedicated to helping address managerially defined problems through action-based, experiential learning and project-based activities.

Academic models currently include those grounded in theoretical social science approaches (such as Chicago); those following a liberal management education agenda advocated by Drucker (1974), Mintzberg (2004) and Colby, Ehrlich, Sullivan, and Dolle (2011), (SMU, McGill); and those oriented towards innovation and a knowledge economy agenda (The Rady School at UC San Diego).

More radical remodelling agendas include the *agora* model of Starkey and Tiratsoo (2007), which argues that the business school should provide a forum and a cultural focus, a centre of political, commercial, social and philosophical activity similar to that proposed by Colby et al. (2011) and Muff et al. (2013).

Durand and Dameron (2008) offer a range of "foresight" scenarios, from shake-out and decline, and the merger of business schools, to the disruption of the value chain of existing business schools by strong competition from online providers such as the University of Phoenix.

Thomas et al. (2013) and Peters and Thomas (2011) believe that some existing business school models are too luxurious and financially unsustainable. They argue that scenarios based either on strategies of drift or "muddling through" or of operating business schools as "cash cows" for university presidents are generally unacceptable.

Summary and Conclusions

The general judgement from all of these books and other literature is that the current dominant business school model must be reevaluated. The business school is perceived to be under threat and at a "turning point" in terms of its future evolution.

The significant criticisms of business schools include the following (Thomas et al., 2013, pp. 66–68):

- the business school lacks identity and legitimacy in the modern university and society in general (Wilson & Thomas, 2012)
- the business school is a socialisation mechanism (Grey, 2005) – a business school is a necessary rite of passage for senior management and more a "finishing school" than an intellectual, liberal-thinking cauldron of activity
- the business school overemphasises shareholder capitalism and does not embrace models of stakeholder capitalism (Locke & Spender, 2011; Muff et al., 2013)
- the business school does not provide a clear sense of purpose, morality and ethics with respect to its role in society (Colby et al., 2011; Ghoshal, 2005; Millar & Poole, 2010)
- the business school focuses on analytics/scientific rigour at the expense of developing wisdom, interpersonal and leadership/managerial skills (Bennis & O'Toole, 2005; Mintzberg, 2004; Schoemaker, 2008)
- the business school produces self-referential research that is seen as irrelevant (Hambrick, 1994; Pfeffer & Fong, 2002, 2004)
- the business school embraces scientific rigour at the expense of other forms of knowledge (Schoemaker, 2008; Thomas & Wilson, 2011)
- the business school has pandered to business school rankings and has become too responsive to the consumer voice (Khurana, 2007)

In addition, Dean Canals of IESE Business School (2011) more recently offered a series of observations on the purposes of the business school. He identified a series of crises (Thomas et al., 2013, pp. 15–16):

- the business school's role in the ethical and moral crisis of scandals such as ENRON and the financial crisis
- the need to take globalisation seriously
- the relationships between the dean and the university and the dean and the faculty

- the sustainability of business models and funding sources
- the perception of the increasing irrelevance of business school research
- the search for stakeholder capitalism and the definition of senior managers' roles and responsibilities in society

Business schools, overall, are seen as competitive rather than cooperative, complacent, conservative, risk averse, resistant to change and lacking in relevance to business.

What then do our experts (see the appendix for a list of those interviewed) feel about the future of management education?

As in Volume 1, the research evidence for this volume is based on as series of 39, two to three hour semi-structured interviews undertaken with experts in the field of management education. Their views have been analysed both intuitively and using quantitative approaches such as N-VIVO analysis to identify key themes, issues and challenges.

The rest of this volume uses insights about the successes and failures of business schools outlined in this chapter and in Volume I (Thomas et al., 2013) as a background for the exploration and evaluation of alternative business school futures.

Volume II, therefore, focuses on future trends and directions for meaningful growth of management education. The plan for Volume II is:

Chapter 2 examines the lessons not learned in management education.
Chapter 3 explores the on-going challenges in management education.
Chapter 4 outlines a set of future scenarios for management education.
Chapter 5 offers a series of conjectures about future patterns and themes in management education.
Chapter 6 explores the "tipping points", blind spots and critical issues for the future. It examines the importance of these issues for change in management education.
Chapter 7 discusses change and the future role and positioning of management education. It also addresses EFMD's future global role in management education.

Appendix

List of Respondents (in Alphabetical Order)

Name	Title
Christoph Badelt	Rector, WU (Vienna), Austria
George Bickerstaffe	Consultant Editor, Global Focus, UK and founder editor of Which MBA, Economist, UK
Della Bradshaw	Management Editor, Financial Times, UK
Jordi Canals	Dean, IESE, Barcelona, Spain
Carlos Cavalle	Entrepreneur and Former Dean, IESE, Barcelona, Spain
Dan Le Clair	COO, AACSB International, USA
Eric Cornuel	Director General and CEO, EFMD, Brussels, Belgium
Sue Cox	Dean, Lancaster University Management School, UK
Rolf Cremer	President, European Business School, Frankfurt and Former Dean, CEIBS Business School, Shanghai, China
Arnoud de Meyer	President, Singapore Management University, Singapore and formerly Deputy Dean, INSEAD, France
John Fernandes	President and CEO, AACSB International, USA
James Fleck	Dean, Open University Business School, UK
Thierry Grange	Dean, Grenoble Ecole Du Management, France
Chris Greensted	Associate Director, Quality Services, EFMD, UK
Jim Herbolich	Director, Network Services, EFMD (Deceased)
Frank Horwitz	Director, Cranfield Business School, UK (Formerly Dean, South Africa)
Mike Jones	Director, Foundation for Management Education, UK
John Kraft	Dean, University of Florida, USA
Peter Lorange	President, Lorange Institute of Business, Zurich, Switzerland
Xavier Mendoza	Deputy Director, ESADE, Barcelona, Spain
Dave Montgomery	Distinguished Professor of Marketing, Stanford University, CA, USA
Michel Patry	President, HEC Montreal, Quebec, Canada

Appendix. (*Continued*)

Name	Title
Kai Peters	CEO, Ashridge Management College, UK
John Peters	Senior Partner, GSE Research, UK
Liliana Petrella	EFMD, Brussels, Belgium
Martine Plompen	Associate Director, Research & Surveys Unit, EFMD, Brussels
Bill Russell	Director of Marketing, Emerald Publishing, UK
Thomas Sattleberger	Board Member, Lufthansa, Germany
David Saunders	Dean, Queens University Business School, Ontario, Canada
Julio Urgel	Director, Quality Services, EFMD, Brussels, Belgium
Ray Van Schaik	Honorary President, EFMD, Brussels; Retired CEO, Heineken
Stephen Watson	European Representative, AACSB International, Cambridge University, UK
	Formerly Director of Judge Business School, Cambridge University
Robin Wensley	Professor of Management, Warwick Business School and Director of Advanced Institute of Management (AIM), UK
Greg Whittred	Dean, University of Auckland Business School, NZ
David Wilson	President and CEO, GMAC, USA
David Wilson	Warwick Business School and University of Warwick, Head of Sociology, UK
Zihong Yi	Dean, Renmin University Business School, China
Phil Zerillo	Professor, SMU and Chairman of Advisory Board of MIM, Thammasat University, Thailand

Chapter 2

Lessons Not Learned in Management Education

Introduction

Chapter 1 and Volume 1 of this study (Thomas et al., 2013) outline the extensive series of debates, discussions and viewpoints about business schools. Mostly it's criticism.

Schools have been criticised for their failure to establish business and management as a legitimate academic discipline (Bennis & O'Toole, 2005; Nussbaum, 1997); for their role in de-professionalising management and promoting managers as "hired hands" lacking ethical standards (Khurana, 2007); for the increasing gulf between business academics and academic rigour and managers and professional management practice (Podolny, 2009); and also for their lack of innovation in exploring the management process and improving the teaching of management (Mintzberg, 2004).

Dominant themes of concern were the lack of innovation and relevance in business schools. In particular the comments about the need for innovation made by two prominent strategy researchers, Gary Hamel and C. K. Prahalad are important and deserve to be examined closely.

They point out: "as we look to the future, we have to consider a totally new way of looking at competition" (Hamel, 1996, p. 113), which will require "a radical rethinking of current management paradigms" (Prahalad, 1996, p. 109).

Indeed, Hamel argues: "What we continue to teach in the business schools is a little bit like being a mapmaker in an earthquake zone. Never before has the gap between our tools and the reality of emerging industry been larger" (Hamel, 1996, p. 113).

> [Hamel] notes that organisations are moving from "command and control" traditional, bureaucratic management forms to more democratic and innovative cultures in which all employees are empowered to express their ideas and recipes for change

More recently, Bisoux (2008), in an interview with Hamel, discusses the "innovation generation" following the publication of Hamel's books on leading the revolution and the future of management (Hamel, 2000; Hamel & Breen, 2007). Hamel provides clear prescriptions about how business schools should adapt to the much more innovative and fast-paced environment of the 21st century.

In discussing the future of management he notes that organisations are moving from "command and control" traditional, bureaucratic management forms to more democratic and innovative cultures in which all employees are empowered to express their ideas and recipes for change.

However, some managers and organisations may exhibit inertia, focusing on the *status quo* and resist changes to their traditional hierarchical, power-oriented governance structures. However, the realities of the new knowledge-based economy means that the current generation — students, faculty and managers — has grown up with the internet, is comfortable with technology and readily accepts new ideas alongside innovation and knowledge as the drivers for change in the global economy.

Business schools, therefore, will have to work better, and more closely, with this innovation generation and adapt their strategies to the reality of the marketplace.

Hamel advises that they should focus on the following themes:

- innovative reinvention
- research conduct
- relevance
- closeness to management

Business Schools Must Reinvent Themselves

Hamel states (Bisoux, 2008, p. 22) that "any field — whether it's medicine, engineering or business — can become stuck in a paradigm trap over time. Everybody's been trained the same way. They think the same way and they take the same things for granted. I think that's where management is today. Business faculty needs to be very conscious of the inherited dogmas that may underlie their views."

In confronting reinvention, the views of Handy (1996), Mintzberg (2004), Tyson (2005) and several of our respondents reinforce the problems of paradigm trap — in particular, the dominance in management education, and particularly MBA programmes, of an obsolete business school model with outdated textbooks and case studies largely reflecting past experiences.

One respondent questioned the generic "me-too" models of MBA education:

"I asked the MBA directors of the top 100 schools on the
Financial Times list how much of the content in their MBA
is from their own faculty and how much is just generic. And
the response was that 90% of it was generic ... there isn't
massive differentiation."

These observations are reinforced by Datar et al. (2010) in their extensive review of MBA programmes. Mintzberg (2004), as noted in Chapter 1,
clearly believes that MBA education is in the grip of a dominant design —
the US logical positivist model — exhibiting little differentiation. It stresses
knowledge of analytic approaches but only scratches the surface of the process of managing and often shows little innovation in the pedagogy of
instruction.

Handy (1996, p. 11) embraces
the idea of a liberal management
education (a viewpoint that is
also echoed by Colby, Ehrlich,
Sullivan, and Dolle (2011) in
the context of undergraduate
business education). He believes

> **Handy embraces the idea of a
> liberal management education ...
> He believes that more time should
> be spent in studying liberal arts and
> less on the more formulaic core and
> specialisation aspects of management**

that more time should be spent in studying liberal arts and less on the more
formulaic core and specialisation aspects of management (Thomas et al.,
2013, p. 28).

As a counterpoint, Laura Tyson (2005, p. 235) argues that business
schools can reinvent themselves:

"I take issue with Professor Mintzberg. The liveliness of the
debate surrounding business schools has long been matched
by the ability of business schools to adjust to changed circumstances and expectations. Like any organisation in a
highly competitive marketplace, business schools are adept at
reinvention."

The question here is whether Tyson's view of change and reinvention
approximates to incremental or sustaining innovation rather than the more
radical or disruptive innovation involving new business models and paradigms as advocated by Hamel (2000), Hamel and Breen (2007), and
Christensen and Eyring (2011). Christensen and Eyring's book on the innovative university addresses the impacts of disruptive e-learning technologies
on teaching pedagogy and research. Both scholars point out that when inertia exists faculty will tend to make incremental rather than radical changes
in their research and teaching processes.

Business Schools and Research Conduct

Hamel believes strongly in the roles that innovation cultures and new processes of idea generation can have in creative debates about future approaches in business schools. He questions whether many people in business schools are asking: "What's the next great breakthrough in management?" (Bisoux, 2008, p. 22)

He challenges business school academics to become more engaged with managers in order to understand their practical problems and thus provide more meaningful theoretical insights and problem solutions. He argues that "deep experimental collaboration between scholars and practitioners is the norm in other professional schools, but it's rare in business schools" (Bisoux, 2008, p. 22).

However, there are notable exceptions. He notes that the dogged pursuit of knowledge through extensive, and determined, exploration with managers was the catalyst that led to "W. Edwards Deming launching the quality movement, Bob Kaplan the balanced scorecard, and Peter Senge founding the Society for Organisational Learning" (Bisoux, 2008, p. 22).

You could easily add the names of Hamel and Prahalad to that list since, through their extensive experience of strategy consulting, they pioneered the concept of the leveraging of core competences as one of the key elements in achieving long-term sustainable competitive advantage for organisations.

But what did it take for academics like Deming, Hamel, Prahalad, Kaplan and others such as Tom Peters, Michael Porter and James Collins to produce path-breaking innovations in the management field?

Certainly, enabling conditions were a curiosity about management problems and practices and a willingness to engage in strong and meaningful collaborations with managers and organisations.

More importantly, these academics broke out of the culture of complacency and inertia endemic in management education and explored the ideas and innovations that will change business schools and managers in the future.

Hamel endorses this view particularly focusing on the ways in which business school faculty must change: "To fulfil our potential as innovators and inventors, we have be willing to look beyond today's best practices and commit ourselves to making a difference in organisations" (Bisoux, 2008, p. 24).

Sadly, the number of business school academics who engage in deep collaborations with manager and management practice is far fewer than those who write theory-based articles in the so-called academic "A-journals" of the business and management field

Sadly, the number of business school academics who engage in deep collaborations with managers and management practice is far fewer than those who write theory-based articles in the so-called business and management academic "A-journals". Typically these theoretical journals have relatively few insights about sound ideas and practice. Consequently, it is unlikely that those practitioners who are willing to experiment with new ideas and practices will build a dialogue with many of the existing faculty in business schools.

Hamel characterises the behaviour and orientation of business school academics as follows:

> "Few faculty see themselves as experimental scientists. They study best practices as they currently exist. They share those practices but they don't see themselves as active participants who are really affecting the future of management practice."

Birkinshaw and Mol (2006) reinforce this view in noting that few, if any, management innovations have their genesis in business school research.

Business Schools and More Innovative Graduates

Business school academics are not embedded in practice as are academics in medicine, law or engineering. As a result it is argued that they are less likely to produce new management innovations, are not heavily engaged with the world of practice and are generating even fewer new innovations in teaching methodologies and pedagogies for business schools than other academic departments.

Consequently it is not surprising that critics such as Colby et al. (2011) point out the curricula and pedagogical weaknesses of our graduates in terms of characteristics such as integrative and critical thinking and preparedness for careers in the world of practice.

Hamel believes that "as management educators we should develop people who can take the lead in inventing new management practices and models that will be critical in the new century. We need to teach them to be management innovators. If we don't start with this generation, I don't know when we start" (Bisoux, 2008, p. 24).

Business Schools and Business School Deans

Hamel does not exempt business school deans from criticism over the education of their students. In particular, he questions whether deans have the stomach, or indeed the confidence, to change the *status quo*.

He points out that in his many conversations with business schools deans, they embrace the principles of innovation and radical change "but when it comes to the practical implications of having to change their own models, they find it enormously difficult to get their heads around that idea" (Bisoux, 2008).

Osbaldeston (1996, p. 215), reaffirming Hamel's concern that faculty may anchor closely around the *status quo* in management education, points out that inertia to change is a real issue: "It could be a combination of the difficulty of escaping from the past, with an inability to create the future, or contentment with a track record of past and current performance."

In summary, this suggests that faculty in business schools are often content with their more discipline-focused and theoretical research-oriented recipes for business school success. As a consequence, not only deans but their faculty are seen as both resistant to change and impeding business model innovations.

> [It] suggests that faculty in business schools are often content with their more discipline-focused and theoretical research-oriented recipes for business school success. As a consequence, not only deans but their faculties are seen as both resistant to change and impeding business model innovations

Hamel notes that "when we look at business model innovation, we learn that the things that ultimately make a difference are more often seen in their inception as practically crazy by the incumbents. If you're not trying at least a few of those 'out there, on the edge' experiments, your business school is not embracing innovation" (Bisoux, 2008, p. 25).

Business Schools and Future Trends

One question that Hamel would pose to business school deans is: "Are you confident that you are preparing your students for the world of business as it will be ten years from now rather than for the world of business as it exists right now?" (Bisoux, 2008, p. 25).

In examining the future Hamel hopes to see business schools and deans exploiting the many opportunities he foresees emerging in the business school environment. They include:

> "There will be more online and diploma programmes that are focused on particular needs, that aren't full-fledged two-year MBA programmes ... There will be more flexibility in the curriculum in terms of the pace at which students earn their degrees ... There will be more emphasis on clinical learning,

on getting out and integrating the theoretical lessons of the classroom in practice" (Bisoux, 2008, p. 25).

Having looked at the relevance of innovation and practical relevance as highlighted by areas of concern and as potential "lessons not learned" in management education, we now examine "lessons not learned" from the perspective of our interviewees.

Are their views similar to those of Hamel, Mintzberg and others we have examined in Chapter 1 and in the introduction to this chapter? What differences are evident? What is the overlap between our interviewees and the criticisms and debating viewpoints expressed in the writings and literature in the field of management education?

Lessons Not Learned in Management Education

Four main themes surfaced in the responses in our interviews. They can be categorised as lessons related to:

- the rationale for, and purpose of, management education
- the generation of research knowledge about management
- curricula, delivery and pedagogy
- the importance of structure and governance in the business school including the roles of university presidents, deans and faculty

Therefore, the following points are reviewed more thoroughly in the next sections:

(i) The need for a revitalised educational philosophy for the business school to overcome the lack of a clear identity and purpose for management education.

(ii) The inadequate generation of knowledge production through management research — the argument that it has little relevance to, or influence on, management practice. Management research is seen as simply too arcane and focused on academic rigour at the expense of practical relevance.

(iii) The seeming lack of innovation in curricula and pedagogical development. Programme delivery and pedagogical processes need curricula enhancement in areas such as ethics, corporate social responsibility

> **In their evolution from trade schools to business schools, administrators have tried to define a clear scientifically rigorous body of knowledge and framework for management education but have arguably failed**

(CSR) and moral values and the "soft skills" of management. The need to achieve a balance between analytic tools and skills of problem solving, critical thinking and integrative synthesis of management issues and problems.

(iv) The adaptation of business school organisational structures and management to new innovations and business models as they are nurtured and implemented by strong and courageous leaders.

Lessons About the Purpose, Rationale and Mission of Business Schools

From the perspectives of our interviewees, business schools do not have a well-defined identity and image. In their evolution from trade schools to business schools, administrators have tried to define a clear scientifically rigorous body of knowledge and framework for management education but have arguably failed.

Their stated aim of seeking to achieve academic legitimacy and peer acceptance, for their business schools, particularly if they operate in a university environment, has also largely failed.

These conclusions are borne out by weaving together selected responses from our experts.

First, the pursuit of academic legitimacy is seen to be a difficult, perhaps unattainable goal:

> "The search (and pressure) for academic legitimacy is intense; however, management is seen as a minor intellectual player."

Second, business schools also have not gained a position at the top table — they are seen as minor players in broad debates about education and corporate/public policy:

> "I don't think that business schools realise or recognise that they're relatively minor players in terms of the things they feel they do influence. They don't have a strong voice in public or private policy [or] in the development of world economics and globalisation, no matter how much they use these words. They are not the slightest influence [on] policy makers and government."

Third, because management is regarded as a minor player by both universities and policy-makers, the issue of the appropriate role of the business school as a professional school in the university inevitably arises:

> "The role of the business school within universities [and] the relationship with the university can be a very difficult one.

I think that it is a major issue ... it is always an issue of how you define the role between what is a professional school and the rest of the university."

Fourth, this logically leads to the examination of whether business schools are clear about their role and positioning in the management education process — indeed, the tensions about roles are evident in the following responses.

"Business schools never defined what management educa-tion is, what a man-ager is, what does managing involve and so on. There is a lot in the leadership literature but I think that management educa-tion took a wrong turn with the emphasis on (quantitative) data collection when it is really about managing people."

"Business schools have been better at ensuring their performance than they have at developing purpose — there is still a lack of understanding of [the] relationship between business and society"

"The urge to develop management as a science (with the quality and attributes of scientific work) and the desire to transform management schools to produce more PhD pro-grammes have exacerbated the tension between the profes-sional and academic sides."

Fifth, as a consequence there seems to be a radical re-thinking of the scope of management education and its future role in society.

"I think there needs to be a clearer sense of purpose and with that I focus on the wider human being."

"Business schools have been better at ensuring their perfor-mance than they have at developing purpose — there is still a lack of understanding of [the] relationship between business and society."

"... We have to take a more humane approach in how we manage a company, what we think management is and the purpose of the corporation. There are other people involved not just the shareholders."

"I think the lessons it can learn are that there needs to be another radical shift ... we have to find new terrain."

Sixth, the question of whether management education has been too inward looking, complacent and self-satisfied is addressed by a Continental European respondent:

> "Business schools have the theoretical ability to be proactive and shape agendas, either by themselves or in consortia or through their societies. But they really haven't seized that at all. They've become, in my view, pretty complacent across Europe and that's not helped by the fact that the top business schools in Europe have remained in the same small grouping for the last 30 or 40 years."

Lessons About Management Research, Its Performance and Its Impacts

The publication of the Gordon/Howell reports on management education in the late 1950s engineered the transition from the vocational, more practical era of business schools into the more academic, scientifically oriented era of research and teaching. This was motivated by a strong desire for academic respectability and the increased generation of high-quality research in the management field. The views of our respondents illustrate the strengths and the weaknesses of this drive for academic values.

First, our respondents recognise the influence of the Ford/Carnegie reports but note the resulting tension the report findings created between sound academic research and their implementation for the practice of management:

> "The Ford/Carnegie reports created a push for academic legitimacy in business schools."

> "The Carnegie report pushed for academic rigour (in the US) although it is hard to argue that the world is better managed because of the push for academic research."

> **"It [management education] should recognise that its research is increasingly considered irrelevant by those it seeks to understand and by that I mean policy makers, senior managers and influential people in business, who are going to shape the future of this world"**

Indeed, one respondent expressed frustration about the search for academic currency:

> "Academic currency is irrelevant (to management practice) research — therefore, there is little, if any impact on practice from academic research."

Second, respondents are clear that the importance of relevance, and practical aspect of research, has not been learned by management educators:

> "What hasn't been learned is that rarefied, irrelevant research just can't be at the heart of the system. That's the big one!"

And another respondent focuses on the weak impact of research on practice:

> "It [management education] should recognise that its research is increasingly considered irrelevant by those it seeks to understand and by that I mean policy makers, senior managers and influential people in business, who are going to shape the future of this world."

Third, there is a feeling that the gap between academic research and practice is widening:

> "Business schools ... have not learned to keep pace with companies; I think they are behind them. And they use as their excuse [not] relevance but rigour. But I think this is an excuse just to slow it down."

Fourth, respondents stress that this gap between rigorous academic research and the needs of a wide range of stakeholders must be bridged:

> "The research we do should ... to some degree engage with the world of management practice ... otherwise you are not a business and management school."

And, it is not just research linkages that are important. Linkages to build networks with management stakeholders are equally vital:

> "You cannot run a business school so disconnected from the business world in terms of programmes [and] research and stay in touch with the real world. And a healthy school is part of a dynamic network of companies, recruiters, graduate students and entrepreneurs. You have to be there and contribute to this network, and somehow benefit as well from it, mainly through ideas."

Fifth, respondents are particularly critical of the linkages between research and technology/innovation. They believe that the areas of communication technology and the management of innovation are under-researched and under-utilised by management educators:

> "I don't think we've been very good about linking management to technology, particularly communications technology; we tend to treat management as a bit isolated and yet what's happening out there is that they're making use of all these technologies in a way that we don't really take into account in business schools."

Sixth, they increasingly question the drive for academic rigour and ask whether this has resulted in an obsession with scientific research (the so-called "physics envy of management education"; Thomas & Wilson, 2011) with associated career incentives for academics and a strong focus on a strategy, or mentality, of "publish or perish":

> "The problem about research [is] the huge demands both from academia itself and for the process of promotion in academia, particularly in the US, for publishing in 'good journals' partly to emulate what goes on in more academic subjects. But against that there's this feeling that there's a lot of rubbish out there, which even though it may be intellectually interesting, doesn't actually do anything."

One respondent reinforces this point about publishing in "good journals" very forcefully:

> "A focus on A-journals has become a focus on arcane journals with no impact. (Academic journal) citations do not equate to impact; they are academic currency. The focus on A-journals impedes debate."

It could, therefore, be argued that the pursuit of academic research and the reward structures of business schools lead faculty members towards research that examines management as a science and not as a practical art.

Another respondent points out that the scientific, academic approach focuses research away from the "soft skills" of management that are important as managers lead, and create, organisations and products:

> "(Academic research promotes) the naïve search for ultimate truths ... we generally thought you could optimise everything. I don't think that one can. (For example) things like emotional capital and so on are important because you can inspire people."

This underscores why the gap between research and practice is of such great importance to management education and, crucially, the ways in which this tension permeates teaching, pedagogy and programme delivery.

Lessons About Management Teaching, Pedagogy and Programme Delivery

There is some concern about whether business schools really understand the content of management education. In essence, the basic proposition is that business schools have not learned, or agreed, about the fundamental knowledge base of management and, even more importantly, how to teach and instil values in managers that meet stakeholder expectations.

> **Respondents raise a contentious issue that concerns the balance between teaching and research activities within business schools and whether the teaching and delivery of management education is seen as less important than research. As one respondent put it: "The push for research has seen pedagogy and teaching take a secondary role"**

Following the corporate scandals and financial crises in the early stages of the 21st century the expectation is that business schools must refresh their attempts to improve management behaviour and play their part in reforming and enhancing the relationship businesses have with their stakeholders.

First, a number of respondents make clear that the curricula and teaching processes of management education are contentious issues, as one respondent argues:

> "Management as an academic discipline really doesn't exist. It is an amalgamation of a number of disciplines."

Which is echoed in the related criticism by another:

> "We haven't learned how to educate our managers, whether they're young managers or mid-career learners, in taking a wider perspective."

This could be due to the *post hoc* development of curricula in management education:

> "A core problem with business school curricula is that they have a 'follower' attitude; they followed the trend into shareholder capitalism and now they're responding by trying to

reach stakeholder capitalism. No business school stood up and said that shareholder approaches are wrong and dangerous until after the financial crisis."

Furthermore, respondents raise a contentious issue that concerns the balance between teaching and research activities within business schools and whether the teaching and delivery of management education is seen as less important than research. As one respondent put it "the push for research has seen pedagogy and teaching take a secondary role".

Second, there is considerable reflection on how properly and effectively to deliver quality management education. Respondents are concerned about the breadth of the management educational experience and the ability of students to "think out of the box" and in an integrative fashion about management issues and problems:

> "We've narrowed down instruction to convergent thinking and have neglected the breadth ... In only a few cases do management problems yield to convergent thinking ... I think the interplay between convergent and divergent thinking is important."

Academics in business schools typically exist in disciplinary "silos" (disciplinary subject areas), which may make their teaching and education inward looking and focused on disciplines.

Another respondent expressed this as follows:

> "Learning should not be teaching in silos/subject areas. We may need to start teaching in silos but we have to be more integrative and paint a much more holistic picture. We need to achieve far more synthesis across the subject areas."

Other respondents expand on how to develop broad-based, and more applied, individuals as the output of management education:

> "We shouldn't just teach the tools, we should teach how to use the tools; to teach responsibly, ethically and for the general good of mankind really, rather than being too narrow."

"I do think that we've lost sight of the teaching of skills … because I think that the role, and purpose, of business schools is to develop the next generation of business leaders. They need to be equipped with the 'how to' experience. We haven't kept pace with that. We've become too research-focused"

In addition, attention was drawn to the theme of teaching the appreciation of models and theories:

> "I think it is about giving people, young people, the ability to apply what they have learned and to give them the ability to learn, not so much in the sense of 'I have my financial model' ... but enhancing the ability to understand and learn."

Third, some respondents believe that global and environmental changes require the development of leadership and other management skills. Their viewpoint is that these facets of skill development are not central *foci* of business school curricula.

> "I do think that we've lost sight of the teaching of skills ... because I think that the role and purpose of business schools is to develop the next generation of business leaders. They need to be equipped with the 'how to' experience. We haven't kept pace with that. We've become too research-focused."

In addition, another respondent points out that there is a challenge to educate global business leaders who understand how to operate internationally with a good background in cultural and contextual intelligence:

> "I see cross-cultural dimensions of managing today as more important than ever. I think that we haven't yet realised how important those things are, particularly the learning, not the teaching, about management in a global environment."

Fourth, respondents reflect further on two areas — the much stronger incorporation of information technology (e.g. e-learning and communication technology) and innovative learning about the practice of management. Their focus is on how they can be handled in business school teaching:

> "I would say that management education is ripe for innovation (and destructive technology)."

> "We seem to downgrade the importance of practice-based learning."

It may be easier to handle action learning as part of a life-long learning process in management education where the awareness of management issues and problems increases with age and experience.

Action, or project-based, learning, may certainly enhance the learning process for young MBAs but will add considerable value, integrative learning and impact to an older student on executive education or an executive MBA programme — an example might be Mintzberg's IMPM programme for practicing managers (see p. 20).

One respondent expressed this idea as follows:

> "I think we have learned something but we can be much better. Something we have to do is to learn what kind of integration is needed at what stage in the career of a person. You need a different kind of integration when you deal with a 40-year-old than when you deal with a 23-year-old."

Fifth, respondents express the view that there is still a lack of understanding of the relationship between business and society:

> "Business ethics and CSR are on the public's mind far more than they used to be; there is a perceived 'ethics' gap in management education. This has acted as a demand-pull force on management education."

To summarise, there is a sense that in programme delivery management education has been far more reactive than proactive, and incremental rather than radical or innovative in the context of changing environments.

Failure to define the discipline of management clearly has led to conservatism and "followership" in management education models; a disciplinary rather than an integrative orientation; a weakness in developing integrative thinking and leadership skills; the slow incorporation of technological skills; difficulty in blending action-learning with traditional teaching models; and a relative absence of ethics, CSR and an ethical and moral framework in the curriculum.

> **There is a sense that in programme delivery management education has been far more reactive than proactive, and incremental rather than radical or innovative in the context of changing environments**

Lessons About the Structure and Functioning of Business Schools

In the strategic management literature, there has been a constant "chicken and egg" debate about whether in the organisational context strategy follows structure or vice versa (McGee, Thomas, & Wilson, 2010). What is clear is that strategy — the strategic logic that sets organisational direction in terms of business models, goals and policies — is inextricably intertwined with structure — organisational systems, culture, leadership, people and so on — in creating an effective strategy implementation process resulting in strong organisational performance.

Ergo, a business school strategy cannot work in practice without a strongly co-aligned organisational structure. As leaders, deans in particular have to manage expectations carefully. They have the tasks of managing faculty and staff, building working relationships with their parent universities (or in the case of private, stand-alone schools with their governing bodies) and determining organisational strategy and specifically the business school's sustainable business model in an acknowledged environment of "hyper-competition" (D'Aveni, 1994) in management education.

However, it is clear (Mintzberg, 1998) that managing in a university/business school context requires a covert form of leadership that preserves, especially, faculty autonomy, critical debate, collegiality and consensus-based decisions.

As Fragueiro and Thomas (2011, pp. 56–57) note, this form of academic leadership may breed values of conservatism and caution, which, in turn, may impede organisational change. Our expert interviewees identify many of these problems, issues and lessons to be learned.

First, our respondents view business school faculty in particular as being too powerful, conservative and resistant to change.

For example, they point out that "the entrenched positions of faculty" make them significant "barriers to change". They further argue that their position is even more "entrenched" because of employee reward and governance systems such as tenure and the tradition of faculty autonomy that reinforce conservative attitudes.

Some respondents see faculty, in their academic ivory towers, as a dominant influence on the conduct of management education:

"Faculty [are a strong influence] because they control the business schools. They control the business schools by the tenure process. You can get them in, you can never get them out. Once they're in, they're basically free to do what they want. They can block any change in a school."

> "Faculty [are a strong influence] because they control the business schools. They control the business schools by the tenure process. You can get them in, you can never get them out. Once they're in, they're basically free to do what they want. They can block any change in a school"

More importantly, they not only influence change but they also set the curricula agendas, often reinforcing disciplinary (silo-type) approaches:

> "The faculty ... have historically defined what is taught, when subjects need to change and how they need to change. They are the dynamic drivers of change."

> "The development of management education is driven by faculty; it tends to reinforce disciplinary thinking in management. If you have the faculty, and you talk about curriculum changes, at least in my experience, you always get a deepening of the curriculum. You don't get things on the outside."

Second, they argue that the conservative posture of faculty, at least, has done little to change the research-oriented context of management education.

> "Faculty find it difficult to think beyond the context; they think of what is being done now, they can't see that down the road management education might be about something different. Academics have the most conservative approach to anything."

And, their focus on research leads them, in large part, to avoid looking at broader issues in management education, including the possibility of interdisciplinary research work:

> "... if you have this huge emphasis on research ... then inevitably it narrows people's focus. They have to publish to get promoted; therefore most often it is not productive to go too far beyond that and to think about linking across to philosophy ..."

The issue of the relative power of faculty and their inertia, resistance and perceived lack of interest in and to change is seen overall as one of the key lessons that has not been learned.

> **Our respondents recognise the influence of the university, university politics and academic legitimacy of the business school in the governance of university-based business schools**

> "I think that we know that some of the things that go on in business schools are mainly for the benefit of the producers,

the faculty, and we know that and we don't seem to do anything about it, so that's a lesson that has not been learned. The business model doesn't appear to be working that well and yet nobody has said how we are going to fix it, [But] let's try to fix it; people [faculty] seem to take the approach that it will all work out in the end."

Interestingly, Osbaldeston (1996, pp. 215–216) (quoted in Thomas et al., 2013, p. 31) points out the combination of faculty inertia and complacency with the *status quo* can result in faculty being impediments to change. He notes that "our core competence is invested in the faculty; so if we recruit the right people, then surely the right people will deliver the right business school of the future."

Third, our respondents recognise the influence of the university, university politics and academic legitimacy of the business school in the governance of university-based business schools.

One respondent points out that a business school is a professional school whose relationship with the university is often ambiguous.

"The role of the business school within universities [and] the relationship with the university can be a very difficult one. I think that is a major issue ... it is always an issue of about how you define the role between what is a professional school and the rest of the university."

Another notes that inertia in this relationship creates a sense that business schools lack intellectual strength and rigour relative to other university departments:

"[There is a] general inertia, which I think has to do with universities and their view of business schools, and the fact that business schools have had it relatively easy for some time as long as they make money. I think that is a bad contract because it does two things: creates complacency among the business schools and creates a very strong bond of trust or mistrust between the university and other departments. I think that is very unhealthy."

Fourth, our respondents also focus on the nature, and requirements of business school leadership in difficult, fast-paced environments. First and foremost, they point out that the "one model fits all approach has gone".

As one respondent put it:

> "I think we need a transition from the old model to a new model ... The old model: faculty meetings, departments, tenure-based vested interests. These all add up to make it not very credible that these types of organisations will be able to adapt ... To create a new model we need to get rid of some over-conservative, narrow-minded ways of thinking ... we need an innovative perspective and to make it happen there has to be a willingness to experiment."

Another respondent takes up the theme that business schools need risk-seeking, innovative, trustworthy and forthright leaders to take the helm:

> **A leader also needs to recognise that the business schools themselves with their silo-ed departmental structures, lack of innovation and narrow non-integrative, disciplinary research can impede creative change**

> "I think that business schools are going to have to professionalise when it comes to the management of their institutions ... it's got to be somebody who understands how a business school operates, who the faculty trust — in any change operation trust is extremely important — and you've also got to have a person who's interested in the job."

As a further respondent points out, a leader also needs to recognise that the business schools themselves with their silo-ed departmental structures, lack of innovation and narrow non-integrative, disciplinary research can impede creative change.

> "Institutions kill creativity — do we have people today who are larger than life in business education? Are we rewarding administrators and bureaucrats? Do we in the academy discourage those who create friction [new ideas]?"

Indeed, other respondents point out the severe business model and financial resource pressures on business schools.

> "Leaders need to evaluate carefully both the business school model and the financial realities involved of building a successful business school."

> "Overall, management education is going through enormous change. Where will the new revenue streams come from to put the school at the cutting edge?"

In summary, a number of respondents point out the need for courageous path-breaking leaders who will attack existing business models and necessary strategic changes:

> "Leaders who are risk takers will trigger change."

> "There is a lack of courage. We are in a world where good schools need good leaders, with the same competence we require of business leaders."

Summary and Conclusions

This chapter has focused on the "lessons not learned" in management education from the perspective, particularly of our research sample of experts, but also the views of key critics and discussants of management education (such as Henry Mintzberg, Rakesh Khurana and Ken Robinson in Chapter 1 and Gary Hamel, a leading exponent in the strategic management field, in this chapter).

We ask at the end of this summary whether there are strong similarities in the viewpoints expressed by the experts and the critics and also examine where differences in viewpoints are evident.

We start with a summary of Hamel's themes on innovation and practical relevance and follow with a summary of respondent viewpoints. Areas of similarity and difference are then highlighted.

Hamel's Observations on Business School Lessons

We summarise his observations in bullet form:

- The need for a radical rethinking of management paradigms. Management educators as innovators, not "mapmakers in an earthquake zone".
- The recognition that management education should be catering for the "innovation generation" — business schools should promote "innovation cultures" (as also noted by Kelley and Littman (2005) and Robinson (2011))
- The endorsement of a liberal arts model of management education (see also Handy (1996) and Colby et al. (2011)), which makes management education more exciting, less boring and instrumental.
- The need to embrace disruptive as opposed to incremental change (see also Tyson (2005) and Christensen (2000)).

- The clear requirement to improve research impact and relevance and hence refresh the linkage with management practice (the need for experimentation and deep collaboration with practice).
- The urgency of curriculum change in business schools. A renewed focus on students becoming "management innovators" and idea creators. Basic disciplinary knowledge should be enhanced through teaching skills in critical and integrative thinking (Colby et al., 2011; Mintzberg, 2004; Moldoveanu & Martin, 2008). Problem-framing and applied learning skills should also be emphasised.
- The problems of dealing with more effective administration and leadership in business schools. The view of deans as conservative, preserving the *status quo* and unwilling to experiment with, or implement, new models is noted. Reticence to contemplate the future is also evident.

Lessons Learned from Our Interviews with Management Education Experts

In a similar fashion, we provide our respondents' observations in bullet form:

Mission, role and purpose of business schools

- In terms of institutional or societal legitimacy, business schools are viewed as minor players with regard to their influence on universities or on corporate/public policy debates.
- As a professional school the business school fits uneasily into the university context (note that Newman (1852) and Veblen (1918) both argue that professional schools should not be part of universities).
- There are "fuzzy" models of management education. Do management educators understand what management is or their relationship to business, government or society?
- Business schools are too complacent and self-satisfied.

Management research

- The Gordon/Howell research model has de-emphasised the linkage to practice and encouraged "A-journal" publication of a "publish or perish" form.
- There is little relevance in, or impact from, management research.
- The gap between academic research and management practice is widening.
- There is sparse evidence of research on the impacts of technological change (particularly the impact of communication technologies on management) or of stakeholder perspectives on management.
- The concern that academic research is about the naïve search for overall truths.

Management teaching and pedagogy

- General problems in the delivery of management education. For example, the context of management education is not well understood and there is a "follower" tendency in teaching models.
- Curricula provide disciplinary depth but lack a treatment of breadth in management education. Students are not taught "how" to apply disciplinary models in a critical, evaluative fashion.
- We have lost sight of the teaching of skills such as critical and integrative thinking and contextual cultural intelligence.
- Practice, or action-based, learning needs more emphasis.
- Advances in e-learning (e.g. blended learning) need faster adoption as effective teaching pedagogies.
- Clear weaknesses in teaching on the interface between business, government and society, for example the (lack of) teaching of ethics, CSR and sustainability.

Business school administration

- Business schools need risk-taking, innovative and creative leaders who can trigger change and explore new models and generate associated financial resources. The best leaders possess the courage to inspire faculty and embrace change.
- Difficult relationships exist between business schools and universities. There is a lack of trust and the sense that business schools are "cash cows" but second-class academic citizens in the university context.
- Faculty influence is too powerful. Faculty are conservative and resistant to change.
- Faculty are "entrenched" — protected by tenure — and control curricula/ programme offerings and disciplinary changes.
- Faculty are anchored in context. They are viewed as narrow, research-focused individuals with a strong disciplinary orientation. They rarely contemplate issues related to the future of management education.

There is clear agreement between our respondents and scholars from the management literature on:

- the need for improvements in management research, particularly the link to practice and the very important task of experimentation/collaboration in research
- the urgency of curriculum reform and the radical re-thinking of management education paradigms and philosophies in an innovative, technologically driven economy

- the need for curricula innovation and a renewed focus on skills development
- the belief that deans are generally too conservative and risk-averse.

If there are differences between the management education observers (Hamel, Colby, Robinson, Kelley and so on) and our respondents, they reflect different emphases. Management educators in the literature stress such things as innovation cultures, the urgent need to re-focus on managers' needs and more liberal views of management education (including the introduction of humanities subjects).

Our respondents worry deeply about the strong influence of faculty, their resistance to change and future developments, and the consequent and growing irrelevance of management research for practical managers in the real world.

We will next turn to a review of our research results about the continuing challenges facing management education.

Chapter 3

On-Going Challenges Confronting Management Education

Introduction

It is clear from Volume I (Thomas et al., 2013) that there are a significant number of issues facing management education. What we seek to address in this chapter is the identification of those issues that constitute on-going challenges for management education.

Many of the well-known and continuing debates that surround the role, purpose and direction of management education undoubtedly relate to the multifaceted challenges the industry faces. A diverse and expert set of respondents (as represented by our interviewees) allows us to deepen our understanding of these challenges. By adding depth, there is an opportunity to identify important and enduring challenges affecting management education. Table 3.1 shows the challenges most frequently mentioned by interviewees.

By grouping these challenges, we can build a more focused view of what the key challenges are and how they fit together in the context of management education. These group categories are

- challenges associated with the *perceived value/success* of management education,
- challenges *external* to the business school environment,
- challenges *internal* to the business school and its operations,
- challenges for business school models and approaches that arise from *perceptual, external and internal* factors.

Volume I drew attention to the complex relationships between stakeholders and the often conflicting interests they have in management education. Indeed, key stakeholders consistently point out that the purpose and perceived value of management education needs continued reflection and debate (Thomas et al., 2013, p. 17). Some stakeholders also favour

Table 3.1: Frequently mentioned challenges.

Challenges	Count of mentions (33 respondents)	Percentage of respondents identifying challenge
Skills demanded (by students/ employers), e.g. critical skills	16	48%
(lack of) Relevance/Impact	12	36%
Rigour in research	9	27%
Faculty	9	27%
Lack of change	8	24%
Competition and reputation	8	24%
Globalisation	7	21%
The relationship between business and society/diverse stakeholder demands	7	21%
Financial sustainability	6	18%
Silos — lack of integration	4	12%
Changes to economic and social context	3	9%
Value of management education	3	9%
Relationship with university	3	9%
Success of management education	2	6%
Poor communication between schools	2	6%
Fees	1	3%
Demand for management education	1	3%

greater breadth, and a more holistic orientation in the business school curriculum allied to an enhanced treatment of societal as well as economic and university responsibilities.

> Some stakeholders also favour greater breadth, and a more holistic orientation in the business school curriculum allied to an enhanced treatment of societal as well as economic and university responsibilities

We have also identified two prevailing positions among the responses that are essentially supply- and demand-driven perspectives about the environment of management education.

The supply-driven perspective is concerned with preferences, terms and conditions of employment and institutional factors surrounding "internal" conditions in business and management schools. Issues that surfaced from this perspective were that faculty are in control of many major issues such as determining what is taught to students and which areas of research are pursued. This highlights the faculty as being the most influential of stakeholders.

An alternative perspective is demand-driven, where either students or businesses are perceived as most influential in shaping management education. As "external" constituents, these "customers" are seen to be actively pressing for their priorities and using their strength to influence how and where courses are delivered and also express demand for specific course content.

Building on these stakeholder perspectives, we categorise challenges identified by respondents as external challenges if they derive from the broad environment of management education and as internal challenges if they reflect the inner workings of a business school.

In turn, the interaction between stakeholders' perceptions of the role and purpose of management education and continuing external and internal challenges gives business school deans and university administrators some policy options to chew on.

Perceived Value of Management Education

The criticisms of management education (see Chapter 1) and the evidence of lessons not learned (see Chapter 2) suggest that the role and purpose of management education is a contentious and controversial issue.

Indeed, in an increasingly pluralistic and global business environment one of the key debates is the role of business and whether the sole purpose of firms is to maximise shareholder wealth.

Contextual and cultural differences will surely influence how the roles of business, business schools and key stakeholders will be addressed around the world. For example: "European business and European management education has developed a balanced relationship with government and society ... business grows not only economically and technically but also with social responsibility and legitimacy" (Thomas et al., 2013, p. 3).

Consequently, alternative regional models of management education may emerge — some more "holistic", some more broad-based emphasising liberal education and some stressing the value of economic and analytic perspectives.

However, whatever the models put forward, many of our expert interviewees are concerned about the perceived value of management education in general and the passive/reactive stance of many business

> **Alternative regional models, of management education may emerge — some more "holistic", some more broad-based emphasising liberal education and some stressing the value of economic and analytic perspectives**

schools and their leaders. One respondent bluntly addresses the low perceived value of business schools and management education:

> "I think that there's a perception problem and I think that something we see so strongly here in the UK is that people do not value it. I think that it's a real, real problem."

A leading academic respondent further emphasises that transformation is needed to provide a viable, value proposition for management education:

> "The biggest challenge is how do you transform yourself; define what a business school is about and what it should teach? ... We need to think really clearly about how to become a 'school for business', where you become a value-adding orchestrator of solutions that businesses need."

Another respondent points out that business schools react slowly and passively to environmental changes:

> "... I see them as passive rather than proactive and with a relatively small voice in some of the major shifts we have seen over the last 20 years."

This view of the "small voice" is reinforced by another expert who stresses that "... unless the [business] schools start addressing what I would count as pressing managerial issues, global issues ... then the disconnect with society grows larger."

And other respondents note that the consistent problem in a fast-paced global environment is understanding the skills of the practising manager:

> "The recurrent challenge is that we don't know what a practising manager needs to do [to succeed]. I think that we'll always have a challenge regarding whether what we do is fit for purpose."

Unfortunately, this lack of focus on practice in their studies may lead students to treat management education in an instrumental, utilitarian fashion rather than as a challenging learning process:

> "The students today seem to accept the fact that they will not be able to know everything ... so they go a sort of utilitarian way of acquiring the knowledge for business education, which is ... 'I just need to know what I need to know at the moment when I need it, so I am no more thinking of education other than as a stock'".

Overall, the clear feedback is that business schools face a perception problem about their value in society. The advice is to become a more proactive "school for business" that not only links the school to management practice so that there may be a clear understanding of management issues but also challenges the students in the teaching and learning process so that what they are taught is exciting rather than sterile and boring.

External Challenges

External challenges arise from the market conditions providers of management education face. The discussion of these challenges will be based on issues and concerns raised by stakeholders as well as our observation of shifts in the operating environment.

Table 3.2 contains challenges, extracted from Table 3.1, which could be considered external challenges. The skills demanded by students and employers, the lack of relevance and impact of business schools and their research, competition, the impacts of globalisation and the business/society relationship emerge as the top external challenges.

We seek to develop a better understanding of the nature of these challenges in the discussion that follows. It should be noted that these challenges must be seen as being closely intertwined with the internal dynamics of management education.

However, we believe that first mapping the external challenges, then the internal ones and finally addressing the relationships between them from a policy perspective will allow a better grasp and a more holistic understanding of the challenges facing management education.

Skills Demanded by Students and Employers

The challenge most frequently identified by respondents concerns the ability of management education providers to equip students with the skills

Table 3.2: Major external challenges.

Major external challenges	Count of mentions (33 respondents)	Percentage of respondents identifying challenge
Skills demanded (by students/ employers), e.g. critical skills	16	48%
(lack of) Relevance/impact	12	36%
Competition/reputation	8	24%
Globalisation	7	21%
The relationship between business and society/ stakeholder demands	7	21%
Changes to economic and social context	3	9%
Value of management education	3	9%
Fees	1	3%

that students, employers and diverse stakeholders require. Nearly half of all our respondents identified this as a challenge and raised the need for business schools to respond to changes in the environment

> **The challenge most frequently identified by respondents concerns the ability of management education providers to equip students with the skills that students, their employers and diverse stakeholders require**

and to adapt their thinking and practice with regard to knowledge/skills that ought to be at the core of management education.

As one respondent argues:

> "[We need to introduce] more of a demand-oriented atmo-sphere in academia; instead of saying here's what we know, take it or leave it ... and if you apply, perhaps we'll let you come in. Modern students, with e-based marketing, are shop-ping around — they are consumers. That having been said, our ivory tower based supply side is, I think, under risk. And of course the servant-oriented demand side is necessary for us; so this is the biggest challenge that I see."

There is a clear message from stakeholders that students, as consumers, will pursue schools that offer relevant skill sets. The challenge for business schools is to manage a transition from an ivory tower-based supply-side approach to management education to one that develops curricula that are deemed relevant to the market.

There is a need to identify and develop skill sets that are in demand. In the previous volume, the fact that 78% of respondents identified students as being the most important stakeholders in management education underscores the pressures for a more demand-oriented atmosphere in academia.

This is no simple undertaking for business schools and university departments engaged in delivering management education. As another of our interviewees notes, this is an immense challenge:

> "The biggest challenge is — and I don't think that any of the other challenges come close to it — is that of building a capable person to operate effectively in a global context. A 'go-anywhere' graduate."

The idea of a "go-anywhere" graduate is an attractive proposition. However, it is not clear precisely what skills are required and how management education ought to respond. Without further engagement with stakeholders, the challenge of providing relevant skills could go unfulfilled:

> "I think that the first part of the job is for companies to determine what it is that they need, and what kind of individual they want us to educate. It's up to them to do that assessment properly. We will deliver the material they ask us to deliver. I am talking more about post-graduate executive education than undergraduate education. Undergraduate education, I think, has a different perspective. In this, we need these corporations and companies to do the job — to determine the kind of people that they want us to prepare for them in the coming years."

Indeed, there needs to be a balance between teaching management as a set of functional disciplines and as the managerial task of inspiring and leading people:

> "The biggest [issue] is not knowing what a manager is and thinking that education in professional disciplines, like finance, marketing etc. would make a manager. And that is a complete error because when you talk about management, it is about bringing people [together] so that they deliver desired results ... it is a pure people issue. How much of people issues are in business school?"

Some of the more nuanced responses that surround the core theme of equipping students with in-demand skills signal areas where there are gaps in current curricula and room for improvement. These are voices calling for educators to emphasise leadership, critical skills, problem solving, listening and other soft skills in their programmes. Again, leadership skills emerge as vital and something that management education should be engaging with, as the following comments illustrate:

> **There needs to be a balance between teaching management as a set of functional disciplines and as the managerial task of inspiring and leading people**

> "It is our role as management educators to educate the next generation of business leaders and we need to ensure that they are equipped with the knowledge and skills that are going to assist them in being successful as future business leaders."

> "What is it that future leaders of businesses and other organisations need to have in terms of knowledge and understanding? The leadership challenges, in other words, are very different today. Today I think that the trends are [related to] 'How do we integrate?' — we still need to teach the functional disciplines but how do we integrate them more effectively?"

> "Management education needs to be developing leaders more than managers. Having said that, people need to understand the basics of management too."

In general, respondents felt that management education needs to become far more responsive in bridging what could be perceived as a skills gap for the average business student. That delivering the right integrative and thinking skills to students is seen to be a difficult task suggests that business schools first need to be better attuned to the skill requirements of modern management.

> **The continuing challenge of relevance is expressed in the parallel play of academic researchers and managers — each in his or her own world — with few, if any, cross-interactions or collaborative relationships between them**

However, it was also clear that a balance must be struck between businesses simply telling management education providers they should become demand oriented and businesses actually engaging with providers to define and enhance the desired skills set of the "go anywhere" graduate.

Lack of Relevance and Impact of Management Research

About a third of respondents identify the lack of relevance in management research as an on-going challenge for management education. Key to this is determining the appropriate balance between theory and practice in management research.

Should we research the problems management actually faces through meaningful interactions and experimentation with managerial practice? Or should we maintain our relative isolation in an "ivory tower" theoretical framework?

> "The biggest on-going challenges have been around for about 100 years and they're still there; which is how do you balance scholarly research and endeavour from a high-quality academic point of view with the need to train and develop a large number of professionals?"

> "I think that one of the reasons is that a lot of the research that is being done by business schools is viewed by the corporates as not useful [in that] they can't understand it. Therefore, they say: 'Why should I have these people come and teach the people in my company if this is what they are going to teach them?' And I think that that is the greatest problem."

> "[The challenge has to do with] how we actually make management education still relevant for participants, companies and future business leaders ... how we make it relevant, how we offer something that is state of the art, useful for the work that those people will have to do over the coming years."

And on the issue of impact:

> "We spend too much time being too clever [in research] with far too little impact."

The continuing challenge of relevance is expressed in the parallel play of academic researchers and managers — each in his or her own world — with few, if any, cross-interactions or collaborative relationships between them.

> "Too often, I've seen a stream of activity that goes into universities and researchers talking to each other and working within their own worlds and the business community working

within its own world and occasionally the two cross over and meet. But ... if you say what's the purpose of a business school, you'd think [it was] actually to make businesses better, to make society as it relates to business better. I don't think that happens very often. So I think that there is an on-going relevance challenge as a major issue."

This final observation links the issues that surround relevance to the question of the mission and purpose of business schools. Indeed, this on-going relevance challenge represents a credibility gap for management education.

How, if at all, can the concerns of organisations, society and management research become aligned more meaningfully and closely?

Competition and Reputation

Several forces including market growth, globalisation and the success of management education have intensified competition among both public and privately funded business schools.

Our interviewees indicate that global, and particularly emerging market, growth has generated not just greater competition but a greater awareness of competition from around the world. This competitive intelligence has led business schools to reconsider and change their competitive positioning:

"Business schools are now closer as a community because of globalisation. [They have become] more aware of the existence and emergence of other institutions with innovative programmes operating everywhere in the world."

"The fact that competition within management education now operates beyond borders has redefined how schools compete."

"Globalisation ... in combination with a general decline in government funding for higher education, has heightened competition in management education. The arrival of for-profit providers has intensified competition for students."

Indeed, the arrival of "for-profits" has engendered differing views about the significance of private competition. For example, the arrival of the University of Phoenix (Apollo Group) has been disruptive in the sense that it has offered a new, and very different, technologically driven learning model for business education that allows for a lower-cost, content-based, quality education in the field. Nonetheless, there is uncertainty about the threat from private competition:

> "I'm not sure whether the threat from the for-profit business school world is going to be that strong. But it might be. Some people say that it will be because it will give people what they want, without paying for what they don't want, which is research."

Moreover, market conditions have created growth in private competition not only from Phoenix and other on-line providers but also from corporate universities who have customised aspects of the business school curricula to fit their own management development and training needs:

> **"Globalisation ... in combination with a general decline in government funding for higher education, has heightened competition in management education. The arrival of for-profit providers has intensified competition for students"**

> "Because university-based business schools have failed to deliver on management education, corporations are starting their own universities and incumbents shouldn't be surprised by this."

One respondent also noted that a number of corporate universities have succeeded because:

> "Customer voice is becoming an increasingly important competitive dynamic — firms want to see 'difference' and customisation in management education to suit their needs."

Competition in management education is now a global phenomenon with an increasing range of public universities, private universities and for-profit private universities jockeying for position in a fluid competitive marketplace. In particular, publicly funded, university-based business schools have had to adapt and refine their programmes and courses to fit the needs of the marketplace:

> "Market circumstances have re-defined competition in management education. Recession and the reduction of public funds in combination with an over-supply of business school courses have prompted business schools to 'sharpen-up' their offerings to customers."

The changes in the dynamics of this competitive landscape have encouraged business schools to build their "brands" and reputations to differentiate themselves and their strategies in the marketplace. As they attempt to build successful competitive differentiation, rankings, such as that run by the *Financial Times*, have provided a new consumer-oriented competitive focus:

> "It is the emergence of the rankings that has influenced heavily the way a lot of business schools think about their strategy."

> "Suddenly, the rankings allowed those significant national players to compare themselves in the international arena, so that was a very significant event."

The increasing pressures of competition have had one quite negative effect, namely that business schools only rarely co-operate, or collaborate, on joint programmes or research and very often do not share information or even co-operate unless there are formal alliances. As one leader from EFMD commented:

> "I like competing as a team towards a certain goal. I don't like the model where killing the other is the objective. In EFMD we ... partner with other organisations rather than fight each other .... There is no single organisation that can do everything."

As we move on to examine the challenge of globalisation, it is clear that business schools have to think internationally about their strategic options and identify ways of attracting students from emerging markets and economies, perhaps through collaborative partnerships and strategic alliances.

Globalisation

Globalisation is an important and critical challenge for management education, not least because, as the previous comments on competition demonstrate, it has changed the dynamics of competition.

It provides faculty and administrators of business schools with the opportunity to define how teaching and research capabilities can be enhanced through global collaboration and experimentation. Such collaborative efforts could potentially lead to the development of new approaches that would present alternatives to the dominant North American model.

"Globalisation [is a challenge] in terms of the resources needed for schools that plan to exploit opportunities

> Globalisation is an important and critical challenge for management education, not least because it has changed the dynamics of competition

beyond borders; this will require them to engage in alliances with other schools and also try to participate in knowledge creation and research, to have a rather more cosmopolitan understanding of developments in other parts of the world — that's a major stretch for people who focus much more on research."

"On a wider front, I think the challenges of globalisation of management education are that ... there's competition emerging to determine which institution can actually understand how to do it internationally in a successful manner. At the same time, because the world's becoming global, there's a clash, a challenge to the perceived American-Anglo model."

Globalisation should also motivate us to reflect on how we can build teaching skills in cultural/contextual intelligence and cross-cultural management. This will provide insights into how the globally sensitive "go anywhere" graduate can be nurtured.

"Globalisation, with the different qualities and attributes that we see in emerging countries, has clear implications ... [for] corporate cultures and management ... I see the cross-cultural dimensions of managing today as more important than ever. I think that we haven't yet realised how important those things are."

Internal Challenges

Internal challenges relate to the internal operations of a business or management school (Table 3.3).

Rigour in Research

Rigorous research was an outgrowth of the Gordon/Howell (1959) reports, which stressed the need for research anchored in the social

Table 3.3: Internal challenges.

Major internal challenges	Count of mentions (33 respondents)	Percentage of respondents identifying challenge
Rigorous research	9	27%
Faculty	9	27%
Lack of change	8	24%
Financial sustainability	6	18%
Silos — Lack of integration	4	12%
Relationship with university	3	9%
Success of management education	2	6%
Poor communication between schools	2	6%
Demand for management education	1	3%

sciences and cognate disciplines. Globalisation is an important and critical challenge for management education, not least because, as the previous comments on competition demonstrate, it has changed the dynamics of competition.

Two viewpoints from our respondents illustrate the tensions between business academics and academia in general and between business academics and professional managers.

The first comment is about the legitimacy, and seemingly unimpressive quality, of management research relative to other social science fields:

> "The legitimacy of our research struck me most — sitting around a table with other actors in social science, questioning the legitimacy of our research, and not being impressed."

The second comment relates specifically to the value of the output of management research for a management audience:

> "Some of the academics that are around don't really under-stand the business world they're talking about."

Indeed, the pressure in academia is characterised as either publish high-quality research in A-journals (the top journals) in the field or perish. They are not

> Globalisation is an important and critical challenge for management education, not least because ... it has changed the dynamics of competition

normally judged on their influence either on organisations or on management practice:

> "The distortion through A-list journals being the measure of academic success rather than what is useful to organisations — the organisations being researched into or the readership — is a major challenge. On that, research materials just do not connect with me."

This "publish or perish" dilemma for academics leads to specialisation and balkanisation of the field into narrower sub-areas and less relevant research output from a societal viewpoint:

> "The way that research and faculty develop, the specialisation, the irrelevance of what people write just drives me up the wall. So the balance has to be to understand and ensure that we remember that the ultimate purpose of this research is ... has to be a societal issue — it could be a social issue, an economic issue or an organisation issue."

However, another respondent counsels that we still must push for rigorous academic research but with the caveat that its appropriateness and relevance should be made more explicit:

> "[The challenge has to do with] how we do relevant research in a rigorous way so that any theory, any model, any point of view about the world has actually some research foundations. I don't think that we should confuse relevance with just superficial reactions about what seems to happen in the real world. I think that we still need research, and rigorous research. But I think that the issue of relevance and how we make it relevant [is a major challenge]."

Yet another worries about the influence of rankings (along with the A-journal focus and the dominant US business model) on the strategies and actions of business schools:

> "The focus is on which journals, how many publications and how that is going to get us up in the rankings, either in

research or a bit less so in teaching ... so there's this homogeneity across Europe of a particular model of education and research and it is that one (the US model)."

Faculty

In our introductory discussion faculty were seen as perhaps being the most influential stakeholder in management education — they have power, they call the shots and often drive the agenda in programme change.

Respondents point out that faculty cultures, practices, governance and tenure are on-going challenges and difficult issues to manage:

> "Faculty are at the front lines of management and in many institutions there's a tradition of family governance ... and they wield a fair amount of power in some ways because of things like tenure."

> "I think that the whole question of tenure needs to be raised because you've got some pretty old people out there."

There are strong respondent views on faculty's emphasis on research and that research quality dominates teaching quality in many situations:

> "I think that the snobbery of academics is not helpful. I think great teachers should be recognised and revered as much, if not more, then great researchers because I think that they have a longer-term impact on people."

> **Faculty [are perhaps] the most influential stakeholder in management education — they have power, they call the shots, and often drive the agenda in programme change**

> "They (faculty) influence the way in which management education has moved very much into a research-obsessed situation. For me, teaching has become very, very secondary to research."

This faculty obsession with research is in part driven by the pressures of reward systems in which expectations of excellent research performance are heavily stressed.

One respondent alludes to the pressure on academics to a produce strong research performance:

> "My sense is that there is more pressure on being an academic; academics are more highly remunerated now in relative terms than they were. [However,] expectations of their research productivity are higher and they're now under more pressure to deliver on that account. But that's only made them less relevant not more relevant to their principal stakeholders (students, business and so on)."

Yet teaching is still tremendously important and respondents argue that the reward systems should recognise teaching and pedagogical quality as much as research quality in creating a strong image and reputation for the business school:

> **Teaching is still tremendously important and respondents argue that the reward systems should recognise teaching and pedagogical quality as much as research quality in creating a strong image and reputation for the business school**

> "I think that there is an on-going challenge in the fact that the evaluation system for faculty is so strongly determined by research performance. Not in terms of what is useful research but in terms of what will get into journals, and yet that's not meeting the actual demand for pedagogy and providing people with the right teachers in front of the students."

> "I think the most difficult and demanding challenges all surround faculty. There is not only one problem — to get them — but also to find the balance between the imperative to develop serious, high-class research for the faculty themselves and for the reputation of the institution for its own sake."

There is also the continuing problem of faculty shortage, driven by global demand and high salaries. Respondents question whether existing PhD programmes will produce enough quality faculty with an appreciation of the real-world business context:

> "There's a generation who are going at some point within the next few years to leave the active practice of management education. Where are we going to find the faculty? And what are the new faculty like? They want $170,000 and $190,000 at

age 28 and they've never worked a day in their lives, having only been at school, and not having written any great research pieces."

"There's not a lot of evidence that they can stand up in front of a class and teach and they don't want to carry a heavy load for the first four years. And so where are we going to find people who can walk into that classroom and inspire? I worry more about getting the right person in front of the class than getting the kids into the class."

Therefore, while high-quality faculty are essential for the success of business schools, faculty and governance processes are conservative forces that may impede change:

"I think the barriers to change are probably ourselves ... mainly probably the faculty. I think it is basically the faculty that is reluctant to see certain changes."

Lack of Change

The reluctance of faculty to change because of conservatism and inertia is matched by the conservative outlook of many schools, which could be a threat to their existence. Indeed, as noted by some respondents, we need to find new business models and understand much better the nature of managerial work and activity:

"Business schools are quite traditional and not ready for a radical change. Unless there is a return to the core business of the schools, which is to develop managers and leaders capable of, let's say, taking risk, that means that the schools themselves should be able to answer the explicit requests for this kind of education. Schools are not anticipating and I think that this is a big thing. And if the business schools are not changing, then others will take that role."

> "The world of work is constantly changing and we need to ensure that we equip our faculty — and this is important — with the knowledge and the skills to deliver much more relevant research and teaching"

"I think that we need to think about a transition from an old model to a new model. The old model with faculty meetings, departments and tenured-based vested interests all add up to making it not very credible. We need to create a new model. We need to get rid of some over-conservative, narrow-minded ways of thinking."

"The world of work is constantly changing and we need to ensure that we equip our faculty — and this is important — with the knowledge and the skills to deliver much more relevant research and teaching."

This is where business schools need strong, business-aware leaders who have the courage to make and inspire radical change. Respondents express their views on the critical role of leadership:

"Leadership — to do strategic change we need leaders to be aware of changes that are needed, are on-going and influence academics."

"Very few business school deans have the courage to say what's actually going on ... they're sitting there and hoping it will come back."

Financial Sustainability

There is clear evidence of the need to ensure the long-term financial sustainability of the business school. Current models may well be hard to sustain in the future because of structural factors such as faculty conservatism and shortages as well as increased competition from other management education institutions.

Some of the respondents' comments are very insightful:

"In the past, the revenue model was very clear. You teach x number of days and you charge your rate per day multiplied by weeks. But now that you have 40% or 50% of the course taught on blended learning, how do you value that?"

"The biggest challenges are financial. The exec ed market collapsed in the recession and nobody knows how it's going to shape up in the future. This is a big chunk of their income. At the same time, degree programmes [have] probably reached their limit in terms of what can be charged and there will be price resistance. In the past, the market has seemed inelastic, but [I] suspect that this is coming to an end."

"Where will the new revenue streams come from to put a school at the cutting edge? There is a need for investment in high-quality faculty based on the mission you're in."

"Because of the pressure, we are all chasing full-time MBA classes as the pinnacle of what we should be doing. In the UK, 93% of full-time MBA students are not from the UK. Lots of really good schools, including ourselves, have trouble recruiting decent-size classes of MBAs. So to make ends meet in a business school in appropriate ways is a big challenge."

These financial realities have shown the need for deans and other administrators to develop new approaches such as, for example, greater programme diversification to attract students:

> **'Resources are not only financial. The shortage of faculty is going to be difficult ... no one has figured out a way yet to run a business school without faculty'**

"I think that there is the financial reality. A school, a dean or a faculty member can have the perfect view of what ought to be done for society but in the meantime there are seats to be filled. It is a reality, unless of course there is extensive funding, that the institution has to attract students one way or another."

And deans have to recognise that despite the reluctance of faculty to change, a business school cannot operate without a sufficient pool of high-quality faculty:

"Resources are not only financial. The shortage of faculty is going to be difficult ... no one has figured out a way yet to run a business school without faculty."

Financial pressures may also mean the "shake-out" of some business schools or, alternatively, mergers of schools such as SKEMA in France and Aalto in Finland. The real issue is that the current business model in many schools is unsustainable — it is too luxurious and its business model is seen as expensive relative to competition from companies, management consultants and for-profit private education providers (Thomas & Peters, 2012).

Other Challenges for Business School Models

Technology

It is quite surprising that technology as a force driving change did not fig-ure significantly in the overall respondents' list of on-going challenges in Table 3.1.

However, in the semi-structured format of the interview process, respon-dents expressed clear and important observations about how technology will alter traditional "bricks and mortar" schools, which currently use faculty-based, "face-to-face" learning and pedagogical approaches:

> "How is technology going to change and how do business schools that rely strongly on 'face-to-face' teaching (which are often the premium business schools) continue to justify their existence when you now can get such high-quality teaching and information through on-line channels?"

Respondents offer a range of views on the changes that may occur in teaching and research in an environment where the students are often much more technologically literate than their instructors:

> "I think that the potential re-definition of the role of the pro-fessor, which can be caused by effective learning technologies and methodologies, again may challenge things."

> "I think widely distributed knowledge through the internet will change the way we think and work and do things and this will push through into management education. The notion of research publishing will change utterly over the next ten to 20 years."

The on-going policy challenge is clearly to determine how technology and the wide range of available communication technologies will change the delivery of management education. New innovations such as MOOCs (massive open on-line courses) and blended learning are already here — how will business schools adapt?

Legitimacy and Value

There is a continuing policy challenge with respect to the legitimacy and value of management education in the broad higher-educational context.

There is a perception that management education is not fit for purpose either in the managerial or the academic domain.

In Volume I, Thomas et al. (2013, p. 134) note that there are a number of reasons for criticisms concerning value and legitimacy:

"First, the pursuit of academic legitimacy has created conditions where business schools are engaged in the study of management rather than studies for better management. This is manifest in the concentration of resources for research (for publication in arcane elite journals) as opposed to teaching and pedagogy.

Second, business schools tend to react to management trends and broader external issues rather than shaping the management agenda (e.g. sustainable management practice).

Third, business schools do not fully understand the role of business in society and are, therefore, ill-equipped to teach better (responsible, sustainable) management practice."

Two comments from our respondents reinforce this perception of the legitimacy of management education.

> "The problem of this [financial] crisis is not a problem of knowledge; it is a problem of conduct."

> "People have to modify their conduct. It is even more than purely ethics so to speak; it is behaviour. And, therefore, I believe that business schools ... should emphasise that the great challenge of management education in the future is emphasising conduct more than knowledge or skills."

This view that conduct is critical is reinforced relative to issues of corporate social responsibility:

> "Philosophically, I think the biggest challenge is that we think that business education is about marketing, strategy, operations, finance or whatever. And that in doing so we do not necessarily answer the questions of companies anymore — I mean their needs in terms of social responsibility and coping with environmental issues."

> 'Business schools ... should emphasise that the great challenge of management education in the future is emphasising conduct more than knowledge or skills'

Conclusions

Many of our respondents are concerned about on-going challenges surrounding overarching issues such as the purpose, value and relevance of management education. They question why the "dominant" US business school model — anchored in the Ford/Carnegie reports — has not undergone much more careful evaluation and revision.

Why, for example, has management education not been examined in as much detail as secondary or higher education in general? They certainly argue that inertia, complacency and conservatism — endemic in the current tenure, faculty governance and business models — raise the same old questions about the role, value and legitimacy of both management education and research.

Their sense is that the faculty obsession with narrow A-journal research and the attendant research-driven model evident in leading public and private business schools largely impedes innovation both in teaching/pedagogy.

It also hinders experimentation between management researchers and managers that might improve both the relevance and interdisciplinary focus of future management research.

Their clear perspective is that many on-going challenges — perceptual, external and internal — remain and create a series of policy challenges about financial sustainability, new business models, the role of technology and the legitimacy of management education to its stakeholders (students, business government and society). And associated questions remain about the identity of the business school as a professional school.

A report card would probably say something like "not a bad effort" in performance terms, but requiring much more evidence of a willingness to address institutional complacency and conservatism and the use innovation and creativity to exploit opportunities in designing a sustainable future for management education.

Indeed, one respondent addressed the change imperative clearly and insightfully by linking the challenges of globalisation and technological change to the need for collaboration between business schools:

> "The future has got to have three things. It has to be global; it has to stop being as American as it was. It's got to embrace technology and technology transfer. And finally it's going to have to work a lot more with alliances … there have to be alliances because there is so much knowledge that is embedded in universities around the world and you have to use technology (and technology transfer) a lot more."

This future orientation provides a guideline as we explore more closely the future of management education in succeeding chapters.

Chapter 4

Future Scenarios for Management Education

Introduction

The previous chapter provided a discussion of the on-going challenges facing management education as perceived by our respondents.

Strong themes emerged from that analysis reflecting to some extent a shared sense of what the problems are and where the tides might be the strongest.

This begs the question of what the future might look like for management education given the current challenges. The range of imagined futures, as one would expect, will depend on how management education as a whole responds to current challenges as well as the particular challenges it chooses to respond to.

At the one extreme, there could be complete inertia, thus allowing the challenges of today to lead management education down a detrimental path. More optimistically, there is a possibility of proactive confrontation of challenges, leading to a positive transformation.

We begin this chapter with a review of possible future scenarios that have been discussed in the extant literature before moving on to present our findings of what respondents believe to be the best case, worst case and most likely scenarios. We round off the chapter with a discussion of several models of management education that have been advocated by their respective authors as being ideal.

Possible Future Scenarios Described in the Extant Literature

Starkey and Tiratsoo (2007) provide a lucid narrative of the current state of affairs in management education, calling it an era of hyper-competition. Business schools today exist in a landscape characterised by an increasing number of competing schools and programmes on the one hand and funding sources that are increasingly uncertain on the other. Endowments have been battered by the financial crisis while governments have scaled back funding for higher education.

The fact that the heyday of booming demand for an MBA degree is behind us does not help. Uncertain demand, and even a fall in applications in some quarters, is making the MBA programme a less than reliable source of income. On the cost side, the sustained shortage of faculty and the concomitant rise in faculty salaries present risks both to the business schools' bottom line and to teaching quality.

> **The heyday of booming demand for an MBA degree is behind us. Uncertain demand, and even a fall in applications in some quarters, is making the MBA programme a less than reliable source of income**

At the same time, as discussed in this volume and by Starkey and Tiratsoo (2007), the legitimacy of the business school is increasingly being questioned, both for the practical relevance of the knowledge it produces and for how it views management through the lens of disciplinary silos. It is against this backdrop that Starkey and Tiratsoo offer possible scenarios for the future of business schools.

The most obvious possibility is one where schools continue on their current trajectory, with attempts to cope with the stresses but with no fundamental shifts to their operating model. Starkey and Tiratsoo refer to this as simply "going with the flow", a situation where the hyper-competition described earlier will likely draw schools towards increasing their income by adding new masters programmes, cultivating alumni donors or cutting staff costs.

There are daunting roadblocks, however, in each of these responses. Starkey and Tiratsoo note the improbability of supplanting the MBA with a new programme that would be as much of a "killer product" as the MBA proved to be. There is also the fact that, outside of top-tier American schools, coaxing contributions from alumni would first require a fundamental change in mindset away from one that regards education as a public good to be provided for by the state.

Cutting staff costs, on the other hand, could have the undesirable downstream consequences of increasing the student–faculty ratio, lowering the quality of education and depressing faculty morale.

The significant downsides of simply going with the flow beg the question of what alternative responses and scenarios there could be. Starkey and Tiratsoo point out that the alternatives fall broadly into the spheres of either moving closer to the practice of management or moving closer to the traditional notion of the academy.

The former would essentially be an emulation of professional schools such as law and medicine where there are clear expectations of the kind of knowledge that those who work in the field must have and where certification by an organisation that represents the field is part of the induction process.

Faculty would have strong links with real-world practitioners (or would be practitioners themselves) and research would be guided by the need for relevance.[1]

To be sure, there are also significant hurdles to this approach, including the fact that there is as yet no strong umbrella organisation that can serve to represent the field of management and no consensus as to the set of knowledge and skills that a manager should have, and ultimately, what management really means.

Starkey and Tiratsoo also foresee that the forging of partnerships with businesses could be fraught with problems of conflicting objectives and loyalties and a "contamination" of the research process by commercial interests. This could devolve into a situation where academic research is co-opted into the business of chasing profits.

The alternative of moving closer to the academy would entail a "back-to-basics" focus on knowledge creation, a path that follows the mantra of "knowledge for knowledge's

> **The defence of research without practical applications, or worse yet, research findings that do not hold up in the real world because of flawed assumptions, can be but a feeble one**

sake" and not bowing to the pressures of immediate practical relevance.

On the teaching side, rather than simply imparting "tools of the trade", a more scholarly, intellectually rigorous approach would be taken. On the research side, there would be investment in PhD programmes and theoretical research.[2]

---

[1]Drawing on Starkey and Tiratsoo's work, Ivory, Miskell, Shipton, White, Moslein, & Neely (2006) (Advance Institute of Management (AIM)) further categorise business schools that move closer to practice into two different models — one labeled "Professional School" and the other "Knowledge Economy". The former describes business schools that are focused on teaching and on improving management practice. Such a school would be oriented towards meeting the needs of managers, employers and governments. The latter describes schools focused on applied research and the commercialisation of discoveries from business schools as well as other departments/schools within universities.

[2]Once again drawing on Starkey and Tiratsoo's work, Ivory et al. (2006) categorise schools that stay close to the academy into two categories. They labeled schools that are focused on teaching and on providing an education that goes beyond simply equipping students with business tools as "Liberal Arts" schools. These schools offer a broader-based education with such aims as developing critical thinking, self-knowledge, leadership and an awareness of the role of business in society. Schools that have as their primary focus basic, theoretical research are labeled "Social Science" schools. The principal concern of such schools would be academic rigour.

This approach, however, also has its difficulties; not least of which is the fact that management doctorates are in short supply these days. The defence of research without practical applications, or worse yet, research findings that do not hold up in the real world because of flawed assumptions, can be but a feeble one. To ignore the chorus of voices calling for research that is relevant, not arcane, would be to bury one's head in the sand.

Durand and Dameron (2008) also present possible future scenarios for management education. Their perspective, however, is very much from that of European business schools and takes the American model that is dominant today as the reference point.

The backdrop to the European situation, as described by the authors, is one where there is under-investment in higher education and where attempts at raising funds through increasing tuition fees have seen significant difficulties.

Competition for faculty is exacerbated by a fall in doctoral enrolment, an increasing number of retiring baby boomers among current faculty and a pay disparity between European and American business schools that gives the latter a significant upper hand in faculty recruitment. More generally, European business schools have traditionally also had weaker links with businesses compared to their American counterparts.

They also note nine challenges internal to the ecosystem of management education that schools face, clustered around the "what", "who", and "how" of management education.

The "what" challenges have to do with:

- establishing management research as a legitimate scientific endeavour
- ensuring the relevance of management knowledge to practitioners and the ability of business schools to equip students with the rights skills to be successful managers
- developing a European brand of management that draws on its current strength of paying more attention to the wider social context of businesses (e.g. ethics and corporate social responsibility, cultural diversity) or that better reflects the idiosyncrasies of the European socio-economic system.

The challenges that belong to the category of "who" have to do with:

- coping with the increasing commercialisation of academia as faculty respond to the competition for talent by capitalising on market opportunities and students behave as "customers" in an environment characterised by a diversity of programme choices
- ensuring competitive agility given the European context of reliance on public funding, central control by a ministry and limited autonomy in

such areas as student selection, tuition fees, and recruitment and promotion of faculty

- grappling with dilution of/conflicts with a school's branding as individual programmes, groups of faculty or individual faculty build their own reputation.

The "how" of management education — the process and method by which teaching is delivered — is confronted with the following challenges:

- determining the balance that should be struck between teaching and research and between different programmes in a school's portfolio (noting that different programmes, to differing extents, help to generate revenue, build reputation and provide a public service)
- responding to the reconfiguration of the value chain, as technology disrupts traditional models of teaching and fundamentally alters the skills demanded of faculty
- addressing managers' need periodically to refresh their knowledge and the increasing trend of interspersing work and study, such as part-time students and internships.

The above challenges provide the context for five future scenarios proposed by Durand and Dameron.

1. The first scenario is what they label "drifting away" and represents a situation where current trends persist — public funding continues to be low, difficulties filling faculty positions remain and the quality of teaching suffers.

   American business schools sustain their dominance and continue to draw top MBA candidates and business executives to their shores. Only the leading European business schools are able to break away from the pack to improve quality. In this scenario, research moves further away from the practice of management and becomes firmly anchored in the world of academia.

   > In the second scenario, European business schools are revitalised by increased funding from EU governments, motivated by the need to compete more effectively in the world economy

2. In the second scenario, European business schools are revitalised by increased funding from EU governments, motivated by the need to compete more effectively in the world economy.

   Some autonomy is granted to universities thereby allowing business schools greater control over admissions criteria, tuition fees charged and how they attract faculty. As an academic career becomes more attractive, the demand for doctoral education increases, more Europeans join the ranks of the academy and European management education develops a more distinct identity.

As a point of differentiation to the dominant American model, some European business schools move closer to the practice of management. This bridging of the academic and the practitioner worlds has the desirable side-effect of drawing interest and funding from businesses.

3. The third scenario proposed is one where technology causes a paradigm shift in the value chain of management education. An unbundling occurs where faculty become knowledge creators in their design of content and universities become vendors of this content.

   Affiliation to one's home university weakens as such faculty market their content to multiple universities and some may go as far as to operate on a private basis outside the confines of a university.

   Other faculty may choose instead to focus on classroom teaching and become, in effect, distributors of content created by others. This focus on e-learning content as the product makes it possible for non-academics to enter the market with their own versions of packaged knowledge, effectively blurring the lines between academia and practice.

   Management education would be corralled into a model where commercial interests become dominant and the traditional notion of the university as a knowledge hub would be undermined.

4. In the fourth scenario, competition puts the spotlight on the need to gain visibility through size, to have an international profile and to reap economies of scale.

   In order to achieve this, mergers and acquisitions, joint ventures and alliances become the instruments of choice. Networks of campuses/schools emerge out of this. By gaining strength through size and visibility, sourcing funding (both public and private) becomes an easier task.

   The greater financial flexibility afforded in turn allows business schools to improve the situation regarding hiring and quality of teaching and research. Their enhanced position ultimately allows them to reinforce their legitimacy as knowledge creators and commercial thinking becomes more muted.

5. The fifth scenario is one that Durand and Dameron refer to as "reactive adaptation". In this scenario, business schools look to multiple avenues to increase funding (by increasing tuition fees, building executive teaching programmes, seeking out donors, building partnerships with companies and so on).

   Improvements to quality are reaped slowly but surely dependent upon institutions' resourcefulness in sourcing funding. Closer ties between business schools and industry are forged but without crowding out the role of the academy. While the gap between European and American business schools is narrowed, the dominant model for management education is still very much the American model.

The set of scenarios envisioned by Starkey and Tiratsoo and by Durand and Dameron are of course quite different, motivated as they are by different concerns and challenges.

Starkey and Tiratsoo's scenarios are largely a response to the criticism that business schools have lost their relevance and they reflect the consequent tension in philosophical inclinations between those who believe in the unfettered pursuit of knowledge and those who believe that management education should serve a utilitarian goal.

Durand and Dameron, on the other hand, consider a larger set of forces that confront European business schools, chief among which are inadequate funding, difficulties in attracting and retaining faculty, and the emergence of e-learning technologies.

Nonetheless, their scenarios are also represented in terms of differing degrees of rootedness in scholarly activity as opposed to a focus on practical relevance. It is this dimension that they have in common with the scenarios of Starkey and Tiratsoo.

We turn now to an examination of the scenarios developed by our expert panel.

Introduction to Scenarios Generated by Our Expert Panel

The exploration of potential scenarios provides an opportunity for our respondents to develop a number of futures for management education. Scenarios are not forecasts but rather an approach to facilitate and map the possible long-term outcomes of a range of trends, events and pathways as the field of management education evolves in the future.

> **It is important, for example, to recognise that there may not be a consensus "ideal future" among our experts simply because they have different subjective judgements and personal evaluations of how the future may evolve**

It is important, for example, to recognise that there may not be a consensus "ideal future" among our experts simply because they have different subjective judgements and personal evaluations of how the future may evolve.

We asked respondents to think of three scenarios — best, most likely and worst — that would cover their perceptions of the breadth of futures of management education in the next decade.

What emerged overall were three scenarios we have described as a "muddling through" scenario (for most likely), a "shakeout" or "stagnation" scenario (for worst case) and an "ideal" scenario (for best case).

The characteristics of each scenario are outlined in Table 4.1 and then examined in detail using selected quotes from our interview experts to explain these scenario characteristics.

Best-Case Scenarios for Management Education Over the Next 10 Years

When asked about the best-case scenario for management education over the next 10 years, responses corresponded to two broad themes.

Figure 4.1 shows that almost three-quarters of responses stressed the need to create more value for stakeholders, while the remaining 26% of responses covered issues related to the structure of the management education field. (Note that this is the proportion of overall responses rather than the proportion of respondents; each respondent can have responses that relate to more than one theme.)

The best-case scenarios for management education over the next 10 years involve significant differences from the *status quo*. The scenarios articulated by our respondents were often quite far removed from the way that business schools and their offerings are currently arranged. They represent, in essence, an "ideal" or aspirational scenario seeking to inspire and drive innovation in management education.

From the two broad themes of creating value for stakeholders and the structure of business schools in the management education field, we were able to identify characteristics of those scenarios that represent a change from the current state of affairs (Table 4.2). While some respondents focused their responses on a specific characteristic, others identified a combination of characteristics in presenting their views.

As can be seen from the Table 4.2, the characteristic most frequently discussed by respondents concerned the nature of pedagogy in business schools. A third of respondents discussed refocusing the purpose of management education and a third talked about bringing schools of business closer to management practice.

Around a quarter of respondents said that adapting to the global landscape was a key issue underpinning the best-case scenario for management education. For 17% of respondents, the structure of the field (predominantly the relationship between business schools, universities and the competitive environment) would be significantly different from the status quo.

Table 4.1: Future scenarios: characteristics.

Name	Characteristics
Best case	
"Ideal"	Improved pedagogy — how and what is taught
— Inspiring	Purpose — seen as valuable in defining and justifying the role of management
— Innovative	Closer to practice
— Valuable	Aligned with public and private management
— High quality	Global — instilling cultural and contextual intelligence
— Practical	High-quality positioning
Most likely case	Follow the market trends
"Still muddling but not yet through"	Incremental change — market-led portfolio management
	Practical relevance
	Market saturation — elite schools win
	Competition — particularly private competition
	Disaggregation of the value chain
Worst case	Irrelevance and illegitimacy for business and society
"Shakeout"	"Sink to the bottom"
"Stagnation"	"Head in the sand" — ostracism
"Knee deep in the big muddy"	"Cash cow" becomes "Starved cow" for universities

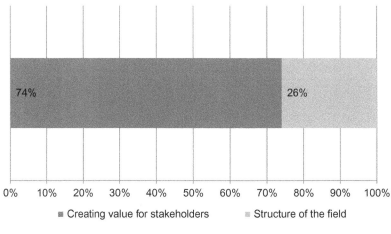

Figure 4.1:   Best-case response map.

Table 4.2: Themes and distinctive characteristics in the "best-case" scenario.

Themes	Distinctive characteristics in the "best-case" scenario	Count of mentions (35 respondents)	Percentage of respondents highlighting characteristic
Value to stakeholders in management education	Pedagogy	13	37%
	Purpose	12	34%
	Move closer to practice	12	34%
	Improve quality	3	9%
Structure of the field	Become global	8	23%
	Structure of business schools/universities	6	17%

Finally, a small number of responses indicate that the quality of management education has to improve beyond current levels of provision.

Improved Value to Stakeholders

Pedagogical Improvements   Thirty-seven per cent of respondents mentioned pedagogical improvement as a significant characteristic. Pedagogy involves the teaching and learning process within management education and encompasses both the content of the body of knowledge disseminated in business schools (what is taught and learned) as well as how it is delivered (the methods by which management education is delivered and how students interface with the subject).

There has been criticism from writers such as Mintzberg (2004), Khurana (2007) and Schoemaker (2008) about whether we have yet identified the body of knowledge that should be taught in management schools. There is still ferment about curricula over-emphasis on business and analytic skills and under-emphasis on skills such as leadership, problem framing, problem solving and integrative thinking.

In other words, critics ask whether we have achieved a curriculum balance between domain knowledge and those skills of problem solving, criticism and synthesis that are necessary to operate in an ambiguous and multi-disciplinary management environment (Thomas et al., 2013, Chapter 3).

> There is still ferment about curricula over-emphasis on business and analytic skills and under-emphasis on skills such as leadership, problem framing, problem solving and integrative thinking

There is a strong belief expressed by our respondents in the development of a broader, more "holistic" and integrated approach to management education. For example, they stress the need for managers to write and communicate well, and for educators to nurture the ethical and moral aspects of the management task.

"Ideally there would be a stronger consensus towards a strong paradigm and a 'holistic' approach to management education. This conceives of management as an integrated discipline and suggests that such a curriculum should foster continued profitable growth of business schools, given the underlying demand for business and management training."

"Business programmes are going to focus less on business disciplines and actually be delivered by creating a lot of other support activities: oral and written communication, ethics, leadership and other things that we can add that make people more productive, more diversified, training them not so much in the disciplines but also in how they can make decisions related to certain core areas such as marketing, finance and so on."

Respondents also envisage a much closer partnership between academia and business to enhance relevance and promote awareness of innovative and entrepreneurial skills.

"I think a blended partnership between academia and business focused on designing relevant programmes of education and training is important. It would equip managers with the ability to think critically, with a good knowledge of society in general and knowledge of the leading edge of business. I also think that we need to work harder at making our managers much more innovative, entrepreneurial and risk taking."

There is also the view that the change initiatives of a major business school or the ideas of a highly respected management educator might generate, and stimulate, important curriculum changes.

"The most transformational and innovative development would be if a major player or role model in the sector 'pulled off' the design of a kind of integrated curriculum as suggested by Professor Teece [University of California, Berkeley]. I think if that were to happen people would pay attention."

Wilson and Thomas (2012, pp. 374, 375) point out that teaching should "develop a strong norm of learning" and inspire students, and Thomas and Thomas (2012, p. 359) also note that business schools must embrace e-learning and blend technology-enabled learning with more conventional face-to-face models of instruction. Our respondents endorse this increased focus on new, more flexible teaching models and approaches.

"We will understand that our focus in undergraduate education is in preparing people for lifelong learning, for learning effectively and

> **Business schools must embrace e-learning and blend technology-enabled learning with more conventional face-to-face models of instruction**

efficiently … . People in careers will move in more directions and will change jobs faster and more frequently than we have seen in the past. Therefore, teaching people how to learn, and adapt to change, will be more important."

"I think it is proper to value and improve teaching and offer a real focus on making the teaching always relevant to the students' upcoming business lives. The use of case studies, group learning, examining the global context and appropriate use of technology are important. And ideally [we should develop] opportunities for learning whether it's internships or different experiences."

"If technology grows, that model of education could be here in 10–20 years and how well those that provide quality management education adapt is critical. We're going to have to come up with standards and evaluation techniques that adapt to that environment because that's where it's going. 'Bricks and mortar' approaches begin to disintegrate — not totally. But imagine a big volume of students — I don't know how else we're going to do it if we don't have a more flexible classroom."

"And I think that probably we will be moving to more flexible learning and more flexible programmes, ones that will have a mixture of face-to-face and distance learning; maybe modular and maybe done in different places with transfer credits. You may study here, continue there; people will have to learn to be more flexible."

(Returning to) the Purpose of Management Education   The respondents certainly feel that proper reflection and review about the purpose of business schools in particular and management education in general is required. This sense of the search for an "ideal" purpose is clear in the following quotes.

"I keep coming back to this purpose. To me the ideal scenario for business schools in the future is that they are viewed in our society, our world, as fundamentally important for the future of the world."

"I tend to think that we can address some of the world's problems through being better managers and good management — a better managed world will be a better world."

"Well, I think that the best case would be a school which has such a strong position that it really creates an atmosphere where the top leaders will be, quote, 'produced'. But at the same time, they will produce research and have a commitment in society and play a relevant role in the solving of problems of society."

Our more pragmatic respondents ask whether we really understand our "end product" and whether we feel confident that we are producing good managers. Do we as educators have the appropriate toolkit?

"We should be more aware of the things we need to do in order to produce graduates who are good at managing organisations but we need a better understanding, a better narrative, of why what we do in management education is actually producing good managers. And we achieve this with confidence so that it's not just the best business schools that are creating successful managers but it is true everywhere in the world. Thus in business education we're actually producing managers who are really running things well."

"I think that we should begin at the end, and there we run into problems. You should say: 'what do we want to have as an end product?' And if you go to management you will

> Our more pragmatic respondents ask whether we really understand our "end product" and whether we feel confident that we are producing good managers. Do we as educators have the appropriate toolkit?

get a very long silence. In general, line management hasn't got a clue about what it wants as a manager in 5–10 years' time. So I think that the schools have a task to identify what are the managerial needs and then address them."

Moving Closer to Practice   Our respondents feel strongly that business schools should be closer to practice and mimic the activities of other professional schools.

"We would have a closer relationship with the business world. The closer relationship means that our research is more relevant to the business world and our graduates are highly regarded and welcomed by the business world. The business world [would] in turn really respect the business school and they would [then] like to sponsor and support business school events and projects."

"There's a need for companies to recognise that management education is good for their managers and that they value it. Therefore, business schools can profit and use their profits sensibly to reinvent their business plans so that they are not dependent on overly expensive faculty, who are themselves over reliant on irrelevant research."

"Management education should be about managing people to be better managers and to create more wealth. And I don't think that the structures that we have in place at the minute permit that."

Improving Quality   There are concerns about whether there is an adequate supply of high-quality human capital (management) faculty to ensure the continued quality improvement and growth of management education.

> "Idealistically, business schools would be populated by really inspiring academics who are broad-based thinkers and who are able to look way beyond their subject areas. It's not things like technology — that will come. Resources will be attracted — that will happen. I am much more worried about the human aspect than the physical."

> "Essentially it is about the underlying quality of what we do in business schools and making sure that this quality actually connects with the needs of the market. But I think that we are an industry in which the quality of what we do in terms of teaching, mentoring students, in terms of research, has to be the driving factor for us. If we improve the quality of what we do substantially, and then we make sure that these programmes somehow meet the needs of companies and graduate students, this would be a fantastic scenario for the next ten years."

Structural Changes in the Field

Structures that Promote Greater Market-Responsiveness, Cooperation and Innovation   Just over a quarter (26%) of responses to the question of the "best-case" scenario relate to the structure of the sector. This comprises two aspects of management education: the organisation of business schools, often as part of a university system, and the capabilities of schools. The concerns relate to the positioning of business schools in both the university and the marketplace and the development of dynamic capabilities through different forms of co-operation among business schools.

> "[Schools] can also use their profits to gain some independence and autonomy. I think that business schools are different from other faculty areas within universities. They have a different, more

> **"I'd like to say [that] in ten years, the best-case scenario would be if we can get all different management education providers who are interested in quality working together collectively to improve standards and models while maintaining their own separate identities"**

market-oriented approach in terms of what scholarship and success means to them. For example, there are few other areas where there is such a marketplace emphasis on getting your students into good jobs. Because doing that attracts good students to come to the school which builds reputation and which then attracts good faculty."

"I'd like to say [that] in ten years, the best-case scenario would be if we can get all different management education providers who are interested in quality working together collectively to improve standards and models while maintaining their own separate identities. For that we don't have a semblance of an appropriate structure."

"Find a positioning for management education that is not hampered by organisational constraints, such as schools having rules that preclude certain strategies and external influences by accreditation and ranking agencies, which tend to foster homogeneity and imitative rather than innovative strategies. The key issue is to identify structures, internally and externally, that can promote innovation and change."

Becoming More Global   Our respondents take up the challenge of making management education a truly global discipline. They stress that the rise of players in Asia and Latin America provides strong diversity and the creation of a range of different models of management education.

"I believe that the great ... global corporations cannot just go to the very few business schools that ... are global. Believe it or not, everybody claims to be global but there are very few business schools in the world that are global. [Being global] has to do with the geography but [it also] has to do essentially with the mentality of people becoming globally aware. Therefore, I believe that there are many big companies in the world that need management education. However, they will not always find in business schools as much global capability as they need for a management education."

"I think in the global economy it's not the US v[s] the rest; it's multiple centres of growth and development in management education. So we are going to see more quality global players and more levelling-out of capability in that middle section. None of the developing country players seem to have endowments of billions to me but they can certainly provide good business education."

"I think that it will be more diverse because I also realise that my frame of thinking is very much Western. I am of course from the West, with all the good and bad things that entails. There will be a new kind of management education in Asia, China, India and Latin America. Africa may be a bit slower. But I know a few things about China and I think the people in the new institutions are not necessarily copying the models and mindsets of what we have been following in the West. I think that they have their own cultural backgrounds and they also have the ability to jump a generation. So I think that there will be new forms of business schools that will emerge, which will become competitively stronger."

Most Likely Scenarios for Management Education Over the Next 10 Years

It is interesting to note from Figure 4.2 that in the "most likely" scenarios respondents place far greater emphasis on the structure of the field (45% responses concern structural aspects of the sector) than in either best- or worst-case scenarios. Competitive pressures (24% of responses) are also

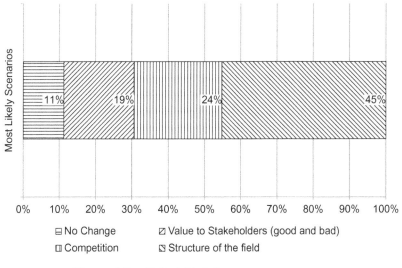

Figure 4.2:   "Most likely" case response map.

Table 4.3: Themes and distinctive characteristics in the most likely case scenario.

Themes	Distinctive characteristics in the "most likely" scenario	Count of mentions (35 respondents)	Percentage of respondents highlighting characteristic
Structure	Specialisation of schools	7	20%
	Globalisation	6	17%
	Private providers	5	14%
	Technology-driven change	3	9%
	Changes to faculty structure	2	6%
	Stable elite	2	6%
	More corporate degrees	2	6%
	Reduced state funding	1	3%
Competition	Increase in competition	8	23%
	Decrease in demand	4	11%
	Shake out	2	6%
	Growing importance of rankings	1	3%
Value to	Increase relevance	7	20%
stakeholders	Improve teaching	4	11%
(good and bad)	Less relevant	1	3%
No Change	No change	7	20%

seen as playing a strong role in how respondents perceive the future unfolding while value to stakeholders (19% of responses) and no change (11% of responses) receive less attention.

For each of the four broad themes of "structure", "competition", "value to stakeholders" and "no change", we identified distinctive characteristics that differentiate the most likely scenario from the status quo (see Table 4.3).

Structural Changes in the Field

One of the key elements in these structural aspects is the decline in government-level funding for management education and the consequent struggle for financial resources that results.

"The most likely outcome is that there's going to be a continuing decline in government support. I don't mean just public universities. Even the private universities will be affected.
For example, Stanford is a private university. However, if
you extracted all the government money or grants, we'd close
up half the university. The engineering school and the medi-
cal school would go. The business school could probably still
operate but they wouldn't get any university support. So I
think that the issue is how fast government funding will
decline. And it is important to recognise that the government,
with declining funding, will probably meddle more than they
currently do."

This lack of funding is seen by our experts as leading to a disaggregation
of the value chain. This will lead to strong review of such elements as technology enhanced learning and a thorough questioning of the "bricks and
mortar" model.

"A likely scenario is a fragmentation of education outside of
the university — I think that if the universities can act as a
sort of gravitational hub around essentially different levels of
management education, we will encourage diversity: some
people doing self-study, some people consuming shorter programmes, some people providing and finding ways of flexible
degree certification."

"If you build a business school what would you start with —
would you start with physical infrastructure? A lot of this
will increasingly be technology mediated. How do private
schools such as Apollo operate? These guys are probably
going to eat the lunches of some of the traditional providers.
I suspect you'll see a move away from that kind of 'bricks
and mortar' operation and there'll be a move towards something else."

"I think in Europe, and in the UK in particular, business
schools have got to get real. They've got to realise that the
glory days are over and that they've now got to adopt a strategy that could change. For example, they might use the
Internet as a vehicle and produce work, which, in my view, is
high quality and matters. And that might mean some of the
larger schools slimming down and reducing numbers, and I
think that is something that will come as a bit of a shock to

> many schools. They've never really had to do that in any significant way and this will be a big transformation."

Our respondents see increasing attempts by schools to change direction. This may involve internationalisation strategies, more specialised (niche) strategies and adoption of lower-cost provision by private providers as they reinforce their market entry strategies.

> "I see in the developed world a stronger specialisation. We will have a stronger push for business schools to be more specific on their positioning and their specialisation. I think the growth of portfolio-type business schools will increase this pressure very heavily. So competition will push things, at least in the most developed countries in which our selling market is more mature ... towards a kind of specialisation."

> "I have no doubt that the leading business schools will be looking at external internationalisation, if the numbers internally begin to decline. So, I think that's an opportunity to be more proactive about internationalising abroad. You know, if the students are not coming to you, you go to them."

> "The top ten, the top 50, top 100 schools — I don't think that anybody is going to topple them. I don't see any real risk there but I do think that you are going to see the proprietary private schools start to dominate the bottom tier and to some extent that will have an impact."

Strong Competitive Pressures

There is a widespread view that competition, particularly from new private competitors, is increasing and creating strong competitive pressures in the field. The most obvious threat is the "shakeout" of weaker schools because of poor pedagogy and under-investment in teaching.

> "The most likely is actually the worst scenario, frankly speaking. That is because business education ... can be done very cheaply.

> There is a widespread view that competition, particularly from new private competitors, is increasing and creating strong competitive pressures in the field

You get a classroom, a few computers and a few breakout rooms and let the students work hard. Further, with a few teachers from industry, you can offer a programme that looks credible. That doesn't mean they're good programmes but they are quite easy to organise. That competition could be very strong, and some of the Apollo Group type of programmes (and also NIAT in India because they are so strong in IT training) could deliver very good, well-organised programmes, and my fear is that this will create huge difficulties for the financial model of many middle-of-the-range business schools."

"I think, really think, that there will be some shakeout of the poor schools, and I think they've got to find ways and means of [training] their faculty to teach better with modern pedagogical approaches and [new] technology."

Our respondents feel that the increased competition will intensify market segmentation and drive schools to search for distinctive, differentiation strategies.

"I think that there will be a continuation of the tendencies of the last couple of years, which means more international competition, including the negative side, which means playing tricks in order to be good in the reputational rankings. More strategic alliances will also occur. Whether or not they are strategic is questionable but at least for the school's letterhead they are strategic, particularly if you can partner with a strong school on another continent."

"We will continue to see incremental change at the top end of our production factory and by that I mean our highest brand names. I don't see the pressure there for change to be anything as pronounced. The innovation will emerge in the second and lower tiers. We will see different models of management education. I think that we could see the corporate sector realising that it does need good-quality management education and research-driven management education. This may lead to a partnership and a new kind of corporate degree-granting university emerging."

"The students will go to the better schools. They've always looked at rankings, particularly with the MBA, and to a lesser extent the MSc programmes. There are many factors that affect the choice of why someone would want to go to one school rather than another. In some countries visa, immigration and employment issues are important. The most important issues, however, would be its brand, its reputation, its rankings, whether it's got accreditations etc."

Finally our respondents note that there is a clear entry pathway into the low-cost, high-quality segment of the field. This may attract for-profit providers such as Apollo and Hult.

"I think that the most likely case is that proprietary [for profit] institutions are going to be stronger, they are going to deliver better and better content, and they'll deliver it in better and better ways and better channels ...."

Greater Scrutiny of the Value Proposition to Stakeholders

Our respondents believe that the value proposition of the research-driven business school will come under increasing scrutiny. University-based business schools will have to justify their positioning and clearly explain their rationale and distinctive features. Their recipe will need to be sustainable relative to efficient, low-cost providers.

"I think that within the business schools themselves the whole pubish-or-perish mentality is going to have to be looked at. The process of spending two years studying something and having it published four years later in some journal that is often not read ... you would think that the researchers or the schools or companies who are funding it would say: 'Wait a minute, why are we doing this?'"

> University-based business schools will have to justify their positioning and clearly explain their rationale and distinctive features. Their recipe will need to be sustainable relative to efficient, low-cost providers

There is also a sense that university/research-based schools are "smart enough" to make the switch to a relevant mode of management education and are in a better position than large-scale for-profit providers:

"I believe that the industry has survived this long [and] that it will make the changes to be distinctly relevant versus the low-cost providers."

No Change

> A number of our respondents made the observation that many schools will fail to grasp the significance of the changing environment and fail to respond in a meaningful way.

> "My mean scenario is business as usual with some frills. I think that my mean scenario also implies one or two, but not very many, institutions getting reconfigured significantly in their business and management schools so that they no longer are just business and management; they may be on to something else or merged with an equivalent group in engineering. But I think that that is at the margin. In general, it is a combination of business as usual and muddling through."

> "I think that many business schools, including some good schools, will completely fail to change and become quite irrelevant. There are some schools that will lose their guard and they will not be able to accommodate that change and to invest in that change."

Worst-Case Scenarios for Management Education Over the Next 10 Years

The worst-case scenarios for management education presented by respondents were grouped around four main "problem" themes: no change; that the field fails to provide value for its stakeholders; that intense competition damages the field; and that the field's structural qualities undermine its effectiveness.

Of course, these are inter-related and complicated issues, which is possibly why some respondents gave accounts of scenarios that involve a combination of issues that span these themes (e.g. that continuity of the current model of management education creates little value for stakeholders).

The responses were grouped as shown in Figure 4.3 for the worst-case-scenario-facing business schools.

Just over a quarter of total responses (26%) were related to the problem of no change and over one-third (36%) were concerned with not providing value to stakeholders in management education. The former showed broad consensus around the lack of change (40% of respondents asserted that no change was the worst-case scenario), whereas the latter represented a constellation of factors that undermined the value of management education.

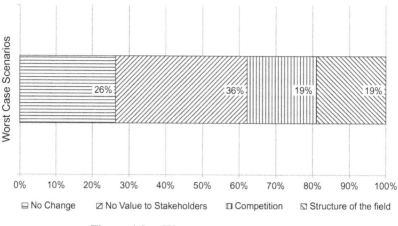

Figure 4.3:   Worst-case response map.

Close to a fifth of responses (19%) discussed concerns about the damaging effect of competition within the sector and the same proportion of responses (19%) indicated that structural issues in the sector would underpin the worst possible case for management education.

We focus next on the intricacies of each of these four themes to deepen our understanding about areas that trouble our expert panel.

No Change

A scenario where there is no change to management education over the next 10 years was mentioned by 40% of respondents as a worst-case scenario. This is a complacent, inertial, "head in the sand" scenario characterised by adherence to the *status quo* and resulting in inevitable decline. For these respondents, maintaining the *status quo* is inappropriate and a future scenario without change is undesirable:

> "The worst case is that we continue to be where we are. That would be awful!"

> "If we just keep going the way we are. The worst case is the "head in the sand" case. You know, we'll just keep going and we see if we can make this work, see if it will come back and see if we stay here long enough."

> "The worst case scenario is insularity [so] that business schools will remain more of the same — they'll hunker down and fight the fight and they'll keep the books and finances going for as long as they can."

"If we continue doing what we're doing, there will be a gradual erosion of the business school."

The idea that stagnation is a worst case for management education is the lynchpin for a number of perceived problems and issues facing the field. Indeed, lack of change from the management education community exacerbates perceived feelings of irrelevance associated

> **It is argued that as business schools fail to keep pace with changes in the business environment, they will become progressively divorced from the underlying business context and hence perceived as increasingly irrelevant**

with the current system. It is argued that as business schools fail to keep pace with changes in the business environment, they will become progressively divorced from the underlying business context and hence perceived as increasingly irrelevant. This undermines the value to stakeholders in management education:

> "Limp along doing what we're doing now. Change presently is incremental and that's fine but the kind of change [that] is happening for our stakeholders is sufficiently dramatic and transformational that, if we are incremental, our lack of relevance becomes even more pronounced."

In addition, change is also perceived as essential in business school programmes:

> "Churning out programmes that have not been revised, updated or redesigned since 20 years ago is unacceptable. There are many schools today that operate on the same philosophy every year."

In one — perhaps extreme — example, one respondent commented that business schools must "... change or they will die".

Indeed, competition also forms the basis for some of the worst-case scenarios put forward in the interviews. A lack of change underpins some of the worst-case scenarios and also provides a common thread that weaves through the three broad themes of value for stakeholders, competition and the structure of the sector.

Failure to Provide Value to Stakeholders

For 43% of respondents, the notion that management education provides no, or limited, value to its stakeholders underpins their worst-case scenario.

Table 4.4: Themes and distinctive characteristics in the "worst-case" scenario.

Themes	Distinctive characteristics in the "worst-case" scenario	Count of mentions (35 respondents)	Percentage of respondents highlighting characteristic
No change	No change	14	40%
No value to stakeholders	No value to stakeholders	7	20%
	Lack of relevance	3	9%
	No legitimacy	2	6%
	Specialisation and fragmentation	1	3%
	Lack of quality	1	3%
	Question of purpose	1	3%
	Too broad	1	3%
	Too narrow	1	3%
	Too much rigour	1	3%
	Lack of specialisation	1	3%
Competition	Competition	4	11%
	Shake out	5	14%
	Race to the bottom	1	3%
Structure	Business school/university structure	4	11%
	Powerful faculty	3	9%
	Become agents of business	2	6%
	Switch to private schools	1	3%

The concern that the value proposition is not articulated well for stakeholders is a more nuanced and multi-faceted argument than the respondents who identified "no change" as a worst case (Table 4.4).

There is a clearly defined perspective and argument in interviewee responses that suggest that the value proposition of management education is no longer present. This ultimately presents a situation where stakeholders choose to ignore or substitute the content of management education. Hence, without a credible value proposition, business schools become somewhat redundant in terms of both business and academia:

> "The absolute worst, and I don't know the probability of this, would be that the MBA and or other [business] education models are finally dead. So people come to the conclusion

that we really don't need this anymore, it's not something that is relevant and not worth what we're paying for it. And I see cracks in that already. The notion of over-shooting, and I think as an industry we have overshot the value, [is evident in the fact] that the price has gone up so much ... ."

"I think you'll see schools disappearing. Pity the poor school in the UK that can't charge £9,000. I don't know how they are going to survive."

"Business schools start to collapse through the failure to convince corporate recruiters of the value of management education, which leads to the failure to attract students because companies start to lose interest in management education as an academic criterion."

"I think that, in the worst-case scenario, we see a kind of social questioning. There is the view of the business community downplaying the role that business schools have played in management education and questioning their value and legitimacy. Therefore, [there is a] switching from business schools as providers of business and executive education to more and more specialised consultants and specialised training firms"

"I think that irrelevance will continue; nobody will want to go to business school; student numbers will drop. The result of that will be the inevitable — not just [the] erosion of some business schools but I think they will become increasingly irrelevant in society and academe. It will prompt the question even more — why do business schools exist?"

Damaging Effect of Competition

Competition presents two types of threats — one arises from the strategies private providers are likely to use and how these strategies will affect the competitive dynamics in the industry. The second focuses on the competition for scarce resources that occurs, particularly in the realm of universities.

In the latter case, this predominantly concerns competition for students and faculty as more global players develop and also a financial transition in some countries away from a state-funded education model.

"I said that competition was on the horizon. I think that it is very threatening because you get competitors with a very different kind of financial business model and there is a risk that this drags business education down to a sort of basic commerce training. Because of that competition we drag

> **"I've been predicting a shake-out for some time. I've figured out that 10,000–15,000 masters programmes in business and economics emerged between 2005 and 2010 and there's not enough room for all of them — there's too much competition"**

down the whole sector and we end up with a few elite institutions who can charge whatever they want because they have a great brand — and lots of bad institutions."

"[My worry is] that management education is simply considered a commodity that anybody can produce and that the Phoenixes and Kaplans of the world become the leaders. Certainly in producing numbers — without disrespect to Wal-Mart — they've become Wal-Mart …"

"Simply a shake-out. I've been predicting a shake-out for some time. Because of the work we have done on the introduction of Bologna in a European context, I've figured out that 10,000–15,000 masters programmes in business and economics emerged between 2005 and 2010 and there's not enough room for all of them — there's too much competition. The shortage in the West in many cases is for students and the shortage in the East in many cases is for faculty members."

"… people don't change, they stay isolated and they think that nothing will change and are not prepared. They believe that this race for the top brand has a greater impact than what [they] are actually doing as an educator. There has to be some kind of balance."

Constraints Imposed by the Structure of the Management Education Field

It is argued that business schools are often constrained by the academic structures within their parent university and hampered by resource competition from other schools in the university context. Hence, continued survival becomes problematic.

"Actually we have a race to the bottom: business schools, because they provide a convenient source of resourcing to their parent universities and so on, start trying to up their volume and cut their costs and in so doing meet BPP, Apollo and other private providers going the other way. They find they've got themselves on a treadmill, which means that they increasingly find it difficult to legitimise their role as genuine academic knowledge providers, as opposed to just low-cost professional development providers."

"Faculty continue to have a stranglehold on resources and business schools continue to produce esoteric research. Parent universities continue to take rents from business schools and strangle them financially."

"I think, from a business education point of view, the worst case is that our great universities will become increasingly irrelevant. It is possible that management education could thrive and survive and universities could die. I don't think that will happen over the next ten years."

Summary of Scenarios

Recall that Starkey and Tiratsoo's scenario of "going with the flow" and Durand and Dameron's scenario of "drifting away" convey a sense of despondence or lackadaisical response to challenges that are unfolding.

The sentiments of our respondents when it comes to the worst-case scenario, interestingly, bear similarity to these two scenarios. The dominant theme in the worst-case scenario is one of "no change", suggesting a sort of strategic drift that permits existing challenges to prevail. Management education becomes increasingly irrelevant to stakeholders under these circumstances.

The best-case scenario, on the other hand, can be summed up as one where attention is paid to developing individuals holistically to become not just good business people but good leaders with strong ethical values.

There would be more flexible models of education as a pure bricks-and-mortar approach is superseded by approaches that leverage technology. At the same time, there is a move closer to practice as research becomes more applied and management education is seen, in fact, as producing good managers.

Thus, respondents' conception of the best-case scenario resembles Starkey and Tiratsoo's scenario of "moving closer to the practice of management" and contains elements of Durand and Dameron's scenario that predicts an unbundling of the value chain brought about by e-learning (except perhaps to a less seismic extent).

The most likely scenario to respondents is a future where competition is intense or, as described by Starkey and Tiratsoo, an era of hyper-competition. The biggest threats would come from for-profit providers with the capabilities to offer the same product or even a higher-quality one at a lower cost as well as increasing numbers of international players.

While the top schools might continue to thrive, others will scramble to differentiate themselves to survive (probably by specialising or internationalising) while still others will be casualties in an industry shake-out.

There would also be a greater push towards ensuring the relevance of business schools, such as by reorienting research towards problems with practical implications. In this scenario, we once again encounter the presaging of a movement towards real-world management.

> **The most likely scenario to respondents is a future where competition is intense. The biggest threats would come from for-profit providers with the capabilities to offer the same product or even a higher-quality one at a lower cost**

It is also evocative of the fourth scenario described by Durand and Dameron, where visibility, having an international profile and reaping economies of scale become an imperative for survival.

What Would Trigger Change in the Most Likely Scenario?

Our experts have characterised the "most likely" scenario as a "muddling through", incremental model with little or no change in an environment of market saturation. It is further suggested that a "follow the market" strategy of market-led portfolio management has been adopted by many schools. We therefore asked our experts to reflect on what would trigger or catalyse change in this scenario.

As shown in Table 4.5, our experts indicate that they perceive three main areas which may modify this scenario. These are discussed in the following sections.

Table 4.5: Triggers for change in the most likely scenario.

	Count of mentions (23 respondents)	Percentage of respondents highlighting area for change
Financial model/lack of demand	11	48%
Faculty	9	39%
Demand-side pressures	6	26%
Technology	1	4%

The Financial Model of Management Education

Thomas and Peters (2012) point out that the current business school financial model, anchored around the US-dominant design model, "is a bit too luxurious" with faculty viewing their main role as publishing in top journals. This is to the detriment of schools in terms of the linkage to practice and the service goals of the business school.

Indeed, there is already evidence that business schools are struggling and seeking alternative models.

An article entitled "Honours without profits" (*The Economist*, June 29, 2013a, pp. 60, 61) reports on a potential alliance between the prestigious Thunderbird school in the United States (reportedly short of students and cash) with the private for-profit Laureate company with its much lower-cost education model. The anticipated benefit of the model and access to more students through Laureate should, it is argued, enable Thunderbird to replenish its balance sheet and cash flow position.

Our experts endorse the view that there is a need for business model innovation to stave off increasing financial pressure.

> "The person who comes up with a better model that actually works is going to be the trigger for change ... how to figure out getting scale economies at lower cost."

> **The current business school financial model, anchored around the US-dominant design model, "is a bit too luxurious" with faculty viewing their main role as publishing in top journals**

> "Some business schools are just not going to make it financially. They are not going to get enough students; they are not going to balance the books."

And our experts also argue that if a top school fails it will be a "wake-up call" for others. They also point out that universities will continue to pressure business schools to produce cash for the benefit of the university as a whole.

> "There might be some financial disarray. Some schools are going to find that they can't function the way they are at the moment. In some sense it would be the business school equivalent of Lehman Brothers going under. If a really good school goes under, others are suddenly going to take notice."

> "Something that triggers change that means [competition] converts to the race to the bottom [which], in turn,

generates pressure from [cash-strapped] parental institutions — typically universities. That would create a potentially very strong downward pressure [on management
education]."

Lack of (Changes in) Demand for Management Education

Respondents note that global demographic and demand patterns are critical change elements. There is evidence, for example, of a shift from West to
East in management education.

"Well, for the degree area, there are demographics. For the
Western world in general there will be not so much growth ...;
people in Asia, for instance, will stay in Asia. They will have
their education there."

"[Change will occur] when students aren't knocking on the
door."

A worst-case driver for change is ostracism through irrelevance to business and society.

"I think that it is also worthwhile to ask our-
selves what society at large and business in particular would miss
if, overnight, business schools disappeared? Answering this question
would define who ... will still be relevant in 20 years.
Management education seems to assume that they play or
may have an important role to play, but how is this evidenced? From my little corner, I do not see, really, what they
do that cannot be done elsewhere. This is a disturbing
thought."

> **Although faculty are recognised as an important source of new ideas and innovations in business schools, they are broadly perceived as entrenched and conservative, "calling the shots" on programme developments and reluctant to change**

Shortage of Faculty

Although faculty are recognised as an important source of new ideas and
innovations in business schools, they are broadly perceived as entrenched

and conservative, "calling the shots" on programme developments and reluctant to change. Nevertheless, because of demographic pressures and a reduction in supply from fewer PhD programmes, there is now a worldwide shortage of faculty that is particularly acute in emerging markets. The consequence is the advent of high faculty costs/salaries and generous reward and incentive systems.

> "There is a lack of sustainability for most business schools within the current faculty model. There is a shortage of supply and the economics of it don't stack up. I don't see the replacement generation of management scholars in the pipeline. I don't see them in the disciplines, never mind in the management discipline."

> "When they (business schools) can't find the professors [because of the] lack of supply of faculty, the good faculty will be 'bought', can 'name their own price' and they will go where they want without any sense of loyalty to their institutions — they are essentially independent contractors. Some providers are doing that now."

> "I think that it's going to be increasingly difficult to recruit staff and continue to grow .... You just can't get the quality of staff today that you could have gotten 20 or 30 years ago. And the reason for that is (a) there is greater choice of business schools to go to and (b) more importantly, there are better careers that are alternative careers and the labour market has changed completely. So again, recruitment and retention are huge issues for business schools, even though they might become smaller and more specialised."

> "... what will define the type of faculty we will have is precisely the issue of to what extent is academic research key for every higher education institution in management. So to the extent [that] it is not, this will imply that you will not need to have people that are prepared to produce that kind of research"

Perhaps working in business schools isn't viewed as attractive as other alternatives.

> "Business schools have got be interesting places to work and, frankly, if you are sitting on an interview panel and you are

looking at some young scholar in front of you and if all you can say is in the next five years I want you to publish four [A-journal] four-star publications. You are not creating excitement about being a management educator."

Demand-Side Pressures for Change (External Threats)

Our experts note that there will be strong demand pressure from stakeholders, particularly students and employers. What students and employers want in terms of the product of management education is an important issue. This entails changing what is taught in business schools to produce "good managers" as opposed to technicians of arcane theory.

"Students themselves will trigger change. In the past, students might have been less vociferous in their own destiny than they needed to be — I always get cross with them if they are like that. They are no longer passive."

"What would [trigger] change would be all these external pressures; the political pressures and the students saying that they want to be well prepared to do a good job and [they] want to be paid well also. So I think that student pressure and political pressure is likely to trigger change."

"Companies need typically two profiles [of employees] — engineers and managers — to run a business enterprise. I think that companies will increasingly say, 'can you provide us with engineers that have a knowledge of business?' and 'can you provide us with managers who are not afraid of technology because they need to use technology, at least IT?' So they will say they need a new type of guy, probably a hybrid manager–engineer type."

And the threat from the new private companies and consulting companies is seen as omnipresent.

"[There is] the rise of external threats from, for example, privates, for-profits or consulting companies taking over in management education. I'm watching, especially on the exec ed side, a lot of different players come in that weren't there before."

We have thus far reviewed the literature and summarised our respondents' views on the possible future scenarios for management education. This contemplation of what the future might be leads quite naturally to the question of what manage-

> **Contemplation of what the future might be leads quite naturally to the question of what management education ought to aspire to; that is, if freed from constraints, what would the ideal management education model look like?**

ment education ought to aspire to; that is, if freed from constraints, what would the ideal management education model look like? We turn our attention to three particular models that have been proposed in the literature.

Ideal Models of Management Education

We include in our discussion, three prescriptive models that have been advocated by their authors:

- The *crucial educational fusion* model of Everett and Page (2013)
- The *agora* model of Starkey and Tiratsoo (2007)
- Vision 50 + 20 of Muff and colleagues (2013)

These models are listed here in increasing order, in our opinion, of innovative transformation. The first of these focuses on the teaching function of business schools and calls for a melding of the liberal arts with management education. It is a model that is more "within grasp" in the shorter term, if pursued.

The second, *agora*, model has research as its focus and calls for a more dramatic change to the *status quo* — a reaching out to various stakeholders to form a network of research partners.

The last of the models would be aptly characterised as path-bending for the radical changes it prescribes to both teaching and research. Its implementation would require a longer horizon before the ideas contained within it are likely to come to fruition. We elaborate on each of these models below.

Crucial Educational Fusion

Everett and Page (2013) note that students (and society in general) justifiably expect business schools to deliver an education with practical usefulness. But they argue that such demands should not mean that business schools single-mindedly focus on imparting practical business knowledge and skills.

They make the case for blending business education with an understanding of the arts and sciences in what they term a "crucial educational

> **"A solid foundation in the liberal arts supports a cognitive dexterity that professionals need to perform well across a fluid range of contexts and challenges"**

fusion", the aim of which is to create well-rounded individuals who have business know-how complemented by sharpened skills in critical and analytical thinking, communications and other skills typically associated with liberal arts programmes.

In their words: "A solid foundation in the liberal arts supports a cognitive dexterity that professionals need to perform well across a fluid range of contexts and challenges".

They also note that the humanities can provide crucial contextual and cultural knowledge that support a higher level of functioning. After all, a manager who pedantically applies business knowledge while ignoring the social, cultural or historical context in which the business is situated is unlikely to meet with much success.

It should be noted that this same idea was concurrently expounded by Harney and Thomas (2013), under the heading of "liberal management education". They argue that an infusion of liberal arts elements is necessary for preparing students to be mature, responsible business leaders and global citizens.

It is perhaps useful to point out at this juncture that if we are to relate "crucial educational fusion" to Starkey and Tiratsoo's scheme of possible scenarios, it represents neither an alignment with the academy nor with management practice since it champions the integration of business and the arts and sciences so that both have rightful places in a novel kind of education.

The challenge, then, is in creating a curriculum that is not too theoretical and not too applied and, more critically, it should not be such that learning in the domain of business and learning in the domain of the liberal arts are experienced as disconnected halves.

As Colby et al. (2011) note, courses in the two domains are often taught by faculty in different departments or schools who have little contact with each other. Consequently, synergies between the two receive little emphasis and students fail to see the relevance of one for the other.

While no recipe has been offered for this "crucial educational fusion", Colby et al. (2011) do note encouraging examples of business programmes that have sought to integrate business perspectives with liberal learning (such as at Bentley University and Santa Clara University).

The **Agora** *Model*

At the beginning of this chapter, we presented the three possible future scenarios of Starkey and Tiratsoo — going with the flow, moving closer to the academy and moving closer to management practice.

These scenarios reflect the tension that exists in universities today; a tug-of-war of sorts between research and professional training and between the search for the "truth" and practical relevance. As noted earlier, each of these scenarios has its attendant drawbacks and none can deservedly be thought of as ideal scenarios.

Starkey and Tiratsoo contend that the best way forward is for business schools to reclaim their place as a centre where new knowledge originates but not in the traditional approach characterised by strict disciplinary boundaries and where research is the dominion of academics.

In describing this scenario, they draw upon the concept of the Greek *agora* — the historical reference for a city's centre of spiritual, political, judicial,

> **In this ideal scenario the business school neither moves towards real-world management nor retreats into itself**

social and commercial activity. It is also a meeting place where citizens gather for various activities.

Using the *agora* as an analogy, Starkey and Tiratsoo make the case for a transformation of the business school into a key player in a new forum, where research is multidisciplinary and where contributions from various stakeholders in society — not just academics — are part of the collaborative landscape.

Thus, rather than constituting a uni-directional movement towards real-world management, it is a movement towards multiple stakeholders and essentially a reaching-out in multiple directions to a network of players. The *agora* is motivated both by a desire to uncover universal knowledge as well as the need to respond to localised and contextualised problems.

Critical to the success of such an enterprise would be factors such as trust between partners, openness to viewpoints from outside of one's discipline and broad representation from stakeholders to ensure that the knowledge produced is "socially robust".

Thus, in this ideal scenario the business school neither moves towards real-world management nor retreats into itself. Rather, there is a blurring of lines between basic and applied research and a conversation that crosses disciplinary boundaries.

Vision 50 + 20

Muff et al.'s (2013) model of the ideal future for management education was the outcome of an exercise that the authors refer to as Vision 50 + 20.

(The name derives from the fact that the exercise comes 50 years after the Gordon/Howell and Pierson reports substantially influenced the world of management education and that it presents a vision for management education for the next 20 years.)

The explicit goal of the exercise was to conceive of a future for management education where there is a shifting of gear from making businesses the "best in the world" to making them "the best for the world".

Implicit in this is the notion that the success of a business must be measured not just on its economic success but also in terms of its impact on society, the environment, its employees and other stakeholders.

The role to be played by management education is expressed by the authors as: "We believe that the mission of business and management educators in the 21st century is to become custodians on behalf of society, to enable and create the business system needed for a world worth living in."

What this vision shares with the *agora* model is the notion of a space or what Muff and colleagues refer to as a *collaboratory* — a space held by management educators for stakeholders to come together to tackle problems in a multidisciplinary fashion.

The three elements central to the *agora* model — the crossing of disciplinary boundaries, broad representation from stakeholders and the creation of a forum — are therefore also represented in Vision 50 + 20.

What Muff and colleagues give particular emphasis to that the *agora* model does not is the issue of service to society. This is reflected in their call to educate students to become

> The relationship between academia and practice would be one where exchanges are robust and where there is unhindered access to each other

globally responsible leaders, to engage in activity that enable businesses to serve the common good and to lead the transformation of the current economic system to one that is congruent with society's long-term interests.

Where Vision 50 + 20 departs from Starkey and Tiratsoo's scenario is its strong call for research to move away from the type of scholarly activity that does not prioritise relevance and that is aimed at the scientific community. (Recall that Starkey and Tiratsoo propose the co-existence of basic and applied research.)

Instead, Muff argues that research should be transformed into an applied field, guided by the purpose of helping businesses better serve society. To do this, business schools need to refocus their research efforts on issues that serve society and to support businesses in terms of finding solutions and providing training as they undertake their broader purpose in society.

Therefore, the relationship between academia and practice would be one where exchanges are robust and where there is unhindered access to each other.

Summary and Conclusions

In our discussion of respondents' responses to the best-case, worst-case and most likely scenarios, the idea that management education needs to improve its relevance to stakeholders was a recurring point.

This is consonant with Vision 50 + 20 as well as the *agora* model in the sense that both advocate the alignment of research to better address the problems that businesses and society need answering. Both call for a movement towards real-world management and away from basic, theoretical research but are differentiated by how far a movement along that path it advocates.

While Starkey and Tiratsoo see complementary roles for the two types of research, Muff and colleagues seem to strongly favour applied research. Regardless of that distinction, it is clear that the call for relevance is a resounding one.

On the teaching side of the equation, the idea contained in Vision 50 + 20 that students need to be groomed to be socially responsible leaders is also represented among our respondents' responses, though perhaps not argued as forcefully.

That the student of management education should be equipped not just with business knowledge but also with skills that allow them to communicate and lead effectively and to be able to think critically, analytically and creatively was also called for by respondents.

This argument and Everett and Page's call for incorporating the liberal arts may differ in shape and form but the underlying essence of each has much in common — simply that holistic development of students, not vocational training, is the way forward. The difference appears to be that Everett and Page see the liberal arts as being an effective instrument that can bring about this change.

Chapter 5

Conjectures: The Road Travelled and the Road Less Travelled

Introduction

In the 1950s and 1960s, as noted by Augier and March (2011), the notion of the business school became a recognisable concept and management education practitioners went through a period of soul-searching. Studies carried out by institutions such as the Ford and Carnegie Foundations proposed that business schools adopt a variation of the model established by the social sciences, generating scholarship with a clear focus on analytical models and scientific rigour.

American and European business schools took this advice to heart and began working towards this model.

The problem, however, is that business schools were never designed to have a purely academic focus. They were always meant to provide pragmatic, real-life management skills to managers, who after business school, would be going back into the marketplace.

Today, we are still struggling to achieve a balance between academic and pragmatic approaches to management education. Business schools also continue to face an image problem. A common perception is that management education is not a serious discipline and it does not result in the professionalisation of management.

Following our discussion of important challenges and future scenarios for the field of management education drawn from our expert panel, we also asked them to reflect on, and provide conjectures about, how change may unfold as they confront the potential routes and pathways that lie ahead.

Using Augier and March's (2011) metaphor of the "rhetorics of change", we identify a number of conjectural rhetorics.

They are the rhetoric of legitimacy, the rhetoric of ethics and social responsibility, the rhetoric of globalisation, and the rhetoric of growing commericalisation of higher education. Below we examine these in turn and conclude with the views of our expert panel on the one thing they would change in management education as they encounter the path ahead.

The Rhetoric of Legitimacy

Our expert panel wrestled with the issues of the identity, image and legitimacy of the business school when we asked them whether business schools can be considered legitimate in the light of recent corporate scandals and global financial crisis.

Our expert panel wrestled with the issues of the identity, image and legitimacy of the business school when we asked them whether business schools can be considered legitimate in the light of recent corporate scandals and global financial crisis

We have grouped their responses in the following way (see Figure 5.1):

- 15% of respondents indicated that business schools have legitimacy
- 42% indicated that the issue of legitimacy was unresolved or too complex to decide one way or the other
- 42% indicated that business schools have lost their way and lack legitimacy in management education

We now provide some of the reasoning respondents used in taking their positions.

Business Schools have Legitimacy

Two over-arching themes support the notion that business schools are legitimate entities.

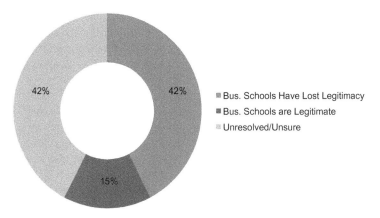

Figure 5.1:   Have business schools lost their legitimacy?

First, legitimacy is justified on the basis that the teaching and research that goes on in business schools is actually of a high standard and beneficial to business.

> "I think that business schools should have been stronger in underlining what they have been doing well. I think that business schools have been doing an awful lot of good things. And I think, again in my personal opinion, that EFMD and many of the educational institutions, or the entire industry, should have spoken up more and said: 'Yes, things have gone wrong but there are still all these managers and CEOs who are doing a good job with our help — in many industries'."

> "In the past several years, business schools, have done very good research in terms of publications and have got funding from some national academies and research centres. In our school we achieved much more respect and legitimacy from our universities because of receiving research grants and awards."

> "I prefer to think that the financial crisis helped business schools find their way. I guess the financial crisis was a wake-up call for business schools, not because they assumed part of the blame, but I think because they now believe they can be part of a better world moving forward — a more responsible business world. They can lead more responsible organisations, they can lead sustainability initiatives; and so I think it was a wakeup call."

"I guess the financial crisis was a wake-up call for business schools, not because they assumed part of the blame but I think because they now believe they can be part of a better world moving forward — a more responsible business world"

Second, the legitimacy of business schools is evidenced by the fact that the media respects and listens to business schools as a legitimate commentator on management issues. As one respondent pointed out:

> "Business schools are genuinely respected — sometimes a bit tongue in cheek maybe — some of the stuff that is being taught is actually old hat. But many people from business schools who talk to the media are definitely listened to. I don't think that they've lost their way in that sense."

While some corners of the media have criticised business schools for being complicit in the financial crisis, the media has in turn been criticised for making business schools the undeserved prime culprit. In this sense, business schools play a legitimate role in helping businesses perform better but are at the same time involved in an image management problem as the media contemplates who contributed the most to the current financial crisis.

Unresolved/Unsure About the Legitimacy of Business Schools

A greater proportion of respondents (42%) were unsure whether business schools have lost their way or were unable to resolve the issue because it is too complicated or still unfolding.

For these respondents, the financial crisis provides a point of reflection and questioning but has not completely eroded the legitimacy of the business school:

> "The situation is not resolved yet; it is on-going. The field is probably in denial regarding the financial crisis and business schools are waiting to see what happens. If it is resolved quickly, then things will not change. Maybe if it goes on for longer they may have to start thinking about how they might need to re-cast themselves or re-engineer themselves in the market."

> "I don't think we knew what was going on [with the financial crisis]; I don't think that we knew how to speak up. I don't think that we were awake and I don't know anyone from academia who stood up stridently and said 'I understand this and here are the immediate implications'."

For others, management education is a work-in-progress where the question of legitimacy is still being tested or simply is not an issue.

> "In a sense, business schools are really technical and professional schools that know everything about the techniques but they are not very good at looking at themselves and positioning their contribution in the whole societal process."

> "Business schools have not succeeded but have not lost their way! However, we have not changed our game much."

> "No they haven't succeeded but I am not sure whether they have really lost their legitimacy. I think this was a very superficial debate."

A further perspective developed by respondents hinges on the notion that schools have been in existence for a long time and have grown significantly. Their resilience through

> **"Despite the criticisms, over the decades, for various reasons, business schools have continued to attract students, survive, and adapt and change and, in some cases, innovate"**

crises and criticism can be interpreted as at least that they are doing "an OK job":

> "Business schools go through cycles. We are told that [they] are irrelevant, that business schools aren't producing what managers want — but that's the managers saying this. What do they know, really? I would say that whatever comes up, we tend to respond to it, [even if] it's a more reactive response. In summary, we probably did an OK job."

> "Business schools, throughout the decades since their inception, have been criticised. And my answer is fairly simple, going back to Peter Drucker. And that is that the purpose of a business is to create a customer and if you don't have any customers who want to buy your product or your service you don't exist anymore. Despite the criticisms, over the decades, for various reasons, business schools have continued to attract students, survive, and adapt and change and, in some cases, innovate. And you have to if you have an organisation that wishes to be sustainable."

Business Schools Lack Legitimacy

Finally, for another 42% of respondents, the situation is that business schools have lost, or lack, legitimacy.

> "We say a lot of things. For example, Andy Van de Ven of the US said at the Academy of Management that we must be rigorous and relevant. Well yes. But do we seem to be moving towards relevance? No. We continue to see a move in the opposite direction ... Have we gotten more practice oriented? No, I don't think so. If anything it's more in the other direction."

> "I'm probably guilty of this myself. But we all know what ought to happen but probably are kidding ourselves that it will happen with the established academic players. Critics in

the *HBR* and elsewhere such as Ghoshal, Podolny, Bennis and O'Toole stressed that we should be relevant. But it's not going to happen. The A-journal reward system for faculty produces high-quality research in academic journals not often read by managers. The reward system endorses A-journals and encourages scholarly writing. In essence, the reward system does not value practical research."

"I don't think that the business schools have succeeded and I think that they're treading water and it is really a criticism of us as a professional association. I think that we're treading water in that we take in as much as we bail out but we've got a big anchor weighing us down in the form of the for-profit business schools that hurts building legitimacy. In addition, we've got internal structural issues from the level of PhD production to maybe the over-accentuation of basic research and then academic structures that deter us from moving forward quickly."

However, if business schools are irrelevant then how can they be held responsible for the negative consequences from bad business?

"I think that the criticisms about the lack of relevance are genuine and valid but if we generally lack relevance, how can we be so instrumental in causing these problems? So I see a bit of a disconnect there. Well, we might be an influence in terms of the culture we create around competitiveness and the pursuit of wealth. I've no doubt that some schools and some faculty pursue those drivers, which are important and powerful. But as an industry, it just doesn't resonate with me."

Perhaps, then, legitimacy may be lacking in the product offered by business schools:

"I don't think that they've succeeded. I would like to see business schools becoming more professional. I

> There is also a widespread notion that the product of business schools may well be destroying good, sound management practices

know that a lot of people see that as going back to the old trade schools. They don't see business schools as a school for a profession. I do think that where business schools are right to seek professionalism, though, is in aligning themselves

> with the professions and ensuring that programmes carry, if
> you like, a professional accreditation because I think that
> that is good for relevance and good for the students. If they
> can go out at the end of their undergraduate programme
> with a degree and a professional qualification — that is
> powerful in the job market."

There is also a widespread notion that the product of business schools
may well be destroying good, sound management practices.

> "There's a growing critique, or criticism, of business school
> students, and in particular MBAs, which I see as a worldwide
> one. And again this is fuelled by social media and the criti-
> cism goes like this ... it says that what the MBAs are taught
> to be is cold-hearted and self-interested, and if you teach peo-
> ple to do that socially and economically, you end up with
> what happened — the current global financial crisis. Self-
> interest rules; it's a Darwinistic survival of the fittest and the
> MBA is a one-size fits all way of educating people through
> self-interest. And you can see that coming through from the
> US to the UK and the rest of Europe."

A counter to that argument is that the MBA is sound and it is organisations that are damaging practice.

> "Well, I think that the MBA is a sound degree but needs re-
> invention. More importantly, I think that the real issue is
> that most people actually want to do the right thing in prac-
> tice, if possible, but the real problem is organisational cul-
> ture. When you take an MBA, you can genuinely say I want
> to be honourable but once you get into an organisation
> where the systems operate differently, you are sometimes
> stuck in a culture — and that's where the problem is."

In summary, those of us who practise in the field have our work cut
out in promoting and establishing management education as a legitimate
discipline.

The Rhetoric of Ethics and Responsibility

How will the field deal with the effects of unexpected events and crises? The
financial crisis of 2008 and the ethical failures of some companies, such as

Enron and World Com, have had an impact on how business schools are perceived.

Media commentators are quick to criticise business schools whether fairly or unfairly. Business schools have been made to appear to be complicit in training the architects of these ethical failures and financial crises. From within the world of management education, the criticism has been that business schools tend to adopt a reactive approach to handling these scandals.

To counter this view we focus on the rhetoric from our expert panel about teaching an ethical and moral compass. Going forward, therefore, it will be important for us to think proactively about how to address the question of ethics in management education.

Our studies show that business school educators have

> **"Something I have learned over the last 20 years is the constant challenge by society of the ethical behaviour of our students and, frankly speaking, we have no good answer to that. We have the easy answer that ethics is something you learn before you come to business school; you learn it as a child. It is a poor answer. It's a cop out"**

become much more aware of issues of corporate social responsibility (CSR) and sustainability.

As one educator on our expert panel explains:

> "Something I have learned over the last 20 years is the constant challenge by society of the ethical behaviour of our students and, frankly speaking, we have no good answer to that. We have the easy answer that ethics is something you learn before you come to business school; you learn it as a child. It is a poor answer. It's a cop out."

Students and businesses are also putting pressure on schools to promote sustainability through organisations such as the UN Global Compact, the Global Leadership Responsibility Initiative (GLRI) and Net Impact, a global student movement on the responsibilities of business.

In response to this demand pressure business schools have started to acknowledge the importance of CSR and sustainability and are increasingly making them a core part of the curriculum. This is a laudable move forward and it is likely to continue in the years to come.

This is emphasised by one of our expert panel in the following terms:

> "Business ethics and CSR are on the public's mind far more than they used to be; there is a perceived 'ethics gap' in management education. This has acted as a demand-pull force on management education to incorporate these topics."

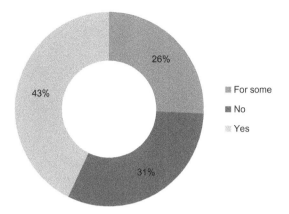

Figure 5.2:   Are criticisms of the lack of CSR, ethics and CSR justified?

Given the presence of an "ethics gap" in management education and expert evidence that some management educators are aware of the problem, we asked our expert panel to reflect further on whether the common criticism of business schools ignoring issues of CSR, ethics and sustainability in their curriculum is justified (Figure 5.2 gives an indication of the results).

The greatest proportion of our respondents (43%) agreed that, yes, the criticisms levelled at business schools are justified. By contrast, just under a third of respondents (31%) reasoned that business schools did not deserve the criticisms received. Finally, around a quarter (26%) of respondents argued that the criticism was, in part, justified but not uniformly across all schools.

This is a fairly stark judgment. Nearly 70% of our respondents believe, at least to some degree, that the criticisms of business schools are justified. However, the reasons that underpin these assertions should reveal more than this general indictment of management education. We therefore examined the reasons given for these responses (see Figure 5.3 for an overview of these responses), which we try to explain in subsequent sections.

Criticism Is Not Justified

Those who argue that the criticism of business schools is not justified (shown in the "No" column of Figure 5.3) produce the most varied set of reasons for why they thought this was the case. One-quarter of those argued that "we've changed", meaning that the sector has embraced changes and answered the critics of business schools.

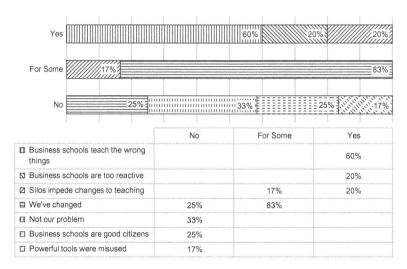

	No	For Some	Yes
▥ Business schools teach the wrong things			60%
▧ Business schools are too reactive			20%
▨ Silos impede changes to teaching		17%	20%
▤ We've changed	25%	83%	
▦ Not our problem	33%		
▣ Business schools are good citizens	25%		
▢ Powerful tools were misused	17%		

Figure 5.3: Detailed analysis of whether business school criticism is justified.

"I don't think that what we do in business schools about [business ethics] is all that brilliant but to say that we have ignored it would not be true. There's been a lot of discussion about this. I think that the public and the media are sticking to their prejudice that of course business schools aren't doing anything about this. However, I think some good things are happening here. But it is difficult to implement. In the early days of being a dean, I wanted to introduce a course called Government and Business Ethics. The only reason I succeeded was because I had just become dean, and they thought they couldn't deny me that. In addition, it was hard to organise and we had no one who could really teach it and so forth. The students thought it was completely mad and wondered why they had to do that kind of nonsense. A resulting internal criticism (not justified) was whether or not we were doing far too much of it."

"Less and less true — business schools have in recent years become pretty responsive."

A second logic emerged which reasons that the connection between management education and the broad conduct of business (particularly events

"Everybody wants to blame business for what's going wrong in the world. I don't believe that the business school is solely responsible for morals ..."

such as corporate scandals or the on-going financial crisis) is somewhat tenuous. For one-third of respondents who reject the criticism of business schools, these issues are seen as so distantly related or so far out of our control that they are "not our problem".

> "[Ethics] is not the responsibility of business schools *per se*. If you care for something and believe it is important, you [should] do it. [For this reason] business schools must integrate ethics and values in the curriculum. [However,] going back to the purpose of a business school education, it is education [and not exclusively ethics education]!"

> "No. Everybody wants to blame business for what's going wrong in the world. I don't believe that the business school is solely responsible for morals, and what have you. After 20 years of teaching on these campuses I have been impressed by how nice the kids are; they really do want to give back to their society. Yet when it comes time to vilify institutions, what happens is that it is usually the corporation that gets the heat and, by association the business school is part of the 'blame game'."

> "We are not evil people. We work hard like anybody else. However, when it comes time to find a scapegoat, the media can always blame business (and business education) because business has a cloudy reputation."

A third logic carries the rationale that business schools are doing a pretty good job and, as one respondent stated, business schools "play as good citizens". However, the focus on such issues as CSR was never seen as a "core" activity:

> "No, I don't think that it is. On the one hand it's not [justified] because business schools were among the first to embrace CSR and ethics to give them their due. US business schools were the first to put on these [courses]. This was a lead that was taken up by the European business schools very quickly."

> "I think not. The bulk of business schools have been aware of the needs of their local environments and their communities. Many of them play as good citizens."

> "My view is that it has never been ignored but it has never been central. And you know I believe that most of what we

teach, or have taught, in business schools, hasn't been driven by an underlying framework that in any way links to social responsibility. I can't name a business school that I can think of that didn't have at least some part of some course that dealt with social responsibility. [However,] It was just never central to school activities."

A fourth group argued that the criticism is not justified because management education provides "powerful tools" and it is not the responsibility of business schools if these tools are misused. However, as one respondent noted:

> **"... it is not a bad idea that [if] we are teaching the use of powerful management tools, we should make managers more aware of the consequences of these tools if they are misused"**

> "... it is not a bad idea that [if] we are teaching the use of powerful management tools, we should make managers more aware of the consequences of these tools if they are misused; we have a role there. And we should also encourage managers to think about how frequently they are going to face trade-offs between doing something that would be to their own individual benefit but may cause broader impacts on other people and society as a whole."

Criticism Is Justified ... for Some Schools

A second group (26% of all respondents) reasoned that the criticism of business schools was justified for some schools but did not apply uniformly across all. This group's reasoning corresponded to two clear themes:

- First, that business schools have attempted to change (83%)
- Second, that disciplinary silos have hampered the ability of some schools to implement change (17%)

It is clear that some respondents believe that schools have changed but have yet to grasp fully how to handle social responsibility and other areas.

> "I think that there has been progress in those areas. Certainly it is now much more evident than it was five and ten years ago. I don't think that we've solved how to handle these issues. Instead, we spend a lot of time focusing on their relevance and value. [For example,] we haven't come up with a

different kind of framework from which to manage. We haven't come up with a different metric than the pursuit of money."

"I think that they are actually paying a lot more attention to CSR and 'green' issues such as ethics. I do think that business schools are paying attention but are not really sure about quite what to do."

"… we've made a lot of progress, but we still have a long way to go. I think that business schools are taking it more seriously because business is taking it more seriously. This was a fringe issue ten years ago for business. It's no longer a fringe issue. Just witness BP."

The structure of business schools also surfaced as a significant barrier to change in relation to whether or not they will undertake or develop courses in ethics/CSR.

"We've always had faculty who've tried to bring those issues individually into curricula. However, when you consider that by their nature they are not discipline-based issues, business schools have by their 'silo-type' construction tended to underplay their significance and importance. It's not that business schools consider that these issues are irrelevant. But their ability to deal with them in an impactful and relevant way has, I think, been challenged by the nature of the beast we are."

Criticism Is Justified

Forty-three per cent of all respondents expressed the view that the criticism of business schools is justified. This is based on three main themes:

First, a dominant opinion is that business schools deserve criticism because they teach the wrong things (60%).

Second, that business schools are too reactive (20%), meaning that they do not provide sufficient guidance and agenda-setting for management practitioners to persuade businesses of the relevance of CSR.

> **"The only thing you have to create is shareholder value and then the shareholders can do with their money what they want … we've ducked the issue and found a very nice academic model almost to justify it"**

Third, disciplinary silos in business schools (20%) serve to maintain the status quo in management education, which means that broader challenges faced in business often go unaddressed in the curriculum.

The notion that business schools teach the "wrong things" featured in several of our responses.

> "Business schools believe in shareholder value in a very simple way. The only thing you have to create is shareholder value and then the shareholders can do with their money what they want, right? Yes, we've ducked the issue and found a very nice academic model almost to justify it. We've seen the limits of that in recent crises."

> "Business schools have not really reacted to ethics issues and have treated it as just another module to be taught. There is too much focus on 'filthy lucre'. And there is not enough [of a focus] on moral philosophy. The philosophical basis of management education [is] lacking — and this is where ethics should fit in."

> "If you look at ethics, for instance, we may have more courses on ethics. However, teaching ethics is about how people actually learn what the classics used to say about having a good life, a life of meaning for oneself and a meaning for others. And I think that sometimes the thinking in business schools over the last 20 years is that this is neither a central nor a relevant issue. The more relevant issue is how you make companies more financially successful. A justifiable criticism is that we are just introducing elements that have more to do with public relations considerations than the intrinsic substance of how you introduce those societal and ethical dimensions into management and strategy. I really think that we are not doing enough in those areas."

There were also respondents who believe that business schools are behind the curve when it comes to dealing with contemporary management issues.

> "My personal view is that they are reacting too slowly and I think that they haven't quite caught up with the fact that their student clientele has shifted in this direction."

> "I don't think that there's a large cadre of schools that want to do much to change their curriculum with the notion of

sustainability being a driver. They're much more market sensitive. Lots of them have put innovation in their course titles in business schools, for example, innovation, entrepreneurship, technology and so on which are much sexier than sustainability."

Finally, respondents again return to the structure of business schools by considering disciplinary silos as part of the problem.

"The existence of the silos in business schools is a constraint on teaching CSR etc. I think that schools want to do it but there is little or no evidence of the development of specific programmes for it. Therefore, it's going to be necessary to embed it more deeply in the curriculum."

"I don't think we have succeeded because of the silo mentality. These issues (CSR etc.) are cross-disciplinary in nature and I don't think that the business schools have worked out how to link these cross-disciplinary elements with the typical disciplinary subject areas present in business schools."

The overriding impression from our expert panel's responses is that business schools need to broaden their curricula and focus on how to embed CSR, ethics and sustainability into the current discipline-based models of management education.

> "... it will be important to include courses that explicitly address ethics and their interaction with critical areas of finance such as risk management"

It is important to recognise that in conjunction with an emphasis on responsible business, it will be important to include courses that explicitly address ethics and their interaction with critical areas of finance such as risk management.

This means more than just studying the consequences of scandals. It means thinking through the everyday ethical choices that managers face when working with other people and other businesses.

It will also be important for the more quantitative branches of business schools to review the complex mathematical models and ethical choices involved in risk management to increase the professionalisation and broad management awareness of the risk management and compliance (regulatory risk) functions in business.

More enlightened mathematical modelling can go a long way to help mitigate the risky decisions that led to the financial crises that we have seen in recent years.

However, it is also important for business schools to articulate that they are not entirely to blame for the corporate scandals that have taken place.

In many ways, it was unfair that business schools were made scapegoats for these crises and scandals. Nonetheless, at this critical turning point for the field, thinking carefully about how to teach future managers how to be more ethical, responsible and sustainable is a valuable step in the right direction.

It will also prepare students to think more broadly about how to prepare for and deal with a wide range of crisis situations. Over time, we trust that the proliferation of courses on ethics and responsibility will change the negative image that business schools have acquired.

The Rhetoric of Globalisation

The other great imperative, and driver, of the future will be to make management education a truly global discipline. Globalisation in its many forms has had a significant impact on management education. It has forever changed the competitive dynamics of business.

> ... specialised knowledge is no longer enough; management students need to be trained to have an integrated international worldview in order to do business in a globalised marketplace

The perspectives of experts from our interview panel illustrate the importance of globalisation for the management education field and the resulting increase in student mobility.

"Globalisation is the overarching driver of demand for management education and the growth of business schools."

"The mobility of students and faculty has reshaped (global) management education."

The reach and particular effects of globalisation are, however, often specific to particular regions and cultural contexts.

In the field of management education, it is therefore important for us to give students the ability to recognise the particularities of individual regions while also giving them the ability to think beyond borders. Within this brave new world, specialised knowledge is no longer enough; management students need to be trained to have an integrated international worldview in order to do business in a globalised marketplace.

Business schools therefore need to move towards a model in which national boundaries no longer matter and in which cultural and contextual intelligence (Fragueiro & Thomas, 2011) are essential.

Our expert panel of respondents recognise the important need for management education to train more deeply the skills required in a "go-anywhere" graduate.

> "Management education has historically not been global and the way that we operated in the past isn't the way we'll operate in the future because it doesn't emphasise collaboration, developing this global-ready graduate. So what we've had in the past is isolation and a lack of co-operation. We've got to move forward towards integration so we can draw on that from the past."

Over the last decade, there has been a marked increase in demand for a uniquely Asian business school model following the shift in the global economy from west to east. This shift provides new options and opportunities for management education to expand in these regions.

There is now more demand for MBA and executive MBA programmes within Asia than ever before. In Japan, following the recession, some managers have chosen to pursue an MBA degree to improve their chances as they enter the job market. Japanese companies seeking to expand abroad are also sending employees to MBA programmes overseas.

In China, Singapore and India business schools are now emerging that will soon rival Harvard, Stanford and INSEAD. Local Asian business schools are attracting students of the highest quality and graduates of these schools are receiving salaries that are competitive with their counterparts in the West.

European business schools are ahead of the curve in terms of their international outlook and there is a distinctive European model (Thomas et al., 2013, p. 4). They have traditionally had a more diverse student body and have incorporated a richer array of cultural perspectives into their curriculum.

The European approach can serve as a valuable point of departure as management education thinks ahead. However, the inexorable shift in the balance of power to Asia means that business schools will need to move away from an Anglo-American focus. There will need to be a much more balanced emphasis on Asian, European and American viewpoints in management education.

> **Students in classrooms from Mumbai to Massachusetts need to be thinking about the cross-cultural dimensions of managing in a global environment**

For business schools around the world to succeed, they need to share resources and exploit opportunities beyond their borders. This will mean forging alliances with other schools and actively engaging in research that has a cosmopolitan outlook.

Students in classrooms from Mumbai to Massachusetts need to be thinking about the cross-cultural dimensions of managing in a global environment.

In today's world, managers need to be able to operate effectively anywhere in the world with a rich understanding of the economic and cultural context wherever they are. One important way to give students this global outlook is to encourage study-abroad programmes and facilitate exchange programmes that allow students to think through business challenges in other parts of the world.

It will also be important for business schools to have a diverse faculty that can provide global perspectives.

There is now more competition between business schools vying for the same group of talented students from around the world. This competition offers an opportunity for management programmes to develop rigorous courses that will appeal to this wider, more diverse range of individuals.

At the same time, the fact that there are more players and greater competition could mean greater innovation and the opportunity for business schools to learn from each other. There is also much localised knowledge that is embedded in universities around the world and great potential for this knowledge to be transferred, particularly as technology continues to make the world a smaller place.

The Rhetoric of Growing Commercialisation of Higher Education

We were particularly interested in the growing commercialisation movement evident in the number of private sector entrants, such as the Apollo Group, Kaplan and Laureate, into the market and sought our panel's view of their future role in management education.

Three dominant themes (see Figure 5.4) emerge from the responses given on the future role of private providers of management education. The first is that private providers are perfectly poised to grow both in terms of expanding global markets and in terms of differentiated offerings to mature markets in the United States and Europe. Forty-five per cent of our respondents indicated growth in private sector providers. A second dominant theme was the issue of perceived quality of the product or service that

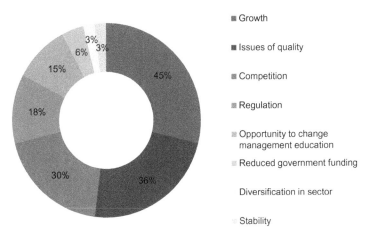

Figure 5.4: Themes associated with private sector players in management education.

private providers offer compared with established, predominantly university, providers. Thirty-six per cent of respondents identified that the quality of service could become an issue for the management education sector, especially in cases where private providers introduce cost-competition to the market. The third theme, mentioned by 30% of respondents, concerns the impact that the private sector is likely to have on competitive forces within management education and the effects this could have on incumbents. (See Figure 5.4 for remaining themes.)

Growth of Private Sector Role in Management Education

Our respondents are clear that there are growth opportunities for the private sector in management education, as seen in the responses below.

> "I would be very, very, very, surprised if the private providers didn't increase greatly in scope and provision. Business education is big business. A lot of people want to be legitimized as managers. [They] want to get certification as a lot of people see it as a meal ticket. I would be very surprised if more commercial operators don't come into the market."

> "The private sector is going to pick up a large section of the educational activity, especially if we move away from degree based programmes."

> "A growth area! I think their goal will be to provide education to a mass market at a cheaper price on a flexible basis."

> "Increasing importance. Look at the OECD data in terms of the increase of private education in higher education. Governments can't fund [higher education]. It is a profit opportunity."

While our respondents see likely growth for private providers, they see its importance as complementing rather than replacing existing models.

> "I think their importance will grow because they will provide alternatives. I believe they will never replace business schools or management education in general, but I think they will become a more important player."

In fact, none of the respondents view private providers as an immediate competitive threat to the established model of management education. This is on the basis that the bulk of growth in private provision will cater to mostly different market segments.

As private provision grows, however, it may not be at an appropriate quality level. One respondent sees the opportunity for growth in private provision, but is uncertain whether entrants will be of high enough quality to grow or sustain market share:

> "I think that, especially if we begin to see growth in the economy, the potential for private providers will surely increase and the market will decide on their quality and value. I have doubts about some of the players, but they must be given the space to prove themselves, to succeed or indeed fail."

Issues with Quality of Private Sector Providers

The real concerns about the quality of private sector provision are evident in the following responses. Is this provision a novel education of high quality or a low quality second-rate, second chance project?

"Companies such as Lorange, Apollo, BPP and HULT are faster, innovative and have fewer institutional impediments. Their big weakness is the whole issue of quality control, admissions, quality of faculty, quality of curricula, etc. All of that needs careful thinking. I'm not sure how that will be done and how fly-by-night operations can be avoided? The worry might be that the large scale providers will attempt to get by with commoditisation and will compromise on quality and innovation."

"The question that comes to my mind is whether in fact it is a more efficient way of offering a good education, or whether in fact it is a con played on people who don't know any better, paying for things which don't actually help them. And I don't know the answer. I don't know if anybody knows the answer. If it's the former, then it's a serious challenge to business education. If it's the latter, then there's a serious government challenge to close it down."

"That's hard for me to say because I think that, on the one hand, their marketing budgets and their business models are so scalable that they'll be well off financially, probably producing mediocre graduates. If that's the case society will pick this up and in the long run people will be less likely to buy from them. So I like to think that they're on this business model peak and then they'll start going down in popularity. They'll appeal to certain people who want a quick degree. In human nature there is the desire to earn something quickly and with not too much effort."

Competition from Private Sector Providers

For some respondents, private providers will clearly increase competition and both broaden and expand their offerings in management education.

> "Some private firms will see this as an area where you can make money, and they will enter the business to make money. It's going to be competitive."

> "[Private providers] will kick the complacency [out] of existing universities. For-profit universities will get a stimulus from government policy and privatisation."

However, others predict that competition will be at the margins of university education and will not significantly challenge the established university model in management education or business schools:

> "Do [private providers] pose any threats to the leading business schools? I don't want to sound arrogant, but at this stage, no! In about 10 years' time I might change my mind. In talking to the leading schools, I think that the private universities and providers will operate at a different level. Maybe they will cater for managers at a lower management level — I don't think that we are playing in the same market yet, but it's not impossible. We need to watch them in my opinion — keep an eye on them."

"Private providers will have a growing market share, but this will not crowd out business schools. Business schools have distinctive expertise, content, credibility, respect, cutting edge capabilities."

"I think they are a threat but not a significant one, so long as we don't lose our way and become totally irrelevant to our practical management audiences. I think that they are predictable. I think they do things differently and they exist for a different purpose. They are not there to generate primary research, or to translate that research into meaningful, applicable and debateable areas. They are there more as a commodification of an industry that's at least reaching maturity. And there'll always be those players who will commodify a product, and they've very good at providing a basic product at a reasonable cost."

This final quote from a respondent illustrates the interplay between all three factors: There is plenty of opportunity for private providers to enter the market and grow and this may impact on universities and business schools either through direct competition for resources or a new dynamic between universities and private providers.

"It's an easy area for the private sector to enter. There is a ready-made market in a sense. If people can do a cheaper degree through BPP on more of a part-time basis ... I think that there will be a continuing growth in that market — and I think that that is actually quite healthy in terms of competition. It will make universities think more about what they are doing."

"There are downsides: I think that they will be teaching institutions so they will not necessarily be advancing knowledge. In a way they are getting it on the cheap. Let the universities create the knowledge and then we'll teach it. But I think for all of that, we'll see growth. That's healthy."

The Road Less Travelled: Unmasking Potential Key Triggers for Change

We asked our expert panel to identify the one thing or issue that they would change as they travel the path ahead.

Their responses to the question relate to two main themes:

- the position of business schools within the university system
- what is taught in business schools (curricula) and how teaching is delivered

The University System

Respondents said that, if they could, they would change the position of business schools within the university system. This encompasses a number of different issues and constraints seen as problematic for management education.

For example, the expectation that business school faculty must produce rigorous research is fundamental to being part of the university system (academic legitimacy). This overarching focus on research poses problems for the mission of management education if that is to produce better managers.

Internally, within the university system, faculty focus on research is seen to undermine the rationale of a business school attempting to provide both strong research output and high-quality teaching. There must be a changed culture in which academic teachers and researchers are equally valued.

> "One of the things that should be changed is the acceptance that not everybody should be expected to do academic research and that you can still be valuable to management education."

> "Business schools should be part of a university but should be given more freedom to develop positioning and legitimacy of management education inside the university context. Business schools have failed in gaining identity/legitimacy in universities."

> "Some of the research has driven teaching out of faculty's mentality, if you will. We have a race of faculty who do not teach. They bargain about how many course releases they can get to facilitate their research output. It would be very nice to change that attitude. I think that a lot would flow from putting the students' education at the centre of the business school. Faculty want reduced course loads for teaching so that they can just focus on research."

Externally, outside the university system, a degree programme in business is sometimes seen as a "soft" option to study relative to science-based subjects.

"I think that I would like to see a more balanced and reasonable view of what management education is. I think in the
UK we are incredibly negative about what management education is. And I think that that is partly due to the fact that
when I was young, you only went to study business if you
couldn't get into a 'proper' university."

At the same time, given the university system's requirement for academic
publishing, the huge increase in the volume of research produced has not
been complemented by a drive to derive useful applications from that
research.

"I think that we have
to realise that univer-
sity is [no longer] the
place that it used to
be ... With knowledge
creation there are too

**"Some of the research has driven
teaching out of faculty's mentality ...
We have a race of faculty who do not
teach"**

many people trying to provide research information and perhaps not enough translating research into relevant information for business and management. We need to [go] deeper in
explaining different forms of research in a palatable manner.
To contribute significant things of value you have to 'deep
dive' in. I think that we need to let some of the best divers in
academia dive together."

The role, power and incentives of faculty under the university system
also emerged as aspects that respondents would change. Our panel believes
that the incentives for faculty are misaligned in terms of providing better
management education. The faculty are seen to "call the shots" in designing
curricula and see academic research as the main rationale for the existence
of the business school.

"You see the point is that [faculty] have been dragged into an
academic system with established values and rewards and
then we criticise them because they are part of the system. I
think they need incentives to make them act differently."

And, faculty inhabit an academic system with established values and
rewards.

"The emphasis on esoteric research, which is only of interest
to academics themselves, has no relevance to what

practitioners do; and there seems to be some peculiar obstacle race to becoming a tenured professor, which is not what one wants in terms of management education."

> "I think that we've hung ourselves up on the notion that the only thing that is important is the creation of knowledge and we've forgotten that the distribution and dissemination of knowledge is of equal importance"

"I think that we've hung ourselves up on the notion that the only thing that is important is the creation of knowledge and we've forgotten that the distribution and dissemination of knowledge is of equal importance. And so ... it's the tenure process that drives it, that's probably projecting the whole notion of the imbalance between knowledge creation and knowledge distribution."

"I would weaken the role of faculty in the running of the school."

The Curriculum in Management Education

The other main concern of our expert panel is that the curriculum in management education and the quality of teaching must also be clear targets for change.

> "Broaden the curriculum. We need a broader base and context in which we teach."

> "I would like to see a focus on leadership. I see that we need to not just give people tools and techniques, but bearing in mind that the role of a manager in the world of work is about getting things done through other people, I would like to see us put much more emphasis on how you get things done through leading other people. And then again, we can't do that because we haven't got academics to teach it ..."

In addition to what curriculum is taught, there are some experts that judge how it is taught as a viable target for change.

> "[There is an] inability of many professors to see that their students probably bring just as much to the classroom experience as they do. To elaborate — not realising that the students, the people who are in front of them in the classroom,

> are resources for each other and for you. You are not the expert in the classroom."

There is also a sense that management education needs to improve its teaching quality and the standard of teaching by faculty.

> "Radically improving teaching."

> "I would change the training of faculty to be good teachers."

It is further argued that training in research alone does not provide, or indeed guarantee, the best management educators.

> "I'd want my faculty to understand — or to have or have had — managerial experience or exposure which would empower them to speak authoritatively both to their research and teaching agenda. I just don't know how we could create that."

However, our experts' perspective is that the focus should be much more on rebalancing the emphasis between teaching and research. Therefore, we also need to get better at communicating the value and relevance of research conducted in management education.

> "Fundamentally, the acceptance that research-led management education is important: we need to be much more able to communicate that. We need better translation of research material. Academic journals must shoulder a lot of the blame because these outlets are not good communicators of the implications of cutting-edge research ... I would hope that we could have better translation of our ideas."

Conclusion

In conclusion, as is clear from these responses, we need to work through basic foundations as we travel the road ahead while framing our identity as a discipline and addressing the challenges of ethics and globalisation. There appears to be a set of key changes our experts call for as we travel the road ahead. They are summarised below.

Teaching and Curriculum Issues

- Teaching is important
- Faculty should rebalance their teaching and research priorities

- Broader curriculum; for example, teaching leadership and people skills
- Faculty as classroom learning facilitators *not* lecturers
- Faculty need teacher training

Faculty Issues

- Faculty need more exposure to business
- There are perverse incentive and reward systems for faculty
- Tenure is a debatable concept
- Faculty power should be reduced

Research Issues

- There is a gap between academic research and its practical impact
- Narrowing the gap between knowledge creation (research) and knowledge distribution (pedagogical delivery)
- Research must be better communicated and translated

Identity and Perception Issues

- Business schools need to establish a clear positioning in universities
- Business is seen as a "soft" university subject

Chapter 6

Blind Spots, Dominant Logics, Tipping Points and Critical Issues for the Future: Unfolding Gaps

Introduction

There is a large, and ever-increasing, research literature on the subject of judgement and decision-making (JDM) and behavioural decision theory (Samson & Thomas, 1986; Schwenk & Thomas, 1983; Thomas, 1984). This was stimulated by the publication of Tversky and Kahneman's (1974) seminal article, "Judgement under Uncertainty: Heuristics and Biases", and by their subsequent paper in 1986 on problem framing and decision making.

JDM studies how people make judgements, statements, opinions and decisions and then assesses how their intuitive judgements about problems and issues can be subject to systematic errors or biases.

Typical judgemental biases include weak premises, availability of appropriate information, overconfidence in judgement, anchoring (on a value or opinion) and insufficient adjustment (around the anchor), confirmation bias (looking for evidence to support a hypothesis) and hindsight bias (a view that what has happened was inevitable).

Our aim here is not to catalogue these biases but point out that they can greatly affect judgements and opinions. Since our research study of management education has relied upon "open-ended" judgements and opinions of experts and stakeholders, we acknowledge that they may not provide complete or, indeed, unbiased perceptions of the future landscape of management education.

Each of these expert judgements may contain inherent biases and reflect the distinctive mental maps and cognitive frames of each of our experts.

They may exclude some important critical issues in the field's development.

We identify critical issues and "tipping points" in management education that may have been largely ignored or perceived either incorrectly or too slowly by experts in the field.

These "blind spots", or perceptual gaps, may have resulted from individual human factors or institutional pressures (e.g. rankings or professional accreditations) that serve to homogenise the perspectives and frameworks of business school deans or university presidents and lead to imitative behaviour and shared external norms.

> An example of a "dominant logic" is the role of the MBA as a general management degree. Despite criticism, it has proved a "killer" product in management education over many years and is still highly valued by business school deans

Such behavioural norms are often described as "dominant logics" — shared views in the management education field that result from the collective experience and common mental models of senior business school and university administrators (Prahalad & Bettis, 1986).

An example of a "dominant logic" is the role of the MBA as a general management degree. Despite criticism (e.g. Mintzberg, 2004), it has proved a "killer" product in management education over many years and is still highly valued by business school deans. Many students regard it as an essential rite of passage if they aspire to reach the C-suite of their organisations.

In succeeding sections we identify the following "blind spots" (or somewhat unfulfilled promises) (Zajac & Bazerman, 1991) that, from our evidence, appear to have received insufficient attention in a field that has been criticised for caution, complacency, conservatism and inertia in an increasingly fast-paced, hypercompetitive marketplace.

They are:

- the impact of technology
- the relevance gap between academia and practice
- the paradigm trap in business school curricula
- the ethics, CSR and sustainability debates
- the importance of entrepreneurship
- the discussion of social and management innovation and business model innovation
- the lessons of leadership
- the localisation versus globalisation rhetoric in the field

We now examine each of these.

The Impact of Technology

Our evidence in Volume 1 suggests that business schools are perceived as failing to live up to their potential with regard to the applications of new technology. While they should be at the cutting edge of technology developments the application of technology in business education is a promise unfulfilled! Business educators are simply not reflecting the reality of the wide application of digital technologies in organisations.

Our students have grown up with these technologies and quite reasonably expect them to be thoroughly harnessed and explored in their business education. As one expert respondent stated (Thomas et al., 2013, p. 163): "I think that students feel that business schools are technologically out of the ark." In their view simply adding PowerPoint presentation slides hardly constitutes a path-breaking innovation.

Equally, "just in time", flexible learning approaches have not been widely adopted using distance or blended learning models and frameworks. These models have not made the headway or impact that has

> **Flexible business education based on distance learning would answer the need for education designed around the work and lifestyle/family commitments of the modern manager**

been predicted. Yet such distance learning approaches would move business education more closely to student demands as they face changing employment and career patterns. Flexible business education based on distance learning would answer the need for education designed around the work and lifestyle/family commitments of the modern manager.

Perhaps the reluctance to change existing approaches, despite the rapid onset of effective learning technologies, has something to do with one of the "dominant logics" of university education — the so called face-to-face "sage on a stage" lecture-based teaching interaction that "has changed little since the middle ages" (*The Economist*, Education, 29 June, 2013b, p. 11).

The challenge of change in this area is to envisage "a potential redefinition of the role of the professor" (Thomas et al., 2013, p. 162). The professor moves from the role of "orator to coach". Technology-enabled learning, transferring lecture materials to high-quality iPad-enabled lectures, for example, should result in a shift from lecture/teaching sessions towards a forum for debate and enlightenment about concepts.

This makes lectures more challenging, participative and much less boring. Students will be more involved in group learning projects, in critically questioning assumptions in their business models and ultimately in refining and enriching their learning processes and insights about the core business curriculum.

It is important to remember that this is the technological age and era of the iPad, the cheap tablet, high-speed mobile networks and adaptive learning software — all of which have the potential to heighten the quality of learning.

As one of our experts puts it: "We fine-tuned our use of technology in the classroom … but I don't see anyone who's been totally revolutionary with technology and pedagogy" (Thomas et al., 2013, p. 114).

And, with an increasingly competitive global economy, technology facilitates the construction of global programmes and associated material through both strategic alliances and the use of blended learning models to enrich the international context of learning (Thomas & Thomas, 2012).

In short, as one of our respondents noted, "management education is ripe for innovation (and disruptive technology)" (Thomas et al., 2013, p. 145).

Gillian Tett, in an essay on the Virtual University (*FT.com/Magazine*, 2/3 February, 2013), wrote that the internet and on-line education are placing "universities on the brink of dramatic disruption". She further argues "these trends have the potential to devastate universities' economic models. If students can now download a course on their iPad anywhere in the world, they might question whether they need to attend an elite college at all."

The counter-argument to the potentially huge transformative effects that distance learning might have on university or business education is that universities provide strong socialisation and networking that are central to current university models. In essence, the "campus experience" with its range of student activities, clubs and active face-to-face learning is promoted as being a distinctive and valuable social, maturation and learning experience.

Nevertheless, other *Financial Times* columnists such as Della Bradshaw (2013) counsel that the advent of MOOC courses (e.g. Coursera) represents a continuing challenge.

> "One of the biggest disruptive forces of the past year has been the rise of educational technology enabling the online distribution of MOOC ... They will bring the teaching of the world's top professors to the desktop for free."

Hommel and Lejeune ("Major Disruption Ahead", *Global Focus*, 2013, p. 10) echo the argument offered by Tett and Bradshaw that "technology-enhanced learning will exert a disruptive influence on management educa-

> **The "campus experience" with its range of student activities, clubs and active face-to-face learning is promoted as being a distinctive and valuable social, maturation and learning experience**

tion". Indeed, they argue that "technological change promises to affect all facets of business school operations — how teaching is designed and delivered, how research is conducted and disseminated and how interactions with stakeholders create value".

As a consequence, we questioned our expert panel closely on the issues of what they perceive will be the impact of technology on management education in the future.

One clear point of consensus among our respondents is that technology has influenced management education and will continue to shape it into the future. However, there are clear differences in opinion about the extent to which technology will drive change in management education.

Four general themes emerge that throw light upon the expected impact of technology on the field:

- technology and the severity of change
- the geography of learning — where students learn
- the modes of learning — how students learn
- technology and the incumbent business school model

Technology and the Severity of Change

An important question here is whether we are sleepwalking our way into the technological future. A key insight is that respondents' views of the impact of technology vary according to their degree of belief about whether it can be a strong catalyst in altering existing practice.

Some respondents view technology as a fairly passive and incremental feature of the management education landscape. For example, they portray technology in a complementary role, enhancing existing arrangements and providing a basis for continuous improvements.

"I think that most of what we've done in business schools — yes, we use simulations and business games and videos much more than we used to in the past, [and] we certainly don't use ... boring and lengthy case studies ... any more and have adopted live case studies — is all quite marginal. There is nobody who says let's do this in a very different way: let's come up with a real innovation! In reality, it is simply continuous improvement."

> **One respondent says "my gut feeling is that it will have tremendous impact" while other respondents labelled the likely impact as "huge"**

"I don't expect very much in terms of the impact of technology on the business of management education ... there are continuous improvements and there will be nice new things but I don't consider any of that to be revolutionary."

In contrast, others anticipate much more profound changes. One respondent says "my gut feeling is that it will have tremendous impact" while other respondents labelled the likely impact as "huge".

Among those who foresee a large impact from technologies, however, there is also some uncertainty over *which* technologies will play a critical role, how they will operate in the context of management education and which portions of the field will be affected the most by an increased application of technology.

Uncertainty was also evident in several responses, suggesting that many respondents may be less aware of — or even comfortable with — many of the emerging technologies. This may be a generational effect!

> "The impact of technology will evolve more and more and more, but we don't yet know what is around the corner. For example, nobody can really know what the impact of social media is going to be but think that it will be strong."

> "I don't know where it will go — I don't think that any of us do."

> "We do not know the technology we are going to have but my guess is that it will continue being a big enabler."

> "I am sure that the trends will continue to a degree which I personally cannot even foresee."

> "If I did know, I would be rich. But I will try to give an answer."

While there is clear indication that technology will drive change, there is much speculation about not only the technologies themselves, but also how these changes will play out in the field of management education.

The Geography of Learning — Where Students Learn

Technology certainly changes the possibilities of expanding education regionally and globally. One of the main impacts identified by our experts was the ability of technology to facilitate and enable distance and distributed learning. This means that students are potentially able to learn from almost anywhere in the world. This in turn allows schools to develop programmes that can unite students and teachers/instructors/speakers across different locations, for example, in a global distance-learning model.

> "Technology already has replaced some of the old-fashioned learning exchanges — some are now electronic instead of face-to-face. I think that what we may well see is the use of

video-based technology instead of just data-based technology."

"I think that we are going to be seeing more distributed and asynchronous learning approaches. These will

> The creation of learning communities that are able to operate globally could provide an enriched learning experience in management education

enable you to run a programme more effectively with a group of people who are in different locations. And with them not necessarily communicating at the same time."

The attractiveness of distributed, virtual learning is even more evident when the opportunities for learning in a global setting are explored.

"We could have much more exciting multi-national projects, with a link-up between schools — there is an element of this happening — but why can't MBA students be working on lots of different projects in lots of different countries through technology? It's all there ready ... it's just not being used."

Similarly, the creation of learning communities that are able to operate globally could provide an enriched learning experience in management education.

"Technology needs to facilitate communication across boundaries of space and time, thereby creating meaningful learning communities, which in turn result in improved use of blended learning technologies."

Among our respondents, there is a clear understanding that, through technology, the catchment for students/customers is essentially global. There is therefore an impact expected from a range of virtual learning models.

Modes of Learning — How Students Learn

Just as technology has enabled the creation of ways of learning globally through distance learning models, respondents also noted that technology has an important impact on *how* students learn.

They identify a fundamental point of departure for the educational strategies of many schools and believe they will innovate and adapt programmes using flexible designs and a range of different timeframes delivered with the aid of educational technology. The principles of distance and online study have been understood for some time and, drawing on our respondents' insight, it is clear that new technological approaches will build on these and drive more flexible ways of learning in management education.

"There will still be face-to-face learning but it will be amended with different learning styles. There will be greater choice, which is a good thing. [Students] will require different learning models. Some people will want a break and focus on the programme while others will want to keep working while studying."

"Through technology we will be able to do more things that will complement, in a more effective way, the traditional interaction between faculty and students."

"You could predict a future where you don't really need traditional classrooms any more. You don't need the three-hour case study any more, you don't need the 'chalk and talk' and by investing in technology you will be able to provide learning that an individual can engage with virtually anywhere they are in the world. So universities and business schools will probably become hubs of activity rather than centres people have to travel to physically to engage in the educational process."

Our respondents strongly support technology developments that help faculty and students interact at different times and through various media. An interesting qualifier is that, in their view, these anticipated changes will supplement, not replace, existing arrangements. There will still, for example, be some face-to-face learning and traditional meetings between faculty and students.

The impact of technology, therefore, will be to extend the reach of business schools globally while expanding their capacity to teach and interact meaningfully through new media. However, this technology-driven shift means that the traditional "chalk and talk" pedagogical approach will be a blended-learning supplement and not the dominant pedagogy.

There is also a strong feeling that the way students use technology to support their learning is different to how current models of education are designed. Further, it is clear that management education has not adjusted to these changes.

"My gut feeling is that it will have a tremendous impact. If you look at kids today, they use the Internet differently — we have not adjusted in a significant way."

> The impact of technology will be to extend the reach of business schools globally while expanding their capacity to teach and interact meaningfully through new media. However, this technology-driven shift means that the traditional "chalk and talk" pedagogical approach will gradually disappear

> "In terms of educational programmes, I think that blended learning will [make up] a higher proportion of turnover in terms of executive education and that we are going to see also much more of it in the MBA and other degrees."

There is clearly a potential mismatch between how students use technology to learn and how institutions in education are configured to use technology in their current learning models. As a consequence there will possibly be an impact on the form and dominant logic of the incumbent business school model.

Technology and the Incumbent Business School Model

The changes anticipated from the movement away from learning *at* a university to technology-mediated learning *with* university oversight were identified in the earlier discussion around the geography of learning.

In the example below, the respondent combines the demand for the "go-anywhere graduate" with the need for a global and collaborative way of working in management education. Technology, so the argument goes, will make this increasingly feasible in terms of both quality and cost.

> "Well, it will reach a point where the cost to develop students and the need for them to be globally ready will spawn much more emphasis on collaborative degree programmes. Even if the home school will give the degree, it will be a collaboration. It's difficult to pull off but we will work together and with technology interventions that will most likely make that programme better and better and cheaper."

Despite near unanimous agreement that technology will impact management education, there is also a sentiment that, at least with the technology available in the short term, it will not produce radical change.

> "In the long run the impact will be enormous but actually in the short run the impact will be much more determined by personal and organisational factors rather than technological capability."

> "It is not changing the essence of management education; it's changing the processes at this point. However, the change in the process is immediate; the change in the essence of the management education model is not immediate. So the impact on the individual is a slow one."

In the short term, different technologies will supplement and enhance the *status quo* through streamlining, making efficiency gains and extending the global reach of business schools. It is in the longer term that technologies will begin to break down the established business school model.

"We don't need to build bigger and bigger business schools. We need to build them bigger in the sense of their global reach using the technology that is available. Why anybody would ... catch a plane and come to [a business school] to be physically there is a big question!"

> In the short term, different technologies will supplement and enhance the *status quo* through streamlining, making efficiency gains and extending the global reach of business schools. It is in the longer term that technologies will begin to break down the established business school model

In summary, it is clear that technology disruption will have discernible long-term effects on the conduct of management education. It will also influence the current "rather luxurious" (Thomas & Peters, 2012) business school models and produce innovations that may lead to high-quality management education at relatively lower costs.

The Relevance Gap between Academia and Practice

The "blind spot" referred to as the relevance gap — often discussed over recent decades but producing few answers — has to do with balancing the production of high-quality, scholarly academic research in business schools with the imperative to engage with practical management in terms of both training management professionals and providing them with useful knowledge to improve management practice. It is often termed the rigour–relevance problem or the twin-hurdle problem in achieving rigour and relevance in management research (Pettigrew, 1997).

In discussing the rhetoric of relevance (2011, p. 217), note that the common response is to call for some form of "balance" or "integration" between experiential and academic knowledge. Debate has centred around the impact of management research (Pettigrew, 2011, pp. 347–354) in terms of its influence on policy and practice.

Indeed, Pettigrew suggests that management scholars should "raise their aspirations and deliver forms and processes of knowledge which meet the double hurdle of scholarly quality and policy/practice impact" (Pettigrew, 2011, p. 347).

Hambrick (1994), in a presidential address at the US Academy of Management, asked the question "What if the Academy really mattered?" thus focusing attention on assessing the relevance and impact of decades of management research. (Note the AACSB *Impact of Research* report (2008) attempted this task much later; refer to Chapter 1 for a discussion of AACSB's findings.)

This seems eminently sensible but, as Augier and March (2011) point out, there are few, if any, significant debates on how to achieve that integration.

More recently, a series of essays in the *Financial Times* has argued that the gap between management theory and practice needs to be bridged more effectively. For example, Kai Peters, the CEO of Ashridge Management College in the United Kingdom (*Financial Times*, 23 April, 2012, p. 11), in an article entitled "Academics Must Bridge the Divide with Business" expressed the general frustration about "the link — or lack thereof — between business school research and business. Academia is slightly conflicted. Rationally, academics recognise that business school research should have intellectual rigour but it must ultimately be useful for business."

However, he notes that while some academics try to address the impact issue, others complain they are increasingly pressured to "publish or perish" in highly specialised academic journals whose output is "patently impenetrable — certainly to practitioners."

> The legitimacy of business schools, certainly over the last two decades, is anchored in rigorous research as an end in itself

Morgan Witzel addresses this complaint in another essay (*Financial Times*, 30 October, 2011, p. 11) entitled the "The Question of Relevance Must be Addressed". He points out that the current espoused purpose of business schools "is the creation of knowledge. That means research, formal empirical research projects with results published in peer-reviewed academic journals … Success in the business school world means having as many articles as possible published in highly ranked journals."

Therefore, the legitimacy of business schools, certainly over the last two decades, is anchored in rigorous research as an end in itself.

Lynda Gratton, a professor of management practice at London Business School, however, offers a partial solution to the relevance gap. She is well known for the successful practical implementation of her "Hot Spots Research" theories on innovation and change, and has pointed out that "there are challenges on both sides of the divide: managers are too busy and professors too focused on academia" (Bradshaw, 2012).

She adds, "I think the challenge is that the bridge between practice and academia is not well-researched", echoing Augier and March's earlier observations about the integration between experiential and academic knowledge.

Given these observations, it seems that we should urgently re-examine and re-design the mechanisms and processes to facilitate translation or transfer of research results and knowledge from business schools to businesses. This should help to ease the tensions at the interface between practical relevance and academic rigour and address the business school's precarious position where the needs of neither practitioners nor academics are adequately fulfilled.

This perceived imbalance between rigour and relevance presents a continuing challenge for business schools. Thomas and Wilson (2011) provide useful insights into the point and counter-point positions about rigour versus relevance that are evident in the spectrum of activities in a business school.

Table 6.1 provides the background for evaluating the opinions and judgements of our experts about the rigour–relevance issue.

> "The urge to develop management as a science and the desire to transform management schools to produce more PhD programmes has exacerbated the tension between the professional and academic sides"

Our experts express their views on the relevance gap around a number of key themes:

- the increasingly academic pursuit of the business school
- weak links to the business community
- the rigour–relevance dilemma in management research

We examine each of these in turn.

An Increasingly Academic Pursuit

Some of our experts continue to question the relevance of current business models that treat management as a scientific rather than practical endeavour. They question whether management education is about teaching and examining the process of management or about focusing on management as a science with a toolkit of theories, research, tools and techniques.

Table 6.1: Conflicting arguments about rigour versus relevance for business schools.

	Lack of practical relevance	Lack of academic rigour
Research	Business school research is too abstract and irrelevant to the needs of practicing managers. It does not attempt to solve current managerial problems	Not enough business school research is grounded in the methodological rigour of the social sciences; it is often too case-based and discursive
Teaching	Business school teaching is too theoretical and not sufficiently focused on problems that managers actually face	Business school teaching is too "customer focused" and not sufficiently distant from, and critical of, management practice
MBAs	MBAs, and business degrees generally, do not produce well rounded managers with leadership qualities	MBA degrees are, or for a long time were, seen as a passport to career progression and greater earning power. The business school is seen as a "finishing school"
Impact for practice	Business education has made almost no impression on practising managers and has failed to impact business performance	Business schools are partly culpable for recent corporate scandals and therefore have had a negative impact on business performance
Output	Many of those taking degrees in management are unlikely to get much benefit from their studies. Their degrees do not prepare them for future careers	Firms cannot simply rely on the university sector to supply the training/education that their managers need. They do not challenge students intellectually and develop creative, imaginative thinking skills

Adapted from Table 1 in Ivory et al. (2006, p. 7).

> "The urge to develop management as a science and the desire to transform management schools to produce more PhD programmes has exacerbated the tension between the professional and academic sides."

> "The one [important] thing is the balance of academic and professional engagement ... We've invested heavily [as business schools] to make business education more academic and we've been quite successful ... But the question is whether we have gone too far towards the academic and not enough towards practice. Is the business school a legitimate school without a significant emphasis on practice?"

> "Management as a practice is not examined. There is too much focus by academics on narrow problems using [arcane] mathematical techniques."

Weak Links to the Business Community

Respondents stress the importance of the link between management education and research and the concerns of the business community. Dialogue and debate between academics and business managers is regarded as essential. This is demonstrated in the following quote.

> "Something which I think we have to do [as a professional association], which I don't think that we are doing well, is serving as a bridge between academics and the business world."

The Rigour–Relevance Dilemma in Management Research

The most pressing concern for our respondents is the gap between the rigorous scientific research advocated by the Gordon/Howell reports (and adopted by business schools) and the practice of management. The gap between research and knowledge production and its relevance and translation to management practitioners is seen as wide and, perhaps, getting even wider.

> "A business school can't be disconnected from the business world in terms of its programmes and research ... A healthy school is part of a dynamic network of ideas from companies, recruiters, students and entrepreneurs."

> "The research we do should to some degree engage with management practice … otherwise you are not a business school."

> "Academic research is irrelevant to management practice … there is little, if any, impact on practice from management research."

The obsessive "physics-envy" (scientific rigour) approach is seen as unfit for purpose in management education.

> **"The research we do should to some degree engage with management practice … otherwise you are not a business school"**

> "What hasn't been understood is that rarefied irrelevant research just can't be at the heart of the business school system."

But as one respondent also points out:

> "I think we still need research and rigorous research. But I think that the issue of relevance and how we make it relevant is very important."

In summary, the critical issue is how we bridge this relevance gap. As noted in an article "Research that Measures Up" (*Financial Times*, 23 April, 2012, p. 11) Della Bradshaw points out, reviewing the work of the UK Advanced Institute of Management, that some professors have bridged the divide.

Apart from Lynda Gratton of LBS, she quotes Professor Michelle Low (Southampton), the author of a much-quoted study of retail giant Tesco, who says that academic research has to be the starting point. "If you're trying to teach people in university the only type of teaching you should do is research-led and research-informed … Otherwise you can read a book."

A similar theme is developed in a forthcoming paper in *Management Learning* (2013) where Paton, Chia and Burt argue that the relevance/irrelevance debate is somewhat misplaced.

> [Academics] offer the proposition that the real task of business schools is to instil the art of making the seemingly irrelevant relevant in order to prepare managers for the challenges they face

Using experiences from a company research case study they point out that by "relentlessly pursuing scholarship, academics can make a valuable contribution to practice by offering counter-intuitive viewpoints that challenge business mindsets".

They offer the proposition that the real task of business schools is to instil the art of making the seemingly irrelevant relevant in order to prepare managers for the challenges they face.

The Paradigm Trap in Business School Curricula

It is important to remember Hamel's observations in Chapter 2 that management as a field has become stuck in a paradigm trap over time with its set of inherent dogmas and dominant logics.

He would agree with Mintzberg's observation (2004, p. 6) (noted in Chapter 1) that following the Ford/Carnegie Foundation reports in 1959 the US dominant design of an MBA programme was established in the 1960s and continues its dominance today.

This "dominant design" has little in the way of pedagogical innovation and not much differentiation from one programme to another although, as Datar et al. (2010) note, there is some limited differentiation in programme design and course sequencing.

Other writers (Augier & March, 2011; Khurana, 2007; Locke & Spender, 2011; Starkey & Tiratsoo, 2007) would also reinforce the ubiquitous presence and dominant logic of the US-focused design, reflecting an obsolete model consisting of outdated textbooks, course materials and case studies based on past experiences.

As a consequence, as pointed out in Volume 1 (Thomas et al., 2013, p. 30), both Hamel and Prahalad believe that business schools must radically re-think their curricula to reflect the realities both of new growing hyper-competitive environments and of the hyper-globalisation of markets.

Indeed, Hamel's comments bear repetition: "What we continue to teach in the business schools is a little bit like being a mapmaker in an earthquake zone. Never before has the gap between our tools and the reality of emerging industry been larger" (Hamel, 1996, p. 113).

The challenge of curriculum change is addressed well by Professor David Teece in an essay (*Financial Times*, 19 July, 2012, p. 11) entitled "Students Blinkered by Narrow Teaching Focus".

He contends that "many [business school] programmes teach from the perspective of single disciplines such as marketing or finance ... but it puts blinders on the students. Such a narrow focus takes us further away from understanding deep problems, most of which require an integrated, multi-disciplinary focus."

He argues that, in today's environment of disruption and fast-paced opportunities, business schools should be teaching how companies innovate, capture value and transform themselves.

This requires introducing an "integrated, multidiscipline focus into the syllabi for all business school courses."

However, the unpleasant truth is that the enemy is ourselves: "the truth is that many faculty members do not know how to integrate the subjects that are the foundation of most business schools' curricula."

We therefore tried to capture the viewpoints of our expert panel on the issue of re-invention and re-framing of the curriculum of the business school. Their views coalesce around *three* themes:

- the perception of the value and purpose of management education
- the problems of the current dominant design
- the need to define new terrain and new models

We examine these in turn.

The Need to Realign the Value and Purpose of Management Education with New Realities

Our experts clearly question the history of management education and its current value and positioning. They worry about the generic, homogeneous current form of the MBA degree and appear to embrace a more integrative, holistic curriculum that addresses a volatile, uncertain and complex environment.

> "We need a stronger context for management education and a stronger sense of purpose about why we are doing it."

> "I think that it is going to be a totally different (information-rich, fast-paced) world. So we need to prepare our students to deal with that. Therefore, I am more worried about the skills for learning we imbue in them than what we make them learn. It will be less important to know marketing and finance well than to teach them [how to resolve problems] and think critically."

> "I frankly think that telling the next generation of students how Canon got it right or about Apple's success with the iPad is pretty trivial ... Unless students start addressing pressing managerial issues, global issues and so on, the disconnect with society will grow larger."

> "The leadership challenges are very different today ... We still need to teach the functional disciplines but how do we

integrate them more effectively? How, for example, do we address the challenges of sustainable development across the disciplines rather than just as add-on courses?"

An Outdated Dominant Design

There is a clear sense that the "one-model-fits-all approach" has gone. They note that we have allowed ourselves to be lulled into a false sense of security with a well-tried curriculum recipe and we need to re-evaluate the design of management education.

> **"I frankly think that telling the next generation of students how Canon got it right or about Apple's success with the iPad is pretty trivial ... Unless students start addressing pressing managerial issues, global issues and so on, the disconnect with society will grow larger"**

"There have been ... incremental, disparate improvements. But I don't think they're paradigm shifting...nor has there been a radical change in curriculum."

"We teach this way because it's the way the curriculum has been for the last 30 or 50 years — this is my course; this is my article — instead of team-teaching and research."

"We became stale by defining management education as the functions of operations, marketing, finance, whatever with a bit of strategy to integrate [it]. We have become so inward looking and complacent — like any business that needs to change."

"We should not be teaching in silos/subject areas ... we have to be more integrative and paint a more holistic picture. We need to achieve far more synthesis across the subject areas."

The Need to Define New Terrain and New Models

Many respondents believe that in an extremely cautious and conservative business school environment we need to identify new ways of structuring curricula and developing new models of management education. There needs to be clear questioning of the roles of pedagogical tools such as case studies and of the relevance of our training in a changing world.

"There needs to be another radical shift ... we have to find new terrain."

"Case teaching harks back to past established practices and identifies them but does not identify how to focus on the future."

"Will case studies still be here? We seem to do it the same as we did 100 years ago — not just 20 years ago. It is still the same stuff. And we should be out there in front of companies not following them."

"I think we can learn by looking back not too far, perhaps to the 1970s and 1980s, when business schools were seen as the future. This was where academic rigour and relevance came together; this was where businesses and organisations of all kinds were able to discuss and develop ideas with academics. I think that it's time, if not revisit that, to have a similar kind of shift."

"The main lesson is that management has to be relevant and that also means in terms of training. For example, history [as a subject] is very important in terms of understanding cycles such as why the banks are making the same mistakes as ten years ago."

In addition, it is clear that our respondents favour experiments with such (relatively) new approaches as action (or experiential) learning.

"I think action learning has a great part to play in our education and we don't use it nearly enough because it is difficult to deliver and assess."

There is increasing evidence of new approaches and paradigm shifts. It is worthwhile noting (see *Bloomberg Business Week*, 3 July, 2013) that Harvard, an elite pioneering leader in management education (see Thomas et al., 2013, p. 111), is beginning a significant overhaul of its MBA that includes a strong element of action learning. This overhaul is to extend the concept of the first-year field course, which includes a trip to a developing country to work with a company to develop a new product or service.

It is for Dean Nohria part of a goal of "translating knowing into doing", engaging in practice and promoting greater integration between the two

> **"I think action learning has a great part to play in our education and we don't use it nearly enough because it is difficult to deliver and assess"**

years of the programme. When Harvard acts in such a forthright way it is inevitable that others will follow with other innovative and creative ways to re-frame the management education landscape.

Ethics, Corporate Social Responsibility and Sustainability

In a *Financial Times* "Soapbox" article (Monday, 4 October, 2010, p. 15), "Schools Sustainability Revolution", Professor David Grayson of Cranfield Management School argues coherently that "business schools globally appear surprisingly slow to spot the extent of the sustainability revolution and the challenges and opportunities it creates".

He goes on to point out despite there being over 10,000 business schools worldwide, only 3% signed up for the UN's Principles for Responsible Management Education and less than 2% signed up for the Aspen Institute's biennial (2011) survey "Beyond Grey Pinstripes", which analyses how well business schools embed social, environmental and ethics materials and courses into their programmes.

On the other hand, in the *Financial Times* (Murray, 2011), the executive director of the Aspen Institute, Judith Samuelson, reports an increasing number of courses of improved quality on topics associated with ethics, corporate social responsibility (CSR) and sustainability.

However, she identifies what she considers a roadblock to adoption of these issues from faculty — "business schools need to do more to shift the belief among some faculty that profit is the sole driver of business strategy".

Milton Friedman's (1970) adage that "there is one and only one social responsibility of business — to use the resources and engage in activities designed to increase its profits so long as it stays within the rules of the game" — is often used by schools and academics to justify notions of shareholder primacy and the enhancement of corporate earnings to the potential exclusion of alternative stakeholder viewpoints.

Another potential faculty problem arises from the structuring of schools in disciplinary silos and an associated incentive system that rewards discipline-based publication in so-called A-journals.

Areas such as CSR are by their very nature interdisciplinary and work in these areas involves faculty involvement in, and the development of, strong partnerships both with other academic areas and businesses. Often this is a daunting and difficult task and precarious career route for young academics.

Therefore, questions about the role of business education in society recur (see Harney & Downing, 2012).

The authors ask whether "business schools do enough to instil a sense of empathy, to say nothing of responsibility, in their graduates, educating them to respond not just to their powerful shareholders but to their many stakeholders in society". They suggest that legitimacy in this area might be achieved by business students offering *pro-bono* business advice to small businesses, NGOs and the like, and "walk the walk" just as law students do with *pro-bono* clinics organised by their professors.

Because of our concern about this ethics, CSR and sustainability "blind spot", we asked our panel for their views and perceptions about how these issues are addressed in business schools.

From their responses (see Table 6.2) we found that there were relatively few positive comments about the treatment

> Areas such as CSR are by their very nature interdisciplinary and work in these areas involves faculty involvement in, and the development of, strong partnerships both with other academic areas and businesses. Often this is a daunting and difficult task and precarious career route for young academics

of CSR and so on in management education. The responses here echo the sense of inertia about business school direction alluded to earlier in this volume.

First, 41% of the responses indicated that business schools have typically adopted a "bolt-on" approach to dealing with issues concerning sustainability, ethics and responsible management.

This finding should be compared with the much smaller 10% of responses that indicate an integrated embedded approach is needed to place these areas firmly within the management curricula. Indeed, the general

Table 6.2: Business school reactions to the "ethics, CSR, sustainability" gap.

Business school reaction	Number of mentions	% of responses
Bolt-on courses	12	41
Paying lip-service to important issues	7	24
Slow to react	4	14
Needs an integrated approach	3	10
Lack of leadership	2	7
No experience or expertise	2	7
Reacted to demand for courses	1	3
Most have not reacted	1	3
Overreaction	1	3

perception is that these issues are not tackled seriously at the pedagogical level because of "bolt-on" courses, which allow little integration with other established themes in management education.

Our experts point out that this exemplifies the field's resistance (or resilience) to change.

Second, 24% of responses suggested that the reaction by business schools was to pay "lip-service" to these important issues through token gestures, not least of which was the prevalence of "bolt-on" courses.

The main themes in Table 6.2 are now discussed. They are:

- "bolt-on" courses
- paying lip service and reacting slowly to important issues
- integrating ethics, CSR, and sustainability into the curriculum
- a lack of leadership in promoting such courses

The "Bolt-on" Approach

Comments about "bolt-on" courses follow.

"In my view they've reacted by adopting various forms of sticking plaster; so far they've covered up the problem."

"[They have done it] slowly and with bolt-on courses, for example in ethics. I'm not sure that there are attempts to teach it across courses."

"With an integrated approach, [such courses] would be embedded in the curriculum, so they would be treated in a more coherent, cohesive way. Many of us have a course in ethics and sustainability. They are very successful and often attractive but they are ultimately 'bolt-ons'."

"Increasingly, this has been brought into our programmes in different ways — some of which are cosmetic.

> **"Many of us have a course in ethics and sustainability. They are very successful and often attractive but they are ultimately 'bolt-ons'"**

Some will say 'we'll have a course in ethics', others have managed to get the faculty at large interested and then it's fed into lots of different courses. I would prefer them to be embedded in different courses."

Lip Service and Slow Reaction

Digging a little deeper, it is clear that the "bolt-on" courses and the somewhat "cosmetic" approach to tackling these gaps in management education fits with a sense of programme continuity rather than change. This is captured in what our respondents refer to as "lip service", a rhetorical and shallow acknowledgement of the need to address these major issues that produces at best an extremely conservative, incremental and cautious approach to curriculum change in business schools.

> "We've probably had many conferences on the subject, produced numerous papers and we've probably added a course to our curriculum and made a definitive change. But in the end it will not make any difference. It's lip service really. Maybe that's because I've been doing this [management education] too long."

> "I think they've given lip service to them basically. I mean you do see ethics appear as a subject in certain curricula but I personally think that ethics itself is not a subject — it should be a hearts and minds subject that permeates right through the whole programme."

> "They should be embedded not add-ons."

> "It's a little more lip service than reality but I think that the more serious problem is that we don't know quite how to do this. And it's a little bit like 20 or 50 years ago, when you had courses in internationalisation popping up."

Integration into the Curriculum

What is clear from the preoccupation with "bolt-on" courses and the perfunctory treatment of ethics, CSR and sustainability in management education is that these (or any other significant changes to curricula) face the barrier of integration within business schools. Certainly respondents indicate that developing integrated curricula is desirable and there is enthusiasm for engaging with these issues yet there seems to be a sense of incompatibility between the principles of integration and the way things are currently done.

"I think certainly that the debates within business schools are focused towards how to integrate issues around sustainability into the curriculum. For example, do we do it by add-ons, such as more electives? I think in part we should do that but more pertinently we should determine how we integrate issues surrounding corporate governance, sustainability and ethics into existing functional courses. That is an interesting challenge which some faculty are very excited about."

"The business schools' reaction has not been strong enough but I also believe that the challenge or the solution is more complicated than it appears to be at first glance. On the one hand you can say that a business school can focus its next academic year on ethics. However, I think that the real solution is integrating ethical behaviour into all the things you do. But that is something that you can't do overnight. So OK, let's show that we are doing something and, at the same time, work conscientiously towards a real solution to the problem."

> **"I think that the real solution is integrating ethical behaviour into all the things you do. But that is something that you can't do overnight"**

"Their reaction has been, I think, to try to address it by introducing programmes with possibly an elective on business ethics. However, I think there is still an on-going debate — should be embedded in the curriculum like the writing in a stick of rock [candy] be a compulsory, detailed programme like marketing or finance study CSR, and properly address it, and write essays on it."

"As we grapple with the model of an integrative curriculum, we will be able to deal with these issues in a much more substantive and meaningful way."

Leadership by Business Schools

A small number of responses once again raised the issue of leadership in business schools. These respondents question directly the ability of business schools to take the lead in thinking about business and society, often due to their reticence to form an opinion. Business schools and their leaders appear apolitical, neutral institutions — bastions of "good science" but lacking the ability to forge identities as thought leaders. This fits with the criticism that business schools are always looking backwards at trends and data — the ever-retrospective leader confronting the future through the rear-view mirror.

> "Business schools could have taken the lead [on] CSR and ethics because this was important long before the crisis. One of the things that has always struck me is why schools, as institutions, and their leaders didn't have the guts to have an opinion."

In summary, our experts believe that business schools reacted slowly to the "ethics gap" but have moved from rhetoric and lip service to a more careful analysis of how to incorporate ethics, CSR and sustainability into their curricula. Some of this is due to student pressure about responsibility (e.g. Harvard's MBA oath) but also through the efforts of such organisations as the Aspen Institute, the UN Global Compact and EFMD.

The Entrepreneurship "Blind Spot"

In examining future pathways for management education, Professor Pedro Nueno of IESE in Barcelona and Madrid has pointed out that manage-

> Business schools must teach the skills and capabilities that enable new ideas and products to be brought successfully to the marketplace

ment education is at a turning point as it enters a new era of innovation, transformation and global growth (see Thomas et al., 2013, p. 29).

This new era requires new ways of doing things, echoing Gary Hamel's stress on innovation, and not on achieving greater efficiency from current operations. Nueno believes strongly that business schools should focus on areas essential to future growth such as entrepreneurship and innovation. This more rapid growth would then be fuelled by the growth in global trade and the global economy.

It is important to re-emphasise, however, that innovation and entrepreneurship are not equivalent (see AACSB Report: *Business Schools on an Innovation Mission*, 2010).

To quote the AACSB report:

"As it is understood today, entrepreneurship is about organisation creation, regardless of whether it is innovative or not, and innovation is about implementing something new, regardless of whether it is through a newly created organisation."

However, innovation and entrepreneurship are strongly linked — organisations are typically created to exploit new ideas, inventions, products and projects and hence create job growth and improved managerial practices. Therefore, it is argued, business schools must teach the skills and capabilities that enable new ideas and products to be brought successfully to the marketplace.

Despite this, media mentions of entrepreneurship education are few and far between though recently there has been an increasing interest particularly in social entrepreneurship (see *Financial Times*, 23 April, 2012, p. 10: "Students Take on the Social Entrepreneurship Challenge" by Anjli Raval).

This chapter suggests that MBA students, faced with uncertain employment prospects and fewer opportunities in consulting and investment banking, are turning their attention to entrepreneurship and particularly social entrepreneurship options.

For business schools, the interest in social entrepreneurship allows them to discuss alternative approaches to business, promote the generation of new ideas about CSR and sustainable business, and hopefully bridge the gap between business and society. It is suggested that by attacking social issues such as poverty, health, illiteracy and so on in an active, team-based learning environment, students will recognise, and empathise with, the growth issues and problems of less developed countries. If they become involved and engaged in this manner, it is hoped that students will develop a stronger moral and ethical compass that will guide them in their future managerial careers.

What is surprising is the general lack of media clamour and business school activity about entrepreneurship — note the emphasis placed on the subject by Professor Nueno and the AACSB report. Globalisation, on the other hand, is much better linked and embedded in curricula through such elements as study-abroad programmes and courses in international business. But entrepreneurship has become somewhat of ignored "stepchild".

Colby et al. (2011, p. 232) point out that there is much less evidence of curricula integration with regard to the area of entrepreneurship. As exceptions they note the contributions of niche schools such as Babson in the United States and Cranfield in the United Kingdom, which specialise in entrepreneurship. They then pose the question: "what would it take to cultivate the level of integration that characterises globalisation (in the curriculum) within the emerging area of entrepreneurship?" (Colby et al., 2011, p. 141). In essence, entrepreneurship is still a niche area with limited traction in business schools.

> The one common theme is rhetoric about the entrepreneurship gap and the value of studying entrepreneurship but there is almost nothing about how to implement this area into the norms and curricula logics of business schools

This "entrepreneurship gap" or "blind spot" is clearly evident in the comments of our respondents. They have not yet heeded the advice of Nueno, AACSB or Colby. The one common theme, not surprisingly, is rhetoric about the entrepreneurship gap and the value of studying entrepreneurship but there is almost nothing about how to this area into the norms and curricula logics of business schools.

> "Innovation in subject areas, for example in entrepreneurship
> and CSR, has come through strongly recently. Some of these
> I see as faddish, although not entrepreneurship."

The contrast with business schools adapting to globalisation is evident in the following remark.

> "I suppose we can say there is more of a change in internationalisation [globalisation], where you have had more students and faculty coming from different countries."

In summary, the entrepreneurship gap has been recognised by our experts but the promise of successful implementation is unfulfilled and not yet achieved despite the increasing rhetoric of its value to the field of management education.

Innovation in Business Models and Management Practices

In Chapter 2 we pointed out, in quoting Hamel, that as management educators we must develop students with the capability to invent new management practices and models. In short, we need to teach them to be management innovators. However, Hamel also suggests that while deans openly advocate the value of innovation and change they find it much more difficult to embrace such innovations in their own business models.

A recent article in the *Wall Street Journal* (12 August, 2013, p. 10) entitled "The Man Who Would Overthrow Harvard" demonstrates how competitive entry may occur in higher education.

A serial entrepreneur armed with venture capital, Ben Nelson has been attracted to the higher education industry and wants "to topple and transcend the American academy's economic and educational model". His business model, the Minerva project, is a re-imagined university seeking to disaggregate the value chain in higher education and, through technology and the selective use of MOOC for introductory courses, to attack the top-end universities — the elite of the educational food chain.

He may or may not succeed but his model will probably attract other competitive imitators or perhaps force some more innovative, entrepreneurial universities to adopt similar principles.

We are already aware of the advent of private competition in higher education from the likes of Hult, Apollo (the University of Phoenix) and Kaplan, which were reviewed in Chapter 1 in the examination of writings on disruptive innovation by Professor Clayton Christensen of Harvard Business School.

Given this background we sought to identify the opinions of our experts about business model innovation. What is clear from their responses is that there are two main themes: the perceived need for new business models and yet another "blind spot", this time on how to design and build new business models. We discuss these themes in turn.

The Need for New Business Models

Our respondents believe two elements are behind the pressure to construct new business models. The first is globalisation, which is driving an urgent need to restructure the organisation of business school operations. The second is the role of technology in facilitating the growth of network-like, perhaps virtual, organisational structures.

> "Because the world's becoming global, there's a clash, a challenge to the perceived [dominant] Anglo-American model."

> "I think that we need to think about a transition from the old model to a new model ... The old model: faculty meetings, departments, tenure-based vested interests ... all add up to make it unlikely that these types of organisation will adapt [in the future]."

> **[There is a] perceived need for new business models and yet another "blind spot", this time on how to design and build new business models**

> "To create a new model we need to get rid of some over-conservative, narrow-minded ways of thinking. I think that the role of traditional management disciplines is quite clear but the world is growing asymmetrically and we really need to think about innovation and change in different ways. And my feeling is that the next wave of innovation will come from Asia. We need an innovative perspective and to make it happen there has to be a willingness to experiment."

Another respondent noted possible innovation in the form of network organisations.

> "I don't know if business schools know that perhaps in 15 years there may not be such a thing as a manager any more in some parts of business. You become a node in the network. The interesting point is how you design/understand how network organisations work."

The Design of New Business Models

What is apparent from our respondents is an absence of insight on how new business models might be developed, given some of the structural barriers and constraints that exist within business schools. One of our experts expressed a particular constraint in the following terms.

> "We know that some of the things that go on in business schools are mainly for the benefit of the producers, the faculty and we don't seem to do anything about it ... the business model doesn't appear to be working that well and yet nobody has said how we are going to fix it. [But] let's try to fix it; people seem to take the approach that it will work out in the end."

It is interesting to note, however, that one of our respondents has developed a network type model as the framework for his business school, the Lorange Institute of Business in Zurich (see Thomas et al., 2013, p. 123). This model involves a radical and extreme alternative to the *status quo* — "with its constituents of part-time faculty, no silos, no offices, no tenure, no academic departments and a fully integrated educational philosophy that links the curriculum to the learning process in the workplace."

In summary, while the Minerva project and the Lorange Institute of Business represent innovative business models, they are clearly exceptions in the current landscape. While there is recognition of the need to innovate, there is far less illumination on the direction a school should take.

The Leadership "Blind Spot"

A recent article (Pincus & Rudnick, 2013) points out "blind spots" in leadership

> "Business schools do not know how to teach the relationship-building skills required for contemporary business leadership"

development such as in relationship-building skills. They quote from Datar et al.'s (2010) study of MBA programmes: MBAs need to understand how to work through people, how to motivate and inspire. MBAs need to ask themselves: How do I engage enough people to accomplish a task while I remain in the background?

The authors favour reconceptualising leadership and organisational change to ground MBA students in relationship building and argue that "business schools do not know how to teach the relationship-building skills required for contemporary business leadership".

We asked our respondents about the nature of leadership and challenges of leadership skills development in the business school context. There were two broad themes in their responses: the need for new approaches to teach leadership skills (echoing Pincus Rudnick arguments) and the leadership characteristics required of business school leaders — deans. We examine each in turn.

Leadership and Leadership Skills Development

There are some suggestions, but not clarity, from our experts about the type of skills — communication skills, creative thinking and so on — that may be required for leaders to manage in practical situations. They also point out the need to be future-oriented in developing leadership.

> "The challenge for business is to figure out the kind of business leaders they will need to meet future challenges. And for business schools, we have to identify what kind of capabilities and skills future leaders must possess."

> "Business schools need to focus more on management development, particularly the skills component … what we've learned is that teaching skills development — leadership development, communication, creative thinking — is really hard and must be improved."

And there are comments about the complexity of leadership in modern organisations — global organisations, network-type organisations or virtual organisations.

> "Leading people has new complexities. For example, how do you influence colleagues who want to be treated as peers while managing an increasingly diverse and ageing workforce? How do you lead virtual or network-type units?"

> "If there's no leadership there's not going to be any change. I don't see any organised changes taking place without good leadership … By leadership I don't mean one single leader on top. I mean leadership in the organisation. I believe that nowadays we need a little bit more leadership to get more impact and make it happen. Hopefully that change will necessarily occur as a result of the financial and economic crisis."

It is clear that respondents are unanimous in emphasising the need to teach leadership skills but are less clear about the specific skills that must be taught and, more importantly, assessing how to teach them.

The Leadership Characteristics of Deans

There is a linkage between the previous discussion on the leadership skills and capabilities and the specific characteristics required of business school

> **"Strategic change leadership requires leaders who can identify needed changes and influence academics to follow them"**

deans. In particular, our respondents point to courage, empathy, trust and risk taking as very important leadership skills of deans as they plan the future pathways and strategies for their schools.

> "A dean must understand how a business school operates [and be someone] who the faculty trust — in any change operation, trust is extremely important — and who has the patience and will to get things done."

> "Leaders who are risk takers will trigger change."

> "Strategic change leadership requires leaders who can identify needed changes and influence academics to follow them."

Indeed, these leadership characteristics are perceived as highly desirable in business school deans (Fraguiero & Thomas, 2011). However, Goodall (2009a, 2009b) points out that business school deans are typically recruited on their academic prowess as a primary concern (by universities) as opposed to their innate leadership qualities. However, the perceptions of leadership in business schools are not always aligned wholly with the characteristics identified above. As we pointed out in Chapter 2, the perception of some is that business school leaders lack courage and a conviction for change.

> "We have had very few... leaders in business schools in Europe who had a clear vision and were able to implement that vision ... George Bain, for his management of London Business School ... Antonio Borges was clearly a very strong leader for INSEAD."

Globalisation in Transition — The "Glocalisation" "Blind Spot"

Martin Wolf (*Financial Times*, 17 July, 2013, p. 7) writing about "Globalisation in a time of transition" points out that despite the global financial crisis, the movement towards integration in the global economy continues unabated. He notes that "foreign direct investment (FDI) and trade have risen far more than global output since 1990 with FDI rising faster even than trade."

Citing a paper by Subramanian and Kessler, "The Hyperglobalisation of Trade and its Future" (2013), he addresses the effects of hyperglobalisation particularly on emerging countries. Hyperglobalisation contributed hugely to emerging countries catching up with the living standards of the high-income nations in the "great convergence" — a trend that has gathered increasing pace since the late 1990s.

This second stage in globalisation since the global financial crisis also surfaces "issues that revolve around the dilemmas of global standardisation versus local differentiation" (Fragueiro, *Financial Times*, 26 April, 2010, p. 9: "Think Local, but from a Global Perspective").

> Fragueiro suggests that business schools can help companies to address the demands of emerging market customers by explaining how to "fine-tune" their products to regional and domestic preferences

Fragueiro stresses that business schools must, therefore, educate students and business leaders about managing in a diverse and multicultural world where it is critical to understand the cultural, social, economic and structural differences across markets particularly when "future growth will unquestionably lie in the fast-growing population of emerging consumers worldwide".

He identifies the trade-off between global standardisation and local differentiation as "glocalisation". As a consequence, he suggests that business schools can help companies to address the demands of emerging market customers by explaining how to "fine-tune" their products to regional and domestic preferences. This drive towards "glocalisation" can enhance integration in the global economy by focusing on methods, and approaches, for handling local differences.

Pfefferman (*Financial Times*, Monday 19 March, 2012, p. 11 "Knowhow Needed for Real-World Problems") also focuses on the growing recognition that there are significant shifts in global markets from the legacy industrial countries to emerging markets such as Latin America and Asia. He notes that "increasingly, companies demand that business schools must prepare MBA (business) students to operate in these new markets".

He puts forward one method of achieving this, namely, through the action learning of teams of students working on specific projects in community development in those developing countries. He quotes examples drawn from the experiences of MBA teams at the Haas School of the University of California, Berkeley.

Other examples include Singapore Management University (SMU), which mandates that students must commit to 80 hours of work on community projects thus applying their business knowledge to real-world problems. Many of these projects are carried out in neighbouring Asian countries and produce a plethora of ideas and infectious enthusiasm for solving messy problems in growing, developing countries. The sense is that these action-learning projects create a set of experiences and lessons that a conventional classroom case study cannot achieve.

Professor Peter Henry (quoted in Knight, 2012), the dean of the Stern School at NYU, is also an advocate of using student projects in countries such as India, undertaken through Stern's Consulting corps programme, to get students out into the real world and doing project work "through the lens of research".

This often provides positive feedback from students about the value of learning from such projects relative to just taking a set of classes on global topics.

NYU, SMU and Berkeley are not alone in using such projects to prepare students for working in the global economy. For example, Harvard's MBA programme has a compulsory field immersion project undertaken in a developing country and MIT has expanded its G-Lab course, which focuses on the project-based management of overseas start-ups.

This brief review of the "hyperglobalisation" trend provides the background on the potential "blind spot" of glocalisation. We, therefore, asked our respondents to reflect on the ramifications and challenges of globalisation. They identify a number of themes: the fact that globalisation is contextually and culturally situated that there is no (global) meaning without (country) context the notion of the globally aware student and the challenge to business school curricula of producing such a student.

First, it is clear that the glocalisation effect is an important issue. In other words, the effects of globalisation have cultural and contextual implications. Hence, it is important to develop skills of contextual (region, regulation or country based) and cultural intelligence (the norms, values and beliefs of a given culture) in conducting business in emerging countries.

> "I see the cross-cultural dimensions of managing today as more important than ever. I think that we haven't yet realised, at least in the west, how important those things are, particularly the learning, not the teaching, about management in a global environment."

Second, the challenge of developing a "go-anywhere graduate" (emphasised by Pfefferman and Fragueiro) from our current curriculum is pointed out clearly.

> "The biggest challenge is that of building a capable person to operate effectively in a global context — a 'go-anywhere' graduate. [The problem is that business schools] are building people through separate disciplines and different emphases. They hope that it pastes and hangs together in the end."

Third, despite the use of project-based action learning in some business schools, there is a prevailing sense that we generally do not know very well how to inculcate global skills in our students or incorporate it in curricula.

> "Management education has historically not been global and the way we operated in the past isn't the way we'll operate in the future because it doesn't emphasise either collaboration or developing this global-ready graduate."

Another respondent expressed quite strongly that the faculty may resist broad curricula changes because of their emphasis on, and comfort with, disciplinary rather than multi-disciplinary perspectives:

> **There is a prevailing sense that we generally do not know very well how to inculcate global skills in our students or incorporate it in curricula**

> "The faculty are brought up to be increasingly narrow and are experts in a narrow part of a particular discipline. How then do we develop those 'globally aware' managers in our programmes if our faculty are narrow and anchored in their disciplines?"

Conclusion

While many of the experts on our panel evinced astuteness in their observations of the challenges, lessons learned and not learned, and possible futures in management education, it was apparent to us that certain "blind spots" persisted. In some cases, these exist not in the sense that business school leaders are oblivious to a particular weakness or challenge but rather that they are superficially treated with a band aid (ethics, CSR and sustainability are possible examples of this).

In other cases, the blind spots get significant share of mind but provoke not action but an on-going rhetoric that fails to focus on viable solutions (e.g. the relevance gap). In still other cases, the issues receive scant attention despite having potentially important consequences (such as entrepreneurship).

As schools are caught up in the momentum of competing within the existing management education paradigm and are faced with the risks of straying from a well-beaten path it is perhaps not surprising that "blind spots" exist.

Yet these "blind spots" represent opportunities that if given proper attention could strongly differentiate a school and strengthen its reputation. It is our hope, therefore, that by putting the focus on them the value inherent in resolving them will also be highlighted.

Chapter 7

Uncertain Futures: What Should Business Schools Do Now?

Introduction

Management education is at crossroads but the path forward is obscure and it is tempting simply to stand still. But we argue that current challenges and those on the horizon require us, as custodians of the field, to reflect on the changes we need to enact to secure the legitimacy and the future of management education.

In this chapter we first examine what the barriers and triggers to change are before turning our attention to what individual schools can do in response to external and internal challenges. We then present our view and those of other commentators on the type of graduates business school we need to produce to enhance the practice of management. We end this chapter with propositions for transformations that we believe are necessary to strengthen the legitimacy of the field.

Consistent Themes

In the earlier chapters of this volume, we discussed the literature and respondents' views on such issues as criticisms of management education, lessons not learned and on-going challenges and blind spots. It is clear from that discussion that there are themes that make recurring appearances. These themes, we believe, represent the compass for change and we think it useful to first revisit them briefly here.

1. The *culture* of business schools is one that is characterised by inertia and a certain resistance to change, owing largely to conservatism, complacency and perhaps a "head-in-the-sand" attitude towards the challenges that confront the field. This is an observation made by

respondents but interestingly this cautious attitude is also reflected in their own responses to the question of what are the most likely and best-case scenarios for management education.

> The current situation is one where the publication of rigorous research in top-tier journals is accorded such paramount importance that the managerial relevance of such findings receives short shrift

2. The *purpose* of management education is an issue that is far from settled, as questions about the value proposition of management education — whether it ought to lean towards enhancing managerial capabilities or towards generating intellectual capital — and its place within the university context continue to be debated. It is likely that its purpose will continue to evolve with time.

3. The *pedagogy* used in business schools is in need of refreshing. The "sage on stage" model of lecturing is being nudged out of popular acceptance by new learning technologies that offer greater flexibility in the delivery of programmes and flexibility in accommodating distances and learning styles of a tech-savvy generation. The case study method might diminish in importance as the value of experiential, action-based learning is increasingly acknowledged.

4. We also need to recognise that *curricula content* in many programmes has failed to keep up with the environment and lost its currency. The development of soft skills and leadership skills and the integration of globalisation, entrepreneurship, ethics, corporate social responsibility and sustainability into curricula are examples of areas of change in need of attention. The argument here is not necessarily that business schools have ignored these areas, but rather that they are often given "band aid" treatment when more invasive efforts are necessary. There are certainly exemplary changes that have been undertaken in some programmes, but these have largely focused on the MBA (e.g. the MBA programmes at Berkeley and Stanford, see Chapter 5 of Thomas et al., 2013).

5. If management education is to regain its usefulness to the practice of management, one needs to take a hard look at current *faculty structures and reward systems/incentives*. As Hamel noted pointedly (Crainer & Dearlove, 1998): "I worry that those of us in business schools spend too much time writing for each other rather than improving business practice." The current situation is one where the publication of rigorous research in top-tier journals is accorded such paramount importance that the managerial relevance of such findings receives short shrift. Teaching is also often sidelined as a role of secondary importance. More generally, activities that compete for a faculty member's time (a scarce resource) but which are not aligned with advancing a narrow research agenda are regarded as low priority. It is tempting to vilify faculty but

surely this points to the need for new reward systems that recognise the importance of applied research and joint projects with industry and, importantly, the need to resist a culture where clinical or practice faculty are perceived as supporting players or second-class citizens.

6. The *funding* of business schools and the *sustainability of current financial models* are becoming increasingly pressing issues. Business schools have already witnessed a pullback in government funding of higher education in the ripple effects of the recent financial crises. As Peters and Thomas (2011) and Thomas and Peters (2012) have noted, an escalation in the tuition fees of the traditional business cash cows, the EMBA and MBA programmes, is unlikely to be sustained as the return on investment is increasingly called into question. Income from executive education and donations are not stable sources nor are they within reach of all business schools. They add that "many institutions are using a faculty model that is very luxurious" — faculty costs account for the lion's share of a school's expenditures with the upward trend in salaries driven in part by a demand–supply gap. "How long can this go on?" is a question that weighs on the minds of many business school leaders and the need for more innovative and flexible organisational structures is clear. Nowhere is this more challenging than in business schools within a larger university system where bureaucratic overload can be a real obstacle to reform.

7. There is a need for a *paradigm* change. Rather than, as Crainer and Dearlove (1998) put it "sleepwalking our way through change", there should be a more serious effort at challenging the current paradigm in each of the following areas. Business schools should propagate an enlightened view of a business' stakeholders as one that includes society, the environment and employees. It should be acknowledged that rankings and accreditations tend to encourage business schools to follow similar policies and actions and out of this should emerge a greater willingness to measure different schools by different yardsticks that are appropriate to these schools' purpose and environment. This should produce greater innovation, differentiation and a smaller concentration of resources at top-ranked schools. While intellectual capital is the backbone of business schools and is essential for knowledge creation and thought leadership, the single-minded pursuit of rigour should be balanced against the need for relevance. Finally, the dominant US model has been resistant to input, particularly from other cultures. Alternative models that better reflect the cultures, history and traditions of different countries and regions and that provide a truly global outlook should be encouraged. Perhaps a good starting point for change would be a critical consideration of models that have been proposed as ideals, such as the agora model (Starkey & Tiratsoo, 2007) and Vision 50 + 20 (Muff et al., 2013).

Adaptability of Management Education and Its Capacity for Change

Many of the critical issues identified as necessary for change coalesce around the tug-of-war between the need to establish the legitimacy of management education as a field where respectable, scholarly research is pursued, and the requirement to be responsive to the needs of industry. The latter is really a collection of needs ranging from equipping students with the right knowledge and skills to be effective managers, developing business leaders with an ethical compass and delivering an education that integrates across the different disciplines of management to providing solutions to real-world business problems.

The time certainly seems ripe for change in management education but, as we noted earlier, any change is likely to face the drag of conservatism and institutional inertia.

> **[The question is] whether management education as a field has the will and the capacity to respond to the challenges that confront it**

This begs the question of whether management education as a field has the will and the capacity to respond to the challenges that confront it. We turn the discussion to what the barriers to change are and what the triggers for change are likely to be.

Barriers to Change

The University System   Business schools embedded within universities must comply with governance policies that limit their agility in responding to challenges. There are, as to be expected, competing interests among the different constituents or schools within a university and an accompanying need for equity and consistency in policies across the university. This typically translates to greater bureaucracy and delays in implementing change.

Autonomy (or the lack of it) in financial matters also limits a business school's ability to change. Treating business schools as cash cows and cross-subsidising other constituents through repatriation of revenues from the business school to the university is not uncommon. But it is often seen as financially burdensome for the business school and an impediment to investing in necessary change.

On the plus side, the broader representation of disciplines within a university has the potential to invigorate academic discourse. A strong scholarly culture is a precondition to the ideal scenarios described in the agora model, Vision 50 + 20 and the crucial diffusion model (see Chapter 4 for a discussion of these models). All of these models call for a multidisciplinary approach to management education (with the latter emphasising in particular an integration of the humanities).

> Faculty can be likened to having two taskmasters — the institution to which they are contractually obligated and the community of scholars to which they look for affirmation

Nowhere is the realisation of these models more feasible than within the environment of a larger university.

Faculty Power and the Tenure System The power structure of business schools is another barrier to change. The preferred style of leadership among academics is far removed from the directive sort that characterises corporate environments. As Mintzberg (1998) noted, a less forceful leadership style and a structure that is non-hierarchical and more conducive to debates and consensus-building is typical of professional settings such as in academia. However, while freeing faculty from the constraints of a strict pecking order and thereby giving them a voice for critical discourse, some argue that these same conditions make it hard to galvanise them to act in the interest of the field, particularly if what is needed runs counter to their own interests. For instance, a change in curricula deemed necessary to develop better managers may be resisted by faculty who see it as a troublesome change to their teaching routine. Thomas et al. (2013) presented a quote from an interviewee that aptly conveys the power wielded by faculty:

"Faculty are at the front lines of management education, and in many institutions there is a tradition of family governance and they wield a fair amount of decision-making power in some ways because of things like tenure."

Faculty who are comfortably entrenched in the system have little incentive to take risks, particularly if the "rules of the game" remain unchanged — that is, if the reward system continues to place the greatest weight on the publication of research in top-tier journals. The solution of changing the reward system may seem simple enough but the business school that does it as a "lone ranger" is unlikely to have much success in changing the behaviour of its faculty. This is because faculty can be likened to having two taskmasters — the institution to which they are contractually obligated and the community of scholars to which they look for affirmation. One's value to the latter group can be an important driver of behaviour (sometimes to the detriment of the former group), particularly if serving the latter guarantees career mobility.

The combination of a balance of power favouring faculty and incentives that are skewed towards research publication creates a fairly imposing roadblock to change. Breaking through this might require the field to act in concert in changing the reward system. It might also be necessary for a certain mindset to be inculcated in PhD programmes.

One can argue that faculty can hardly be blamed for conducting arcane research targeted at top-tier journals when the emphasis on such a pursuit can be traced back to their very first day as a PhD student. Few PhD programmes devote much attention to developing teaching capability or building links between academia and industry and it is therefore little wonder that PhD students persist in doing "what they are trained to do" even after they transition to becoming faculty members.

The tenure system tends to exacerbate this situation.

Faculty working towards tenure are made to focus their energies in the early years of their career on producing rigorous research. The "publish or perish" dictum puts immense pressure on faculty to publish in top journals with tenure criteria leaving little room to incentivise pedagogical or practice-related efforts.

One might think that faculty granted tenure or freed from the tyrannical constraints of tenure would be more willing to step outside their comfort zone to respond to real-world problems faced by practitioners. More often than not, however, there is persistence in doing the same type of research, perhaps reflecting the fact that the familiar route is also the path of least resistance. The greater powers vested in tenured faculty can make it more challenging to get buy-in when change is needed.

Faculty Structure As we have noted elsewhere in this volume, the effective practice of management requires the integration of knowledge and skills across disciplines and it is therefore necessary to train students

> **The mismatch between how faculty are organised and the multidisciplinary approach that is needed in management education presents an immediate problem**

in a multidisciplinary approach. Research, if it is to address effectively issues faced by companies and society in general, ought also to draw on knowledge across disciplines. This argument is, in fact, central to the ideal models of the agora model (Starkey & Tiratsoo, 2007) and Vision 50 + 20 (Muff et al., 2013).

Faculty, unfortunately, are typically organised along disciplinary lines in terms of the research that they undertake, the courses that they teach and for administrative purposes within business schools. The mismatch between how faculty are organised and the multidisciplinary approach that is needed in management education presents an immediate problem. The present paucity of dialogue across disciplinary silos means that few faculty can claim to be knowledgeable outside of their own silos and are therefore ill equipped to train others.

Leadership   While change can be initiated at the grassroots level, more often than not strong leadership is needed. Business school deans need to be forward thinking and willing to take on risks but this quality is unfortunately not abundant.

This can be attributed to a number of factors, among which is the fact that the median tenure of a dean is three to four years — a time horizon that does nothing to encourage long-term strategic planning. Within that fairly short tenure, deans often find themselves unwilling to implement drastic and potentially unpopular (given the conservatism of faculty) changes that might disrupt stable revenue sources or that might have negative repercussions on rankings or accreditation.

Even if a dean is willing to go out on a limb, he or she is likely to find it difficult to secure buy-in from a conservative faculty body. The slow process of achieving that, coupled with a dean's short tenure, is a formula for incremental changes to the status quo.

Triggers for Change

While the barriers to change described above seem formidable, our respondents acknowledge that certain situations are likely to compel action and trigger change. We discuss these triggers below.

Funding Issues and the Sustainability of the Current Financial Model   Business schools face increasing pressures on both the revenue and cost sides of their financial models. Where higher education has traditionally received government funding there has been a steady decline in that support brought about partly by flagging economies in the wake of the financial crisis and also by changes in philosophical leanings on higher education as a public versus private good (see Peters & Thomas, 2011; Thomas & Peters, 2012).

Universities have had to increase tuition fees to compensate for the decline in funding but face limits as to what the market is willing to bear. MBA programmes in particular have seen such an increase in fees that some have questioned their return on investment. At the same time, there is evidence of a downward trend in applications to MBA programmes.

We have noted earlier that other sources of funding — from executive education and donations, for example — have not proved reliable substitutes.

> [The fight to survive] may well prompt schools to find innovative solutions to this dire situation, perhaps by turning to industry for partnerships and consulting revenue or by leveraging learning technologies ... to cut costs and expand geographic reach

A shortage of faculty and the concomitant increase in faculty salaries has also contributed to increasing financial pressures.

There is much pessimism among our respondents about the sustainability of the current financial model of business schools. The likelihood of a shakeout, with marginal schools going bust, is seen as a high probability.

If anything, it is the fight to survive that may well prompt schools to find innovative solutions to this dire situation, perhaps by turning to industry for partnerships and consulting revenue or by leveraging learning technologies (such as MOOCs) to cut costs and expand geographic reach.

Competition Starkey and Tiratsoo (2007) have aptly described the management education landscape as one of hypercompetition. Hard data are not easy to find but it is likely that there are now more business schools around the world than ever before. The competition is magnified by the fact that the market place is a global one. Business schools compete across national boundaries and even continents for faculty talent as well as students.

One might think that emerging markets would increase demand for management education sufficiently to keep the old machinery going. But business schools in places such as China and India have seen such an uptick in quality that indigenous students are increasingly choosing to attend their own local business schools. There has also been an increasing trend for students drawn to Asian business schools from other parts of the world as they sense a shift in the economic centre of gravity to Asia.

Add to this mix the fact that for-profit providers, such as Kaplan University and the University of Phoenix, are increasingly making their presence felt. According to Starkey and Tiratsoo, the combined market share of these for-profit providers stood at 10% of all US MBAs in 2003/ 2004. A decade on, they have in all likelihood made even greater inroads in capturing market share.

This hypercompetition may well compel business schools to examine their competitive advantages and their business models more critically. Some schools, such as INSEAD in France, have already responded to globalisation and increasing competition by extending their market reach with satellite campuses. It is likely that more distinctive and innovative business models will emerge in response to this greater competition.

Leadership While business school leadership is characterised as largely risk-averse, respondents also noted that an important trigger for change is a dean who is willing to break the mould. Without a courageous and risk-taking attitude from a strong leader, there would be little impetus for faculty to stray from "business as usual".

Responding to the Challenge of Change

So how might schools respond to the challenge of change? What are some of the strategic alternatives and considerations? We review in this section other authors' take on the challenges that confront the field and their

> The fact that many countries around the world face an ageing population has profound implications for what the future will look like on many fronts, including the demand for education

insights on the responses that might serve business schools well.

External Challenges

Jessup and Laing (Bisoux, 2013), citing declining funding, increased competition and stakeholders demanding more options, easier access to services and value for money, have called attention to the urgent need for new financial models.

As Laing puts it: "We can no longer continue to try to squeeze efficiencies from existing models."

Turpin (2013) similarly notes declining government funding as one of four major forces to contend with. In addition, the present economic problems in the United States and many European countries have serious repercussions on job opportunities for young graduates. The fact that many countries around the world face an ageing population has profound implications for what the future will look like on many fronts, including the demand for education, the type of education demanded, the strength of the economy and the amount of public funding available in the face of potentially falling tax receipts.

Finally, technology-enabled learning, such as MOOCs, can dramatically change the management education landscape though schools that choose to join the fray of offering e-learning will have to grapple with issues of pricing, ensuring quality and the like.

Like Jessup and Laing, Turpin observes that executive education "customers" are becoming increasingly demanding — they are more cost-sensitive, look for the best deal and are concerned about impact.

Hill (2012), who also notes the game-changing potential of e-learning, argues that young people are no longer beholden to the traditional approach of a business education, given the myriad of online courses available.

It is now possible to take charge of one's education by downloading lectures from YouTube, completing online courses provided free by organisations such as Khan Academy and even earning certificates of mastery for online courses provided by universities through platforms such as Coursera and edX.

What should schools do in the choppy waters of such an environment?

Differentiate Jessup and Laing and Turpin argue that differentiating one's offer is an imperative for survival. This can come about by adding new features to existing programmes such as in the case of Loughborough University's School of Business and Economics and its yearlong undergraduate internship in the United Kingdom.

One can differentiate by repositioning a programme such as when Audencia Nantes School of Management in France relaunched its MBA as an MBA in Responsible Management. Differentiation can also come by way of adding new programmes with a distinctive value proposition such as the World Bachelor in Business programme offered as a collaborative effort between the University of Southern California in the United States, Bocconi University in Italy and the Hong Kong University of Science and Technology in China.

Differentiation requires, of course, a keen understanding of the competitive landscape and the points of difference that will be valued by the market and is particularly important when attempting to bolster revenues by increasing tuition fees.

Re-engineer the Mix of Programmes and Students Citing his own experience at the University of Arizona's Eller College of Management, Jessup suggests that growing one's profit centres can be a viable strategy. This might entail adjusting the admissions mix in a school's programme portfolio to focus on growing the enrolment in the most profitable or adjusting the proportion of international to domestic students.

Turpin notes the potential in offering recurring short-term courses as part of lifelong learning to executives instead of one-off packaged programmes. Such a format, along with offering courses in different parts of the world, caters to executives' preference for flexibility.

Merge and Establish Partnerships Mergers present opportunities for increasing scale, boosting visibility and leveraging complementary strengths. French schools, which have historically been organisations that served local interests, have, in recent years, taken this route to increase their global competitiveness.

> **[Growing a profit centre] might entail adjusting the admissions mix in a school's programme portfolio and focusing on growing enrolment in the most profitable**

Rouen Business School and Reims Management School, for example, announced their merger in April of 2013 and before that Ceram

Business School and ESC Lille merged in 2009 to become Skema Business School.

For-profit organisations have also been growing their presence in the higher education market through acquisitions and partnerships.

Career Education Corporation, a US-listed company, now owns American InterContinental University, Colorado Technical University, the International Academy of Design & Technology, Le Cordon Bleu North America, Inseec, and more recently, the International University of Monaco. Laureate Education is another example of a for-profit organisation with a vast reach of 780,000 students in 29 countries that has grown tremendously through acquisitions and partnerships.

Thunderbird School of Global Management in the United States, the most recent addition to Laureate's portfolio, pursued this route to resuscitate finances in the face of plunging enrolments. The partnership gives Thunderbird access to Laureate's network of campuses and allows it to expand its online and undergraduate offerings.

The latest alliance forged between a business school and a for-profit organisation, in August 2013, is between Ashridge Business School and Pearson, an educational publishing group as well as owner of the *Financial Times* and part-owner of *The Economist*. The product of this partnership is a jointly offered undergraduate business degree. As Ashridge chief executive Kai Peters, explains: "From the business school side we just don't have the resources and the reach [of Pearson]" and hence the reason for the partnership.

Leverage Technology   Hill notes that there is a gap between what young people demand and what traditional schools offer. One need only contemplate how much of a young person's life revolves around technology to appreciate how much catching up schools need to do in terms of incorporating technology to bridge that divide.

Laing similarly cautions that schools ignore MOOC platforms such as Coursera and edX at the risk of their own demise. MOOCs offer the flexibility in pace and mode of learning that is consonant with the preferences of young adults and brings with it potential cost efficiencies.

How MOOCs are integrated into programmes, what proportion of a programme they should account for and the pricing model for programmes involving MOOCs are issues that need close examination. But leveraging technology-enabled learning is no longer a fringe activity that can be disregarded.

Internal Challenges

So far we have discussed challenges brought on by external forces and we turn out attention now to challenges that are internal to the business school.

Durand and Dameron (2011) argue that business schools have lost their way, as they pointedly described the flaws inherent in the way the typical business school is run today.

> **Research, and esoteric research in narrow areas at that, is prioritised and young PhDs with publication potential are pursued with high salaries**

Their argument centres on business schools' pursuit of legitimacy and reputation through mechanisms such as accreditation, rankings and number of publications in top-tier journals.

The last of these, no doubt, feeds into performance on the first two and has become the focus of any business school that wants to be considered a serious player. Hence, research, and esoteric research in narrow areas at that, is prioritised and young PhDs with publication potential are pursued with high salaries.

Never mind that these PhDs are often recruited into programmes with hardly any working experience and may even balk at requests to show the managerial relevance of their work. Many view research as their reason for being and teaching as a necessary annoyance.

As a consequence, many such faculty have very little appreciation of the issues faced by practitioners and are uneasy in front of an audience of seasoned executives.

Schools have found a way out of this quandary by relying on adjunct faculty and external parties to teach, while counting on research faculty to churn out top-tier publications research.

Therein lies a dissociation between the research and teaching functions of a business school — they exist as if they are mutually exclusive spheres.

If knowledge gained through research is meant to be disseminated to the wider community through teaching, the process has surely been circumvented by such a system. Durand and Dameron refer to this as a "business school bubble", a state of affairs that cannot be sustained in the long term.

Turpin (2013) made a similar observation, as reflected in the following quote:

"Companies often ask how relevant the academic world is today. Last summer I was in America talking to deans of major business schools and some of them believe that the academic world is indeed becoming more and more academic. What impact do we want to have on the businesses of tomorrow?"

Despite this awareness, Durand and Dameron note the same inertia that we described earlier:

"Business schools have lost their way. Something needs to be done about it. Interestingly enough, many retiring business school deans who deliver their last speech as they leave tend to say something of that sort. Yet, their successor immediately keeps going as before."

The challenge for business schools is, therefore, to build reputation through research that is valuable to the wider community and not arcane research read only by fellow researchers.

One might argue that the distinction between relevance and rigour is a false dichotomy that presumes one necessarily comes at the expense of the other.

Another challenge is to draw the two spheres of teaching and research closer together so that research and teaching capabilities are developed within the same individual faculty. Business schools that have both research faculty and clinical or practice faculty have an implicit contract of division of labour, creating a situation where either teaching or research is likely to be given short shrift depending on which faculty bucket one falls into.

How might a business school respond to these challenges? For one thing, tenure and promotion criteria ought to be revised so that decisions are not made based on mere bean counting of publications in top journals. In addition to broadening the set of journals to include those that publish applied work, measures of research impact should be developed.

Programmes that increase contact between faculty and practitioners, and help faculty develop an appreciation for problems faced by practitioners, should be formalised. Examples would include executive-in-residence programmes, corporate immersion programmes for faculty and joint projects with practitioners. Doctoral programmes targeted at practitioners with significant work experience (often called Doctor in Business Administration, or DBA, programmes) and differentiated from traditional PhD programmes with their focus on applied research ought to be given serious attention in a school's portfolio.

What Must Management Education do to Produce Better Managers?

The previous section was about how individual business schools can respond to external and internal challenges. If we revisit the question of what the purpose of management education as a field is, the answer will inescapably include elements of improving management practice and producing better managers. And if that is true, then what must the field collectively do to fulfil that purpose?

For one thing, the world has undeniably changed in the post-financial crisis era — many economies are in tatters; there is a greater consciousness of the dangers of unbridled capitalism and the need for social responsibility; and many are looking to emerging economies (including what has been termed the "double MIT" clusters of Mexico—Indonesia—Turkey and Malaysia—India—Turkey) for growth.

Soft Skills

In this changed environment, what can we foresee about the qualities and attributes that managers must have to be successful and in what new areas must management educators focus their energies?

One view that resonates with us, and many others, we are certain, is Turpin's (2013). He places the emphasis on softer skills over the domain knowledge, as seen in the following quote:

> **The challenge for business schools is to go beyond one or two ethics courses tacked onto curricula like an after-thought and attempt to weave ethics consistently across curricula**

"The ultimate goal of business schools, I believe, is to produce responsible leaders who can deal with an increasingly volatile, uncertain, complex and ambiguous world: the so-called VUCA market. At the top of any corporation, people are smart and have proven that they can run a business and be successful. In the end, authentic leadership and personal values will increasingly make the difference."

There has been an appeal for business actions to be guided by strong moral and ethical values post-crisis and this is unlikely to be a passing fancy. Personal values, as reflected in ethics and social responsibility, will certainly continue to be important markers of good management. As we noted in Chapter 6, the challenge for business schools is to go beyond one or two ethics courses tacked onto curricula like an after-thought and attempt to weave ethics consistently across curricula.

One example of how values can be integrated in undergraduate training is a programme called SMU LifeLessons at Singapore Management University. Values-based education is implemented through co-curricula activities such as orientation camps, community service initiatives, intra- and inter-varsity competitions and internships through the years that students spend at the university.

These activities are used as platforms to develop such qualities as awareness of one's value and purpose, awareness of social issues and the ability to manage conflict. SMU uses a variety of instructional methods for this including case studies, journaling, self-reflection and group discussions.

The quote from Turpin begs the question of what "authentic leadership" entails and how one might nurture that quality. Thomas Robertson, dean of the Wharton School, has made the case for diversity in a given setting being an important enhancer of learning ("Leadership Gains from Diversity in Education", *Financial Times*, 2012).

Diversity, which we can define as an environment with participants of different ages, races, genders and cultures, moves people out of their comfort zone and encourages more rigorous debate and self-reflection. Out of this emerges more creative problem solving.

As Robertson puts it: "Innovation is born out of friction". Sharpened leadership skills are also presumably born out of this process.

Another likely prerequisite for strong leadership is emotional intelligence. There can be no leaders without followers and emotional intelligence is the lubricant of interpersonal relations.

Santiago Iniguez, dean of IE Business School in Madrid, Spain, argues that traditional measures of intelligence such as the GMAT, GRE and IQ tests overlook other forms of intelligence that can be just as important for professional success ("We Must Find New Ways to Identify Talent", *Financial Times*, 2012).

Contrary to the popular belief that emotional intelligence is innate, Iniguez, citing scholarly work in the area, notes that emotional intelligence is a skill that one can acquire through practice. This makes room for management education to cultivate stronger management abilities by paying closer attention to developing emotional intelligence.

The need for renewed emphasis on the softer skills is echoed by Peters ("Kindness Can be the Hardest Word of All", *Financial Times*, 2010), who notes that the quality of relationships is often the lynchpin of organisational success. In fact, Peters distils it to a single word — kindness — and argues that it is kindness (as expressed in decency, courtesy and thoughtfulness) that brings about repeat business and profits.

As he puts it: "If people and relationships are the *sine qua non* of enterprise success ... then decency, thoughtfulness and the likes of attentive listening should know no peers in the management canon."

Business schools must therefore find a way to instil in students the value of kindness and, perhaps ironically, a sense of servitude as it aims to produce better managers.

Globalisation is often assumed to have the effect of homogenising the world when in fact what it has done is make economic, political, cultural, religious and regulatory differences between countries more important.

Edward Snyder, dean of Yale School of Management, believes that business schools need to teach core competencies in three areas: how markets work; how organisations work; and the context in which business operates (Bradshaw, 2011).

He contends that the last of these is the challenge. Management students need to be equipped with better contextual knowledge and a greater sensitivity to differences in how different countries and different sectors operate.

Indeed, the idea of a "go-any-where" graduate was a refrain in the responses of our panel of experts. To be future-ready in a globalised world, the graduates we produce need to have global exposure, cultural intelligence and the ability to manage the unexpected in unfamiliar environments.

> **To be future-ready in a globalised world the graduates we produce need to have global exposure, cultural intelligence and the ability to manage the unexpected in unfamiliar environments**

Thinking Skills

There have been calls for integrative thinking to be given more serious attention in curricula. Teece, for example, argues that managers cannot afford to approach problem solving through the lens of single disciplines, such as marketing or finance ("Students Blinkered by Narrow Teaching Focus", *Financial Times*, 2012).

Today's dynamic business environment presents challenges whose solutions come from integrated, multi-disciplinary approaches. The predominant model of teaching along disciplinary lines, it is argued, "puts blinders on students".

A similar argument is made for melding the liberal arts with a management education by authors such as Hardy and Everett (2013) and Harney and Thomas (2013). A liberal arts education is said to provide the breadth of knowledge and the ability to view a problem from multiple perspectives and hence better equips the manager. The humanities, in particular, have been touted as providing much-needed training in analytical thinking, critical thinking and communication as well as developing a greater awareness of self and of society.

On top of this, Edmundson ("Why Major in Humanities? Not Just for a Good Job — For a Good Life", *The Washington Post*, 2013) argues that the true value of the humanities resides in the fact that they provoke informed and thoughtful dialogue about the way we ought to conduct life, a point that is particularly poignant today given the recent failures by businesses to take account of the larger interests of society.

Roger Martin, former dean of the Rotman School of Management at the University of Toronto in Canada, has been a vocal advocate for the merits of applying design thinking to management practice.

Design thinking mimics the approach that designers use to tackle problems — designers find creative solutions to a problem, a process that typically involves a combination of inductive, deductive and, more importantly, abductive reasoning skills (a logical process whereby one attempts to make sense of an observation through hypothesis generation). Design thinking is also about the mindset or attitude that is brought to the process.

As Dunne and Martin (2006) explain: "In conventional management thinking, constraints are seen as an undesirable barrier to the generation and implementation of ideas; for a designer, however, constraints are embraced as the impetus to creative solutions."

Martin argues that design thinking is all the more important in a highly competitive context, where merely refining and honing a competitive position is not enough to create or maintain a competitive edge. It is the creation of solutions that do not currently exist — solutions that let a company leapfrog its competitors — that offers a better chance of success.

New and Not-so-New Domain Areas

There is no denying that we are in an era of "big data" — shorthand for the vast amounts of data that companies accumulate and which require complex analytical methods of processing. Increasingly, insights gained from analysing this data will form the basis of competitive advantage, whether it is in customer relationship management, supply chain optimisation or financial modelling, and hence the growing importance of being comfortable with the use of data for effective decision making.

In fact, the growth in data is far outpacing the talent available to deal with it. McKinsey Global Institute predicts that by 2018, the United States will face a 1.5 million shortfall in managers and analysts who have the necessary skills to make effective use of big data.

In light of this, business schools would be well advised to integrate data analytic skills into their curricula. Terry College of Business at the University of Georgia at Athens in the United States and the Singapore Management University are among the few schools to have developed a concentration in analytics and more schools will likely follow suit as employers increasingly demand these skills.

The 2008 financial crisis has led to a reflection and a questioning among finance scholars of the utility of financial models, the uncritical use of which has been blamed for the meltdown. For example, Didier Cossin, professor of finance and governance at IMD in Switzerland, writes that "most financial models taught today rely on false mathematical assumptions that create a sense of security even as failure approaches" ("Financial Models Create a False Sense of Security", *Financial Times*, 2011). Complex decisions are made on the basis of models with simplified assumptions to potentially disastrous effects.

However, Salvatore Cantale, also a professor of finance at IMD, cautions that "the world still needs financial models: they are useful analytical tools for understanding complex business situations. It is up to managers to learn how to steer them properly and avoid crashes" ("Financial Tools Must be Handled with Care", *Financial Times*, 2012).

What is needed is not the abandonment of these models, as called for by Cossin, but that business schools deliver a more thorough understanding of these models, including their assumptions and potential flaws. A refocus in finance courses is necessary so that students are not merely taught the utility of the models but also the circumstances under which they are valid and the risks associated with their application.

Transforming Management Education

Reviving the Professionalisation Project

It would not be an exaggeration to say that public trust in managers, business leaders and business institutions has taken a beating during and following the financial crisis. This has precipitated some soul searching among academics about what management's obligations to society are and what is needed to mend the cracks in that relationship.

To restore faith in managers, Khurana and Nohria (2008) argue that the way forward is to make management a profession, like other professions overseen by a governing body with the power to set

> [The financial crisis] has precipitated some soul searching among academics about what management's obligations to society are and what is needed to mend the cracks in that relationship

rules and policies that guide the development of the field. Members inducted into the profession, through formal education and certification would be required to adhere to a code of conduct and face possible sanctions in the event of violations. They further add that membership in the profession would give one a shared ethical orientation and sense of responsibility. The fact that moral values are integral to a profession's image would provide the necessary motivation for vigilant self-monitoring.

In order for professionalisation to be possible, as we noted in Chapter 1, certain conditions will have to be satisfied. To recap, Khurana (2007) lays out these conditions as:

(1) there must be an agreed-upon body of knowledge
(2) there must be a consensus about managerial status and legitimacy

(3) there must be a governing body that sets policies, standards and examinations for entry into the profession

Detractors of the position that management should be professionalised have argued that these conditions cannot be met. Barker (2010), for example, argues that setting the boundaries on what management constitutes is an impossibility, considering that the manager relies on a range of inputs to perform his/her job and his/her work is not marked by discrete starting and end points as in other professions. As he put it: "The role of a manager is inherently general, variable and indefinable."

He argues also that a good manager is made not simply through the imparting of technical or functional knowledge but is nurtured in an environment that develops the softer skills such as greater thoughtfulness and awareness. These qualities outweigh the role of functional knowledge and by their very nature cannot be examined by standardised exams.

The ability to integrate across functional areas, moreover, cannot be taught but is learned "in the minds of the students". Consequently, managerial ability cannot be satisfactorily predicted by academic assessments.

Martin (2010) takes a similar stand on professionalisation. He takes as a starting point the fact that professions are characterised by information asymmetry, with the professional possessing specialised knowledge that the layperson does not.

While features of that asymmetry can be argued to be present in management, he points out that from a regulatory point of view failures of management can seldom be traced to a lone actor since management tends to be a group activity. Hence, the entity held accountable for failures is often the company. Moreover, the cost of failure in management, with some exceptions, is seldom considered to be high. These conditions make it unlikely for management to attract regulation and therefore unlikely for it to be considered a profession.

This debate can only be viewed as a healthy response to an important question and it provokes thought on a number of questions, such as how high must the cost of mismanage-

> **[Soft skills] are necessary but not sufficient; such skills do make for a good manager in combination with good functional knowledge but on their own they do not**

ment be for regulation to be "worth the effort"? Martin's statement that "more often than not a bad manager is thought to cause short-term damage from which the company in question can recover after the bad manager is fired" seems to suggest a viewing of cost from the company's perspective.

We would argue that the very thing that instigated this debate is the view that bad management can exact too high of a cost on society and can unleash damage that reverberates across the world.

As for whether responsibility for mismanagement can be traced to an individual, we believe that it is possible. The fact that a bad manager can be fired, as described by Martin's statement above, suggests that individuals can be held accountable, even in an activity that is deemed a "group activity". Shared culpability has never been a basis for the forgiveness of wrongdoing.

We agree wholeheartedly with Barker's assessment that soft skills and skills of integration make for better managers but like Martin we disagree that these skills cannot be taught or that they cannot be improved with formal training. In the previous section we noted evidence that emotional intelligence can be acquired with practice (Goleman, 1998) and we believe that other skills, such as leadership and the ability to deal with uncertainty, can be similarly nurtured.

That these skills are teachable does not, however, necessarily mean that they are amenable to testing and this is where the viability of a standardised test to certify managers might be questioned. If these soft skills are thought to be so important to being a good manager, can a professional certification process escape assessing candidates on these skills?

The answer to this question depends very much on whether we believe soft skills to be a necessary and/or sufficient condition for effective management. Our view is that they are necessary but not sufficient; that is, such skills do make for a good manager in combination with good functional knowledge but on their own they do not.

This amounts to claiming that the functional knowledge (or what Khurana and Nohria refer to as a formal body of knowledge) that is imparted in management education does add value. It is contrary to other claims that assert that the practice of management does not require formal training or that management education is merely a signalling device or that its value rests solely in the network of contacts that students acquire.

Khurana and Nohria suggest that denying the value that this formal body of knowledge brings would be a wholesale denial of the legitimacy of management education. In summary, we believe that, while soft skills are important, this does not automatically preclude the utility of a certification test for managers based on functional knowledge. The test would represent the minimum standards in terms of functional knowledge that can be expected of managers.

This, however, begs the question of whether there is an agreed body of knowledge that would-be managers could be tested on.

Certainly, curricula at most business school programmes are broadly similar and agreement on the competencies that define that body of knowledge ought to be within reach. Barker's stand, however, is that the body of knowledge should be defined by the knowledge that managers need to draw on in discharging their responsibilities. The fact that it

> "I don't think you need to maximise profits because I think when you maximise profits you go down the route where you can become criminal in your activity"
> — Anita Roddick

is hard to set the boundaries on what a manager does leads him to conclude that it is not possible to define that body of knowledge.

This view has intuitive appeal but perhaps the fact is that we currently have only a poor definition of what it means to be a manager leads to (or perhaps reflects) the generalist nature of the job.

According professional status to a manager could have the desirable effect of re-defining and bringing clarity to what being a manager entails, steering it away from the jack-of-all-trades perception that currently prevails. We believe that this question is far from being settled and deserves vigorous debate.

Is the professionalisation project an impossibility or does it simply entail heavy lifting? We believe that its impossibility has not been clearly established as yet and an investigation of its viability ought to be a matter for serious consideration. To be sure, the professionalisation of management will be a massive endeavour but the rewards in terms of the higher standards of conduct that the practice of management will be held to and the legitimacy that comes along with it may be well worth the trouble.

Reinstating Stakeholder Primacy

The late Anita Roddick, founder of The Body Shop, found herself defending her business model — one that takes a broad definition of stakeholders — in a TV interview on an Asian news channel.

As the journalist challenged her on the accountability of The Body Shop to shareholders and what he perceived as the side-lining of the imperative to maximise profits to make room for the interests of the community, a bemused and even seemingly annoyed Roddick retorted: "Why is that a dilemma?" She went on to say: "I don't believe that shareholders hold all the cards. They're just one of the stakeholders. What about the environment, that silent stakeholder? What about your employees, who give their lives to a company? Don't they have a say in things?"

When pressed on the notion of maximising profits, she said: "I don't think you need to maximise profits because I think when you maximise profits you go down the route where you can become criminal in your activity."

That interview was recorded in 2004, making that last statement seem almost a prescient warning of the financial crisis that was to come. The dialogue is also illuminating for the fact that shareholder primacy has carved out such a stake in the collective consciousness that a departure from maximising shareholder profits is viewed as something that needs to be vigorously defended.

Business schools are in no small part responsible for such a deeply entrenched mindset. For the last three decades, finance and economics professors have subscribed to "agency theory", or the belief that companies are best served when managerial actions are guided by the maxim of increasing shareholder value. Business students have consequently been indoctrinated with that same principle.

We believe that such a view is becoming increasingly hard to defend in today's climate (both economic and weather-wise). Global warming and changing weather patterns, sustainable

> **If tenure is about allowing one to pursue the truth without fear of reprisal, the pre-tenure years have, ironically, been subverted by the very fear of not getting tenure**

food production, health risks from pollution and the food supply, economic malaise and unemployment are but a few of the issues that the world needs to deal with.

Business schools cannot afford to ignore these larger societal issues. They ought to seek legitimacy by taking up the challenge of serving societal, not just shareholder, interests. This requires that we change the language that is used in classrooms from shareholder- to stakeholder-speak, that curricula are revised to include content on managing (not just managing businesses but managing in a broader context) and that journals take a stance in encouraging research that has not just profit implications but policy and welfare implications as well.

Rethinking Tenure

Tenure is a sacred cow. While there may be grumblings in some quarters about the failings of the tenure system, the criticisms have seldom drawn enough attention for tenure to be at risk. To be sure, tenure has its merits. Academic freedom, as argued by many authors (e.g. Brown & Kurland, 1990), has always been central to the argument for tenure.

The short version of the argument is that tenure has the noble purpose of providing protection to academics as they seek the truth, even if that means taking positions that are unpopular, counter to conventional wisdom or anti-establishment.

Tenure today is seen as such a prized status that the pre-tenure years are often marked by tremendous pressure to publish. If tenure is about allowing one to pursue the truth without fear of reprisal, the pre-tenure years have, ironically, been subverted by the very fear of not getting tenure.

What the deafening ticking of the tenure clock does to academic integrity and the willingness to venture outside the expectations of journals and senior faculty may be a matter of debate but we can be sure that it is not conducive to a whole-hearted, unbridled pursuit of the truth.

Granting that tenure has its place in business schools, the question that the field ought to seriously contemplate and perhaps re-evaluate is the basis on which tenure is granted.

At the moment, the prioritisation of rigour over relevance means that publications in journals with narrow specialisations are what clinches the deal.

If management education is to seek legitimacy by reconnecting with the business community, its incentives for tenure ought to mirror that endeavour. That is, we cannot tout the need for relevant and managerially impactful research while continuing to reserve the biggest rewards for those who engage in esoteric research.

In particular, schools that hire "practice" or clinical faculty on term tracks need to confront the question of why such faculty are not also deserving of the academic freedom afforded by tenure. Schools that offer applied PhD programmes (such as DBA programmes) need to answer the question of why they engage in the effort of producing such doctorates while perpetuating a tenure system that rewards basic research.

Resisting the Paradigm Trap

Western business schools have for a long time enjoyed a position of strength, having a reputation for higher-quality programmes, faculty and research. As a result, talent, in the form of both faculty and students, has always converged on the West from the rest of the world.

There are now signs that the dynamics have changed as business schools from emerging economies such as China, India, Singapore, Hong Kong and Brazil see their reputations rising. This is largely driven by the surging growth of emerging economies compared to the lackadaisical performance of the West, which has fallen behind in terms of job and market opportunities and investment in education.

As a recent article in the *International Herald Tribune* reported (Saalfield and Appel, "Emerging Economies Attract Local Talent", *International Herald Tribune*, 2012), more students in Asia are choosing to pursue their business degrees at home. The reasons cited include the fact that there is a growing perception that indigenous business schools have improved markedly in quality (certainly there are now more Asian business schools represented in the *Financial Times* Global MBA ranking) and that not only are domestic degree programmes less costly but career prospects are also seen to be brighter at home.

This is accompanied by the trend of more students from the West opting to study at Asian business schools. Some are drawn to Asia because they have aspirations to break into the Asian market with their businesses while others are simply responding to employers' demand for those trained in Asia in order to staff growing Asian operations.

Faculty, too, are increasingly moving from West to East because of greater investments in education, the concomitant accretion in reputation of Asian business schools and the fact that the very different context throws up interesting research questions.

This shifting landscape, one might think, sets the stage for innovation to occur in the business school world. With so many business schools emerging in different parts of the world, one would expect a variety of different business school models and perhaps greater experimentation with running things differently. Thus far, sadly, there is little evidence of this.

Across the world, business schools have tended to mimic the model of their American counterparts, perpetuating the dominant logic. To some extent this is also driven by the implicit belief that doing things the way the top schools do signals one's intention of being a serious player. Hence, business schools from around the world compete for faculty largely trained in US doctoral programmes, incentivise publication in the same collection of top US journals and teach broadly similar curricula along the lines of functional disciplines.

Where there have been new programmes or new models, the changes have been incremental rather than radical, with some exceptions such as Mintzberg's International Masters in Practicing Management (IMPM) and the Lorange Institute of Business.

> **With so many business schools emerging in different parts of the world, one would expect a variety of different business school models and perhaps greater experimentation with running things differently.**
>
> **Thus far, sadly, there is little evidence of this**

Another possible reason for the lack of innovation has to do with the fact that it requires resources while most schools around the world currently face resource constraints, albeit of differing natures and to differing degrees.

India, for example, faces an acute shortage of faculty, the result of academic salaries that lag far behind local practitioner salaries and academic pay in other parts of the world. This has had the unfortunate consequence of stifling research and creating a vicious cycle where the lack of research hampers schools' ability to recruit high-quality faculty.

In China, business schools benefit from significant investments in education but face strict regulations that constrain autonomy. Business schools in Singapore benefit from similar strong government backing and healthy public funding of higher education. However, there is significant government oversight and the larger goals of the nation, such as the manpower needs of the economy, impose performance expectations on business schools and have an influence on their strategic direction. In contrast, business schools in the United Kingdom face the challenge of drastic cuts in funding and a limit on how much tuition fees can be raised to increase revenues.

These constraints have largely led to a cautious attitude. In some instances, business schools seeking funding have had to adopt a positioning that is palatable to a risk-averse funding agency. This has the unfortunate effect of dampening the spirit of innovation in service of constructing a proposition that is an easy sell; hence, the tendency to look to existing models of success based in the United States.

We argue that a sustained pre-occupation with the dominant logic can only be detrimental to the field and schools need to resist being caught in this paradigm trap. The ecosystem cannot support a growing number of business schools all competing for the same limited pool of faculty, limited numbers of pages in journals and a limited pool of MBA candidates.

As with design thinking, business schools need to negotiate around constraints and allow barriers to be an impetus for creative solutions. Otherwise schools risk being driven out of the market and falling under the wheel of for-profit competition.

Though they may lack strong brand names and high-quality faculty, for-profit competitors are thriving by providing a reasonable quality education at a lower cost and building on a base of private capital.

A partnership in undergraduate education such as that between Ashridge Business School in the United Kingdom and Pearson Education may arouse scepticism but business schools desperately need creative models and solutions to compete effectively in this changed environment.

Conclusion

We believe that now is the time for a new Ford Foundation/Carnegie Foundation report on new models and directions in management education. The committee that oversees this should encompass insights from key schools, authorities and individuals across the global management education landscape. It must also exhort deans and university presidents to take up the challenge of innovation in their business models.

Afterword: Transformation and Future Change in Management Education

We have presented here a mapping of the uncertain futures of management education. For example, the most likely scenario outlined by our experts can be characterized as "business as usual" with incremental change, owing to the culture of inertia and conservatism that is often prevalent in business schools. However, there is a genuine belief among the same experts that innovation in new business school models should be undertaken in the light of concerns about the long-term financial sustainability of some business schools and the ever-increasing forces and pressures of globalization, and technology-enhanced learning (often described as "blended learning").

We point out a range of barriers to change including the important influences of the university system, faculty power and tenure, faculty structure, and business school leadership. We note that while these barriers may be difficult to overcome, we predict that increased competition, particularly from private providers, and pressure from funding issues and the consequent sustainability of the current financial model, will trigger change. In particular, we expect to see debates about transformation in management education, focusing on issues such as reviving the professionalisation project; reinstating stakeholder, versus shareholder, primacy; rethinking tenure; and resisting the paradigm trap (i.e. the dominant logic of the current business model).

We believe, in conclusion, that a new set of thought leadership proposals for the future of management education should emerge from the research leadership initiatives of EFMD and, perhaps, a new commission on management education embracing global thought leaders and promoted by EFMD, in association with AACSB and GMAC.

References

AACSB. (2003). *Sustaining scholarship in business schools.* Tampa, FL. Retrieved from http://www.aacsb.edu/publications/researchreports/archives/sustaining-scholarship.pdf

AACSB. (2005). *Why management education matters.* Tampa, FL. Retrieved from http://www.aacsb.edu/publications/researchreports/archives/why-management-education-matters.pdf

AACSB. (2008). *Impact of research.* Tampa, FL. Retrieved from http://www.aacsb.edu/publications/researchreports/currentreports/impact-of-research.pdf

AACSB. (2010). *Business schools on an innovation mission.* Tampa, FL. http://www.aacsb.edu/publications/researchreports/currentreports/business-schools-on-an-innovation-mission.pdf

Adams, J. (2001). *Conceptual blockbusting: A guide to better ideas.* Cambridge, MA: Perseus.

Altshuler, A., Anderson, M., Jones, D., Roos, D., & Womack, J. (1984). *The future of the automobile: The report of MIT's international automobile programme.* Cambridge, MA: The MIT Press.

Augier, M., & March, J. G. (2011). *The roots, rituals and rhetorics of change: North American business schools after the second World War.* Stanford, CA: Stanford University Press.

Barker, R. (2010). No, management is not a profession. *Harvard Business Review,* *88*(7/8), 52−60.

Bennis, W. G., & O'Toole, J. (2005). How business schools lost their way. *Harvard Business Review,* *83*(5), 96−104.

Bhide, A. (2008). *The venturesome economy.* Princeton, NJ: Princeton University Press.

Birkinshaw, J., & Mol, M. (2006). How management innovation happens. *Sloan Management Review,* *47*(4), 81−88.

Bisoux, T. (2008). The innovation generation. *BizEd,* *7*(5), 17−24.

Bisoux, T. (2013). Cornering the market. *BizEd,* *12*(4), 18−25.

Bloom, N., Sadun, R., & Van Reenen, J. (2012). Does management really work? *Harvard Business Review,* *90*(11), 76−82.

Bloom, N., & Van Reenen, J. (2007). Measuring and explaining management practices across firms and countries. *The Quarterly Journal of Economics,* *122*(4), 1351−1408.

Bloomberg Business Week. (2013). Changes at Harvard. *Bloomberg Business Week,* 3 July.

Bower, J. L. (1986). *The resource allocation process.* Boston, MA: Harvard Business School Press.

Bradshaw, D. (2011). If you get the right people, they will build the school. *Financial Times,* 17 October, p. 14.

Bradshaw, D. (2012). Research that measures up. *Financial Times*, 23 April, p. 11.

Bradshaw, D. (2013). The fifty ideas that shaped business today. *Financial Times*, June, p. 49.

Brown, J. (2012). *Enrollment trends at AACSB-accredited schools*. AACSB Business Education Data and Research Blog. Retrieved from http://aacsbblogs.typepad.com/dataandresearch/2012/10/enrollment-trends-at-aacsb-accredited-schools.html. Accessed on 29 October.

Brown, R., & Kurland, J. (1990). Academic tenure and academic freedom. *Law and Contemporary Problems*, *53*(3), 325−355.

Brown, T. (2009). *Change by design: How design thinking transforms organisations and inspires innovation*. New York, NY: HarperCollins.

Canals, J. (Ed.). (2011). *The future of leadership development*. Basingstoke, UK: Palgrave Macmillan.

Cantale, S. (2012). Financial tools must be handled with care. *Financial Times*, 19 February, p. 11.

Cheit, E. (1985). *Business schools and their critics. business and public policy*. Working Paper No. BPP-5. Center for Research in Management, University of California, Berkeley Business School, CA.

Christensen, C. M. (2000). *The innovator's dilemma*. New York, NY: Free Press.

Christensen, C. M., & Eyring, H. (2011). *The innovative university*. San Francisco, CA: Jossey-Bass.

Christensen, C. M., Horn, M. B., & Johnson, C. W. (2008). *Disrupting class*. New York, NY: McGraw-Hill.

Clark, B. R. (1998). *Creating entrepreneurial universities: Organisational pathways of transformation*. Oxford: Pergamon Press.

Colby, A., Ehrlich, T., Sullivan, W. M., & Dolle, J. R. (2011). *Rethinking undergraduate business education: Liberal learning for the profession*. San Francisco, CA: Jossey-Bass.

Collins, J. C. (2001). *Good to great: Why some companies make the leap ... and others don't*. New York, NY: HarperCollins.

Cossin, D. (2011). Financial models create a false sense of security. *Financial Times*, 5 September, p. 11.

Crainer, S., & Dearlove, D. (1998). *Gravy training: Inside the world's top business schools*. Oxford: Capstone Publishing.

Cyert, R. M., & March, J. G. (1973). *The behavioural theory of the firm*. Englewood Cliffs, NJ: Prentice Hall.

D'Aveni, R. (1994). *Hypercompetition: managing the dynamics of strategic maneuvering*. New York: The Free Press.

D'Aveni, R. (1996). A multiple constituency status based approach to interorganisational mobility of faculty and input−output competition among top business schools. *Organisation Science*, *7*(2), 166−189.

Datar, S., Garvin, D. A., & Cullen, P. G. (2010). *Rethinking the MBA: Business education at a crossroads*. Boston, MA: Harvard Business Press.

Davies, J., & Thomas, H. (2009). What do business school deans do? Insights from a UK study. *Management Decision*, *47*(9), 1396−1419.

Delbridge, R., Gratton, L., & Johnson, G. (2006). *The exceptional manager: Making the difference.* Oxford: Oxford University Press.

Drucker, P. (1974). *Management: Tasks responsibilities and practices.* New York, NY: Harper & Row.

Dunne, D., & Martin, R. (2006). Design thinking and how it will change management education: An interview and discussion. *Academy of Management Learning & Education, 5*(4), 512–523.

Durand, T., & Dameron, S. (2008). *The future of business schools: Scenarios and strategies for 2020.* Basingstoke, UK: Palgrave Macmillan.

Durand, T., & Dameron, S. (2011). Where have all the business schools gone? *British Journal of Management, 22,* 559–563.

Edmundson, M. (2013). Why major in humanities? Not just for a good job — For a good life. *The Washington Post,* 8 August.

EFMD. (1996). *Training the fire brigade: Preparing for the unimaginable.* Brussels: EFMD Publications.

EFMD. (2012, January 24). *The future of management education.* Brussels: EFMD Publications.

Everett, D., & Page, M. (2013). The crucial education fusion: Relevance, rigor and life preparation in a changing world. In G. Hardy & D. Everett (Eds.), *Shaping the future of business education: Relevance, rigor, and life preparation* (pp. 1–18). Basingstoke, UK: Palgrave Macmillan.

Fraguiero, F. (2010). Think local, but from a global perspective. *Financial Times,* 26 April, p. 9.

Fragueiro, F., & Thomas, H. (2011). *Strategic leadership in the business school: Keeping one step ahead.* Cambridge: Cambridge University Press.

Friedman, M. (1970). The social responsibility of business is to increase its profits. *New York Times Magazine,* September 13.

Ghoshal, S. (2005). Bad management theories are destroying good management practices. *Academy of Management Learning and Education, 4*(1), 75–91.

GFME. (2008). *The global management education landscape.* Bingley, UK: Emerald Group Publishing.

Goleman, D. (1998). *Working with emotional intelligence.* New York, NY: Bantam.

Goodall, A. (2009a). *Socrates in the boardroom: Why research universities should be led by top scholars.* Princeton, NJ: Princeton University Press.

Goodall, A. (2009b). Highly cited leaders and the performance of research universities. *Research Policy, 38*(7), 1079–1092.

Gordon, R. A., & Howell, J. E. (1959). *Higher education for business.* New York, NY: Columbia University Press.

Grayson, D. (2010). Schools ignore sustainability revolution. *Financial Times,* 4 October, p. 15.

Gregg S., & Stoner, J. R. (Eds.). (2008). *Rethinking business management: Examining the foundations of business education.* Princeton, NJ: Witherspoon Institute.

Grey, C. (2005). *A very short, fairly interesting and relatively cheap book about studying organisations.* London: Sage.

Hambrick, D. C. (1994). What if the academy actually mattered? *Academy of Management Review, 19*(1), 11–16.

Hamel, G. (1996). In EFMD (1996, pp. 113–115) (op. cit.).

Hamel, G. (2000). *Leading the revolution.* Boston, MA: Harvard Business School Press.

Hamel, G., & Breen, B. (2007). *The future of management.* Boston, MA: Harvard Business School Press.

Handy, C. (1996). In EFMD (1996, p. 113) (op. cit.).

Hardy, G., & Everett, D. (Eds.). (2013). *Shaping the future of business education: Relevance, rigor and life preparation.* New York, NY: Palgrave Macmillan.

Harney, S., & Dowling, E. (2012). It is time that business schools learnt to walk the walk. *Financial Times*, 28 May, p. 13.

Harney, S., & Thomas, H. (2013). Towards a liberal management education. *Journal of Management Development, 32*(5), 508–524.

Hill, A. (2012). Business education is ripe for reinvention. *Financial Times*, 20 November, p. 12.

Hommel, U., & Lejeune, C. (2013). Major disruption ahead. *Global Focus, 7*(2), 10–13.

Iniguez, S. (2011). *The learning curve.* London: Palgrave Macmillan.

Iniguez, S. (2012). We must find new ways to identify talent. *Financial Times*, 30 July, p. 10.

Ivory, C., Miskell, P., Shipton, H., White, A., Moeslein, K., & Neely, A. (2006). *UK business schools: Historical contexts and future scenarios.* London: Advanced Institute of Management.

Jensen, M. C., & Meckling, W. H. (1976). Theory of the firm: Managerial behavior, agency costs and capital structure. *Journal of Financial Economics, 3*, 305–360.

Kelley, T., & Littman, J. (2004). *The art of innovation: Lessons in creativity from IDEO, America's leading design firm.* London: Profile Books.

Kelley, T., & Littman, J. (2005). *The ten faces of innovation: IDEO's strategies for beating the devil's advocate & driving creativity throughout your organization.* New York, NY: Doubleday.

Kets De Vries, M. (2006). *The leadership mystique.* London: Pearson Education.

Khurana, R. (2007). *From higher aims to hired hands: The social transformation of american business schools and the unfulfilled promise of management as a profession.* Princeton, NJ: Princeton University Press.

Khurana, R., & Nohria, N. (2008). It's time to make management a true profession. *Harvard Business Review, 86*(10), 70–77.

Khurana, R., & Spender, J. C. (2013). Herbert A. Simon on what Ails business schools: More than 'a problem in organizational design'. *Journal of Management Studies, 49*(3), 619–639.

Khurana, R., & Spender, J. C. (2013). What skills do MBA students really need. *Financial Times*, 21 April.

Knight, R. (2012). Using research to solve real world problems. *Financial Times*, 16 July, p. 10.

Knights, D. (2008). Book review: From higher aims to hired hands: The social transformation of American business schools and the unfulfilled promise of management as a profession. *Academy of Management Review, 33*(4), 1020–1022.

Locke, E. R., & Spender, J. C. (2011). *Confronting managerialism.* London: Zed Books.

Lorange, P. (2008). *Thought leadership means business: How business schools can become more successful.* Cambridge: Cambridge University Press.

Lorange, P. (2010). *Leadership in turbulent times.* Bingley, UK: Emerald Group Publishing.

Martin, R. (2010). Management is not a profession – But it can be taught. *HBR Blog Network,* 1 July.

Martin, R. L., & Milway, J. B. (2007). *Strengthening management for prosperity.* Institute for Competitiveness and Prosperity, Toronto. Retrieved from http://www.competeprosper.ca/uploads/ManagementPaper_May07.pdf

McGee, J., Thomas, H., & Wilson, D. C. (2010). *Strategy: Analysis and practice* (2nd ed.). London: McGraw-Hill.

Millar, C., & Poole, E. (2010). Ethical leadership in a global world – A roadmap to the book. In C. Miller & E. Poole (Eds.), *Ethical leadership: Global challenges and perspectives.* Basingstoke, UK: Palgrave Macmillan.

Mintzberg, H. (1973). *The nature of managerial work.* New York, NY: Harper & Row.

Mintzberg, H. (1998). Covert leadership: Notes on managing professionals. *Harvard Business Review, 76*(6), 140–147.

Mintzberg, H. (2004). *Managers not MBA's: A hard look at the soft practice of managing and management development.* London: Pearson Education.

Moldoveanu, M. C., & Martin, R. L. (2008). *The future of the MBA.* Oxford: Oxford University Press.

Muff, K., Dyllick, T., Drewell, M., North, J., Shrivastava, P., & Haertle, J. (2013). *Management education for the world: A vision for business schools serving people and planet.* Northampton, MA: Edward Elgar.

Murray, S. (2011). Sustainability lessons from the boardroom. *Financial Times,* 31 October, p. 10.

Newman, J. H. (1852). *The idea of an university.* London: Longmans Green.

Noorda, S. (2011). Future business schools. *Journal of Management Development, 30*(9), 519–525.

Nussbaum, M. C. (1997). *Cultivating humanity: A classical defense of reform in liberal education.* Cambridge, MA: Harvard University Press.

Nye, J. S. (2008). *The powers to lead.* Oxford: Oxford University Press.

Osbaldeston, M. (1996). In EFMD (1996, p. 25) (op. cit.).

Paton, S., Chia, R., & Burt, G. (2013). Relevance or 'relevate'? How university business schools can add value through reflexively learning from strategic partnerships with business. *Management Learning, 44*(1), 1–22.

Peters, K. (2012). Academics must bridge the divide with business. *Financial Times,* 23 April, p. 11.

Peters, K., & Thomas, H. (2011). A sustainable model for business schools. *Global Focus, 5*(2), 24–27.

Peters, T. (2010). Kindness can be the hardest word of all. *Financial Times*, 24 August, p. 10.

Pettigrew, A. (1997). The double hurdles for management research. In T. Clarke (Ed.), *Advancement in organisational behaviour: Essays in honour of D. S. Pugh* (pp. 277–296). London: Dartmouth Press.

Pettigrew, A. (2011). Scholarship with impact. *BJM, 22*, 347–354.

Pfeffer, J., & Fong, C. T. (2002). The end of business schools: Less success than meets the eye. *Academy of Management Learning and Education, 1*(1), 78–95.

Pfeffer, J., & Fong, C. T. (2004). The business school business: Some lessons from the U.S. experience. *Journal of Management Studies, 41*(8), 1501–1520.

Pfefferman, G. (2012). Knowhow needed for real-world financial problems. *Financial Times*, 19 March, p. 11.

Pierson, F. C. (1959). *The education of American businessmen*. New York, NY: McGraw Hill.

Pincus, J. D., & Rudnick, H. E. (2013). Leadership blind spot. *BizEd, 12*(3), 41–46.

Podolny, J. M. (2009). The buck stops (and starts) at business school. *Harvard Business Review, 87*, 62–67.

Porter, M. E. (1990). The competitive advantage of nations. *Harvard Business Review, 68*(2), 73–93.

Prahalad, C. K. (1996). In EFMD (1996, pp. 105–109) (op. cit.).

Prahalad, C. K., & Bettis, R. (1986). The dominant logic: A new link between diversity and performance. *Strategic Management Journal, 7*, 485–501.

Raval, A. (2012). Students take on the social innovation challenge. *Financial Times*, 23 April, p. 10.

Robertson, T. (2012). Leadership gains from diversity in education. *Financial Times*, 5 March, p. 13.

Robinson, K. (2011). *Out of our minds*. Chichester, UK: Capstone Publishing.

Saalfield, P., & Appel, R. (2012). Emerging economies attract local talent. *International Herald Tribune*, 18 May, p. 11.

Samson, D. A., & Thomas, H. (1986). Subjective aspects of the art of decision analysis. *Journal of the Operational Research Society, 37*(3), 249–265.

Schoemaker, P. J. H. (2008). The future challenges of business: Re-thinking management education. *California Management Review, 50*(3), 119–139.

Schwab, K., & Martin, X. (2012). *The global competitiveness report 2012–2013*. Geneva: World Economic Forum.

Schwenk, C., & Thomas, H. (1983). Formulating the mess, the role of decision aids in problem formulation. *Omega, 11*(3), 239–252.

Simon, H. A. (1997). *Administrative behaviour: A study of decision-making processes in administrative organisation*. New York, NY: Free Press.

Spender, J. C. (2008). Book review: From higher aims to hired hands: The social transformation of American business schools and the unfulfilled promise of management as a profession. *Academy of Management Review, 33*(4), 1022–1026.

Starkey, K., & Tiratsoo, N. (2007). *The business school and the bottom line*. Cambridge: Cambridge University Press.

Staw, B. M., & Epstein, L. D. (2000). What bandwagons bring. *Administrative Science Quarterly, 45*, 523–536.

Subramanian, A., & Kessler, M. (2013, July). *The hyperglobalisation of trade and its future*. Working Paper Series, WP 13-6. Peterson Institute for International Economics, Washington, DC.

Teece, D. (2012). Students blinkered by narrow teaching focus. *Financial Times*, 19 July, p. 11

Tett, G. (2013). The virtual university. *Financial Times*, 2–3 February.

The Economist. (2009). Business schools in the recession: Resilient Wreckers. *The Economist*, 15 October.

The Economist. (2010). Business education: Case studies. *The Economist*, 8 May, pp. 65–66.

The Economist. (2013a). Honours without profits. *The Economist*, 29 June, pp. 60–61.

The Economist. (2013b). Teaching and technology: Education. *The Economist*, 29 June, p. 11.

Thomas, H. (1984). Strategic decision analysis: Applied decision analysis and its role in the strategic management process. *Strategic Management Journal, 5*(2), 139–156.

Thomas, H., Lorange, P., & Sheth, J. (2013). *The business school in the 21st century*. Cambridge: Cambridge University Press.

Thomas, H., & Peters, K. (2012). A sustainable model for business schools. *Journal of Management Development, 31*(4), 377–386.

Thomas, H., & Thomas, L. (2011). Perspectives on leadership in business schools. *Journal of Management Development, 30*(5), 526–540.

Thomas, H., Thomas, L., & Wilson, A. (2013). *Promises fulfilled and unfulfilled in management education*. Bingley, UK: Emerald Group Publishing.

Thomas, H., & Wilson, A. D. (2011). Physics envy cognitive legitimacy or practical relevance: Dilemmas in the evolution of management research in the UK. *British Journal of Management, 22*, 443–456.

Thomas, M., & Thomas, H. (2012). Using new social media and web 2.0 technologies in business school teaching and learning. *Journal of Management Development, 31*(4), 358–368.

Turpin, D. (2013). Challenges & opportunities in the new education school world. *Global Focus, 7*(2), 8–11.

Tversky, A., & Kahneman, D. (1974). Judgement under uncertainty: Heuristics and biases. *Science, 185*, 1124–1130.

Tversky, A., & Kahneman, D. (1986). Rational choice and the framing of decisions. *Journal of Business, 59*(4), 251–278.

Tyson, L. D. A. (2005). On managers not MBA's. *Academy of Management Learning and Education, 4*(2), 235–236.

UK. (1960). *The Robbins report on higher education*. London: Her Majesty's Stationery Office.

UK. (1965). *The Franks report on british business schools*. London: Her Majesty's Stationery Office.

Veblen, T. (1918). *The higher learning in America: A memorandum on the conduct of universities by business men*. New York, NY: BW Huebsch.

Wessel, M., & Christensen, C. M. (2012). Surviving disruption. *Harvard Business Review*, *90*(12), 56—64.

Wilson, D. C., & Thomas, H. (2012). The legitimacy of business schools: What's the future? *Journal of Management Development*, *31*(4), 368—376.

Witzel, M. (2011). Question of relevance must be addressed. *Financial Times*, 30 October, p. 11.

Wolf, M. (2013). Globalisation in a time of transition. *Financial Times*, 17 July, p. 7.

Zajac, E. J., & Bazerman, M. H. (1991). Blind spots in industry and competitor analysis: Implications of interfirm (Mis)perceptions for strategic decisions. *Academy of Management Review*, *16*(1), 37—56.